THE INTERNAL WORLD OF THE JUVENILE SEX OFFENDER

FORENSIC PSYCHOTHERAPY MONOGRAPH SERIES

Series Editor: Brett Kahr
Honorary Consultant: Estela V. Welldon

Other titles in the Series

Violence: A Public Health Menace and a Public Health Approach
Edited by Sandra L. Bloom

Life Within Hidden Walls: Psychotherapy in Prisons
Edited by Jessica Williams Saunders

Forensic Psychotherapy and Psychopathology: Winnicottian Perspectives
Edited by Brett Kahr

*Dangerous Patients: A Psychodynamic Approach to Risk Assessment
and Management*
Edited by Ronald Doctor

Anxiety at 35,000 Feet: An Introduction to Clinical Aerospace Psychology
Robert Bor

The Mind of the Paedophile: Psychoanalytic Perspectives
Edited by Charles W. Socarides

Violent Adolescents: Understanding the Destructive Impulse
Lynn Greenwood

Violence in Children: Understanding and Helping Those Who Harm
Edited by Rosemary Campher

Murder: A Psychotherapeutic Investigation
Edited by Ronald Doctor

Psychic Assaults and Frightened Clinicians
Edited by John Gordon and Gabriel Kirtchuk

Forensic Aspects of Dissociative Identity Disorder
Edited by Ada Sachs and Graeme Galton

*Playing with Dynamite: A Personal Approach to the Psychoanalytic
Understanding of Perversions, Violence, and Criminality*
Estela V. Welldon

THE INTERNAL WORLD OF THE JUVENILE SEX OFFENDER

Through a Glass Darkly then Face to Face

Timothy Keogh

Foreword by Stanley Ruszczynski

Forensic Psychotherapy Monograph Series

KARNAC

First published in 2012 by
Karnac Books Ltd
118 Finchley Road, London NW3 5HT

British Library Cataloguing in Publication Data

A C.I.P. for this book is available from the British Library

ISBN 978 1 85575 862 9

Edited, designed and produced by The Studio Publishing Services Ltd
www.publishingservicesuk.co.uk
e-mail: studio@publishingservicesuk.co.uk

Printed in Great Britain

www.karnacbooks.com

CONTENTS

ACKNOWLEDGEMENTS   vii

ABOUT THE AUTHOR   ix

SERIES EDITOR'S FOREWORD by Brett Kahr   xi

FOREWORD by Stanley Ruszczynski   xv

INTRODUCTION   xix

PART I: THE FORENSIC FOCUS

CHAPTER ONE
The nature of juvenile sex offending   3

CHAPTER TWO
The characteristics and differences of juvenile sex offenders 9

PART II: THE LENS

CHAPTER THREE
Attachment and juvenile sex offending   21

CHAPTER FOUR
Psychopathy and juvenile sex offending   43

CHAPTER FIVE
Malignant narcissism, psychopathy, and perversion   53

CHAPTER SIX
Epigenetics and aspects of the neurobiology of attachment   73
and sexual behaviour

PART III: MAGNIFYING THE LENS: RESEARCH FINDINGS

CHAPTER SEVEN
The study and its findings   93

CHAPTER EIGHT
A closer view into the internal world of the juvenile   109
sex offender

PART IV: PRACTICE AND APPLICATION

CHAPTER NINE
Implications for the assessment of the juvenile sex offender   123

CHAPTER TEN
The tale of two psyches: case histories of juvenile   141
sex offenders

CHAPTER ELEVEN
Mentalization based therapy (MBT) and other   157
psychoanalytic treatment

EPILOGUE   171

REFERENCES   177

INDEX   215

ACKNOWLEDGEMENTS

In thinking about those who helped me with this book, I am mindful of how fortunate I am to know and to have known so many knowledgeable, kind, and generous teachers, supervisors, mentors, and peers. I realize how enriched I am from my relationships with them.

In terms of the direct help I have received with the completion of this book, I am particularly grateful to three people who gave me extensive content feedback and advice: first, my former PhD supervisor (who encouraged me to write the book), Professor Susan Hayes (University of Sydney); second, my colleague, Professor Dianna Kenny (University of Sydney); and third, my former supervisor during my psychoanalytic training, Maria Teresa Hooke (Past President of the Australian Psychoanalytical Society). Their editorial advice was both rigorous and generous.

I am extremely appreciative of the technical advice that I received on particular sections of the book, specifically from Professor Peter Fonagy, Dr Thomas Ogden and Dr Ian Harrison. I also wish to thank Georgina Emanuel, Maria Kourt and Elizabeth Emnauel for other assistance.

viii   ACKNOWLEDGEMENTS

I am also particularly indebted to Thomas Murphy for his comprehensive editorial support.

Moreover, I wish to acknowledge the young offenders and young people who gave of their time to facilitate my research, which substantially informed the ideas in this book.

Finally, I would like to acknowledge the suffering of the victims of sexual abuse (including those offenders with backgrounds of sexual and other abuse), and hope that this book will help in some way to reduce its incidence.

ABOUT THE AUTHOR

Timothy Keogh currently works full time as a psychoanalyst and forensic and clinical psychologist in private practice in Sydney, Australia. He is a full member of the Australian Psychoanalytical Society, a research fellow of the International Psychoanalytical Society and an associate faculty member of the Centre for Behavioural Sciences in Medicine at the University of Sydney. Dr Keogh was formerly statewide Director of Inmate Services and Programs with the New South Wales Department of Corrective Services (Australia). Prior to this he held the post of Director of the Collaborative Research Unit within the New South Wales Department of Juvenile Justice, where he was also Director of Psychological Services and Programs. He has published and co-authored numerous journal articles, monographs, and chapters on juvenile offending, sex offending, adolescent mental health, and psychotherapy. He is immediate past President of the Couples and Family Psychotherapy Association of Australasia (CAFPAA), and National Convener of the Psychoanalytically Oriented Psychology Interest Group (POPIG) of the Australian Psychological Society.

*In writing this book, I am thankful for all of
the people in my life whose love sustains me,
especially my family and close friends.*

*In addition I wish to express my profound gratitude
to my analyst, Dr Ronald Spielman.*

I dedicate this book to all of you.

SERIES EDITOR'S FOREWORD

Throughout most of human history, our ancestors have done rather poorly when dealing with acts of violence. To cite but one of many shocking examples, let us perhaps recall a case from 1801, of an English boy aged only 13, who was executed by hanging on the gallows at Tyburn. What was his crime? It seems that he had been condemned to die for having stolen a spoon (Westwick, 1940).

In most cases, our predecessors have either *ignored* murderousness and aggression, as in the case of Graeco–Roman infanticide, which occurred so regularly in the ancient world that it acquired an almost normative status (deMause, 1974; Kahr, 1994); or they have *punished* murderousness and destruction with retaliatory sadism, a form of unconscious identification with the aggressor. Any history of criminology will readily reveal the cruel punishments inflicted upon prisoners throughout the ages, ranging from beatings and stockades, to more severe forms of torture, culminating in eviscerations, beheadings, or lynchings.

Only during the last one hundred years have we begun to develop the capacity to respond more intelligently and more humanely to acts of dangerousness and destruction. Since the advent of psychoanalysis and psychoanalytic psychotherapy, we now have access to a much deeper understanding both of the aetiology of aggressive acts and of their treatment; and nowadays we need no longer ignore criminals or abuse them—instead, we can provide compassion and containment, as well as conduct research that can help to prevent future acts of violence.

The modern discipline of forensic psychotherapy, which can be defined, quite simply, as the use of psychoanalytically orientated "talking therapy" to treat violent, offender patients, stems directly from the work of Sigmund Freud. Almost one hundred years ago, at a meeting of the Vienna Psycho-Analytical Society, held on 6 February 1907, Sigmund Freud anticipated the clarion call of contemporary forensic psychotherapists when he bemoaned the often horrible treatment of mentally ill offenders, in a discussion on the psychology of vagrancy. According to Otto Rank, Freud's secretary at the time, the founder of psychoanalysis expressed his sorrow at the "nonsensical treatment of these people in prisons" (quoted in Nunberg & Federn, 1962, p. 108).

Many of the early psychoanalysts preoccupied themselves with forensic topics. Hanns Sachs, himself a trained lawyer, and Marie Bonaparte, the French princess who wrote about the cruelty of war, each spoke fiercely against capital punishment. Sachs, one of the first members of Freud's secret committee, regarded the death penalty for offenders as an example of group sadism (Moellenhoff, 1966). Bonaparte, who had studied various murderers throughout her career, had actually lobbied politicians in America to free the convicted killer Caryl Chessman, during his sentence on Death Row at the California State Prison in San Quentin, albeit unsuccessfully (Bertin, 1982).

Melanie Klein concluded her first book, the landmark text *Die Psychoanalyse des Kindes* [*The Psycho-Analysis of Children*], with resounding passion about the problem of violence in our culture. Mrs Klein noted that acts of criminality invariably stem from disturbances in childhood, and that if young people could receive access to psychoanalytic treatment at any early age, then much cruelty could be prevented in later years. Klein expressed the hope that: "If every child who shows disturbances that are at all severe were to be analysed in good time, a great number of these people who later end up in prisons or lunatic asylums, or who go completely to pieces, would be saved from such a fate and be able to develop a normal life" (1932, p. 374).

Shortly after the publication of Klein's transformative book, Atwell Westwick, a Judge of the Superior Court of Santa Barbara, California, published a little-known though highly inspiring article, "Criminology and Psychoanalysis" (1940), in the *Psychoanalytic Quarterly*. Westwick may well be the first judge to commit himself in print to the value of psychoanalysis in the study of criminality, arguing that punishment of the forensic patient remains, in fact, a sheer waste of time. With foresight, Judge Westwick queried, "Can we not, in our well nigh hopeless and overwhelming struggle with the problems of delinquency and crime, profit by medical experience with the problems of health and disease? Will we not, eventually, terminate the senseless policy of sitting idly by until misbehavior occurs, often with irreparable damage, then dumping the delinquent into the juvenile court or reformatory and dumping the criminal into prison?" (p. 281). Westwick noted that we should, instead, train judges, probation officers, social workers, as well as teachers and parents, in the precepts of psychoanalysis, in order to arrive at a more sensitive, non-punitive understanding of the nature of criminality. He opined: "When we shall have succeeded in committing society to such a program, when we see it launched definitely upon the venture, as in time it surely will be-then shall we have erected an appropriate memorial to Sigmund Freud" (p. 281).

In more recent years, the field of forensic psychotherapy has become increasingly well constellated. Building upon the pioneering contributions of such psychoanalysts and psychotherapists as Edward Glover, Grace Pailthorpe, Melitta Schmideberg, and more recently Murray Cox, Mervin Glasser, Ismond Rosen, Estela Welldon, and others too numerous to mention, forensic psychotherapy has now become an increasingly formalized discipline that can be dated to the inauguration of the International Association for Forensic Psychotherapy and to the first annual conference, held at St. Bartholomew's Hospital in London in 1991.

The volumes in this series of books will aim to provide both practical advice and theoretical stimulation for introductory students and for senior practitioners alike. In the Karnac Books Forensic Psychotherapy Monograph Series, we will endeavour to produce a regular stream of high-quality titles, written by leading members of the profession, who will share their expertise in a concise and practice-orientated fashion. We trust that such a collection of books will help to consolidate the knowledge and experience that we have already acquired and will also provide new directions for the future. In this way, we shall hope to plant the seeds for a more rigorous, sturdy, and wide-reaching profession of forensic psychotherapy.

We now have an opportunity for psychotherapeutically orientated forensic mental health professionals to work in close conjunction with child psychologists and with infant mental health specialists so that the problems of violence can be tackled both preventatively and retrospectively. With the growth of the field of forensic psychotherapy, we at last have reason to be hopeful that serious criminality can be forestalled and perhaps, one day, even eradicated.

References

Bertin, C. (1982). *La Dernière Bonaparte*. Paris: Librairie Académique Perrin.

deMause, L. (1974). The evolution of childhood. In: Lloyd deMause (Ed.), *The History of Childhood* (pp. 1–73). New York: Psychohistory Press.

Kahr, B. (1994). The historical foundations of ritual abuse: an excavation of ancient infanticide. In: V. Sinason (Ed.), *Treating Survivors of Satanist Abuse* (pp. 45–56). London: Routledge.

Klein, M. (1932). *The Psycho-Analysis of Children*, A. Strachey (Trans.). London: Hogarth Press and The Institute of Psycho-Analysis (first published as *Die Psychoanalyse des Kindes*. Vienna: Internationaler Psychoanalytischer Verlag).

Moellenhoff, F. (1966). Hanns Sachs, 1881–1947: the creative unconscious. In: F. Alexander, S. Eisenstein & M. Grotjahn (Eds.), *Psychoanalytic Pioneers* (pp. 180–199). New York: Basic Books.

Nunberg, H., & Federn, E. (Eds.) (1962). *Minutes of the Vienna Psychoanalytic Society. Volume I: 1906–1908*, M. Nunberg (Trans.). New York: International Universities Press.

Westwick, A. (1940). Criminology and psychoanalysis. *Psychoanalytic Quarterly, 9*: 269–282.

Brett Kahr
Centre for Child Mental Health, London

FOREWORD

Even at the best of times, adolescence is a time of turmoil. It is a developmental phase distinct from that of childhood and from that of adulthood and is defined by the young person's struggle between dependence and independence, the oscillation between a sense of isolation and the need to be part of a peer group, the turning away from parents, the rapid development of the body and the emergence of sexuality, the increasing awareness of physical prowess, and the more public acknowledgement of intellectual achievement or failure. These are all struggles of both the mind and the body.

Each of these developmental struggles, if successful, leads to maturational gains, but they are also accompanied by losses and the pain that accompanies loss. Winnicott refers to adolescence as a developmental phase which significantly requires a "struggling through the doldrums" with only one cure, he says, "the passage of time" (Winnicott, 1961) and the move into adulthood. The Latin word *adolescere* means "to grow up".

The adolescent process is one fundamentally driven by the complex psychic project of searching for and establishing a personal identity. As Waddell describes it, "one of the main undertakings of adolescence is that of establishing a mind of one's own, a mind which

is rooted in, and yet also distinct from, the sources and models of identification that are visible within one's family, or in the wider school
and community setting" (Waddell, 1998, p. 158).

All of these processes are psychosocial, by which I mean that they
are experienced both internally and externally by the young person,
but also have an impact and meaning for the young person's family
and community. The turmoil of change, experienced by the adolescent
is, to some degree, also experienced by those around him or her.
Parents have to accommodate letting go of their children, often aided
by the young person's rejection of them, adults have to sometimes
enviously witness the newly found sexuality of adolescence, and
parents and the community have to contend with the adolescent's
sometimes rebellious testing out of aggression and potency. As adolescents develop into young adults, they inadvertently remind their
elders of their own ageing and mortality.

So, even at the best of times, the adolescent process has a powerful impact both on the young people themselves and on those around
them.

It is, therefore, not at all surprising that juvenile offending and
especially juvenile sex offending evokes such intense emotions. The
already disturbing turmoil of ordinary adolescents is now writ large
by the impact of delinquent, criminal, and violent enactment.

Inevitably, delinquency, criminality, general violence or sexual
violence—physical acts involving others—affects us all, not only in its
physical outcome, but very often by also arousing strong feelings of
condemnation, anger, fear, disgust, outrage, among others: toxic emotions which disturb our thinking and our responses, and from which
it is often difficult to distance oneself. As Hinshelwood tells us, people
who behave in this way are often described as difficult, but this is
mostly because they arouse difficult feelings in us and, hence, affect
us in our attitudes towards them (Hinshelwood, 1999).

Because of the power of this intrusion and emotional disturbance,
the failure in the capacity to think about the perpetrator often results
in the offender's actions simply being *reacted* to, for example by
condemnation, the quick use of punishment, or physical incarceration.
Sometimes there is an active demonization of the perpetrator.

Of course, the need to manage and control the perpetrators of such
behaviour sometimes might well be required. The author of this book,
however, passionately argues for there to be an emphasis on focusing

on the juvenile offender's internal world. He promotes the view that behavioural management and physical containment, if not accompanied by the application of psychological interventions directed in depth at the young person's internal world, will usually be futile and possibly destructive. At worst, society's concrete reaction to the juvenile offender's actions perpetuates the cycle of mindlessness that is likely to be the root cause of such juvenile offending behaviour.

The lack of benign attachment figures and the resulting lack of psychological and emotional containment results in a failure to develop a mind that can reflect on itself or on others. Bravely, but accurately, the author shows that the controversial concept of psychopathy, which he links to the concept of malignant narcissism, continues to be a useful lens through which to explore violating and violent behaviour, be that more or less overtly sexual.

I write "bravely" because this is now a term that tends to be avoided, but perhaps if one follows the clinical understanding offered by Glover, the term reminds us of the complexity of what we are dealing with. Glover describes how essential it is for the clinician to understand and, more importantly, "to endure the psychopath's assaults on his most cherished possession, namely his capacity to heal. In other words, the prerequisite of any (such) therapy . . . is a capacity to endure repeated disappointments" (Glover, 1960, p. 149). As argued by Stoller, most sexually perverse or sexually violent behaviour is actually "an erotic form of hatred", and its underlying violence has to be taken very seriously (Stoller, 1975), both the violence against the body and also the violation of the capacity to think and reflect. Sexualization is often employed to control the object and their mind so as to protect against fears of core complex anxieties of engulfment or abandonment (Glasser, 1998).

This book is the first in the Karnac Forensic Series that takes up the issue of juvenile sexual offending. The author provides us with many tools with which to examine the internal world of the juvenile offender. Though he comes from a psychoanalytic, object relations perspective, he gives equal emphasis to other parameters, resulting in a text which is a treasure trove of psychoanalytic, clinical, neurobiological, and research-based concepts, well illustrated by clinical examples. With this range of perspectives, each explored in some detail, we are helped to navigate that which might otherwise feel like impossibly stormy and dark waters . . . waters which indeed might be felt to be ". . . inhabited by strangeness, things no one identifies with", as he quotes, at the head of Chapter One, from the American poet, Sheila Murphy.

This is an impressively scholarly and comprehensive text, as well as being clearly written and accessible, and is obviously the product of someone who has a deep appreciation of, and concern for, the subject matter. In addition, although the book presents us with conceptual and clinical thinking relating specifically to the juvenile sex offender, the reader will learn about concepts that are also applicable to the forensic and personality-disordered adult patient. With offending behaviour, disturbing and damaging in its impact, there will always be a tension between the need for physical constraint and punishment and that of seeking meaning in the behaviour and the need to understand its causes and, hence, promote the possibility of development and change. This book is a very serious attempt to help us in that latter task.

Stanley Ruszczynski
Clinical Director, Portman Clinic,
Tavistock and Portman NHS Foundation Trust
Full Member, British Psychoanalytic Association
Full Member, British Association of Psychotherapists

Introduction

This book presents a series of ideas and concepts formulated over the course of more than twenty years of clinical and research experience with juvenile sex offenders. The ideas and concepts I propose stem from a psychoanalytic view of juvenile sexual offending which suggests that it represents, in the broadest sense, a failure to achieve a capacity to love maturely. Juvenile sex offenders are seen as only being capable of a *sexualized* or *violently sexualized* mode of relating to others as a consequence of having *internalized* an inadequate *blueprint or mental representation* of a mature, loving, reciprocal relationship.

The book, therefore, aims to demonstrate how understanding the *internal world* of juvenile sex offenders can inform their assessment and treatment. A focus on the internal world is what distinguishes psychoanalytical approaches to the assessment and treatment of juvenile sex offenders from other contemporary approaches, such as cognitive–behavioural and learning theory models. The particular psychoanalytical view I present is through the lens of their capacity for attachment and "human relatedness", their level of psychopathy (level of detachment), and the associated empirically based correlates of their mental representations of self and others (their "object relations"). In particular (and with reference to my own research), I explain how these provide a view into the emotional experience of juvenile sex offenders, which not only reveals them as a group to be psychologically maladjusted, but also suggests that *there are sub-groups of such offenders who are differentially motivated in their offending* and who need to be treated accordingly.

The central concept in this book, the internal world, is thus psycho-analytical in origin. Psychoanalysis is essentially a method for investigation of the mind, especially the unconscious mind. It explores the underlying motivations of behaviour and provides a method for treating mental disorder. While psychoanalysis originally identified the existence of an unconscious mental life (an internal world), it was with the development of *object relations theory* that the notion of internalized mental representations of the self, and its experience with significant others during infant development, became a particular focus. The central notion in object relations theory is that mental representations operate like a type of "shadow play" and influence our perception and associated behavioural and emotional responses to others (in the external world), that is, they shape our experience. The idea that there is transferability and modifiability of such mental representations, via unconscious processes with others, has been at the heart of the concept of transference in psychoanalysis and accounts for the importance placed on the therapeutic relationship in effecting change in psychoanalytically based treatments.

In terms of the development of these ideas, Freud, in his classic paper "Mourning and melancholia" (1917e), attempted to distinguish normal mourning from the pathological process of melancholia. In doing so, he proposed the idea that the ego could split in order to avoid mental pain and to protect an internal object (mental representation) from being lost. Ogden (2009) noted how, in this paper, "Freud made use of this seemingly focal exploration of these two psychological states (mourning and melancholia) as a vehicle for introducing – as much implicitly as explicitly – the foundation for his theory of internal object relations" (Ogden, 2009, pp. 124–125). The idea that the ego could split and that the split-off parts could have an unconscious relationship with each other paved the way for the elaboration of an object relations theory, which described how the self and its relationships with its objects become psychically represented.

Object relations theory was developed further during the 1940s and 1950s, notably by Fairbairn (1944, 1952), who coined the term, and by Klein (1946). It was a theory that suggested, in departure from Freud's view, that the key motivation for humans was a need for relationship, not primarily a response to instincts (drives). Object relations theorists argue that it is our primary (attachment) relationships, in interaction with unconscious fantasy (referred to as *phantasy*), which primarily influence the development of internalized psychic representations. When developmental conditions are favourable (secure and loving), the development of a positive and secure sense of self and a belief in the value of interdependency in relationships are fostered (Diamond & Blatt, 1994).

Fairbairn (1944) liberated himself from Freud's *Sexualtheorie* (libido theory) and elaborated an *Endo-psychic* structure. Fairbairn explained the complex processes involved in the splitting of the self and its relationships with its objects as part of the development of an autonomous self. Klein (1946), like Fairbairn (1944), built on what Freud had outlined and stressed "object seeking" as a prime motivator in human behaviour, but still acknowledged the importance of instincts and drives. Klein (1957) also articulated the psychic processes (such as projection and splitting), which could both facilitate and retard the growth of the ego.

A central tenet of this book is that an impoverished sense of self and a poor mental representation of relationships with the other are fundamental aetiological factors in juvenile sex offending. Object relations theory explains how the self develops as a result of its experiences with significant others. The self is seen to move from a state of psychic merger with its objects to a gradual differentiation from them. This involves stages in psychological development in which, first, the self is merged with its object, to a stage where difficult to manage aspects of the self are split off and projected into the object of attachment, until a point of later maturity, when all aspects of the self can be integrated, resulting in a relatively autonomous self. In the infant, such development is normally linked to neurological maturation, which gradually facilitates integrated perception and more complex information processing. This development is also dependent upon emotional factors. As such, an emotionally responsive containing environment facilitates development from more primitive modes of ordering experience.

The development of this internal world is not linear, but dynamic, and regression to earlier developmental levels, triggered by stress, can occur. For this reason, object relations theory describes developmental positions rather than stages.

Following the elaboration of the experiences and psychic processes involved in the earliest ("autistic–contiguous") stage of development articulated by Ogden (1989), the developmental progression described can be seen as one encompassing an autistic–contiguous (AC) (Ogden, 1989) through to a "paranoid–schizoid" (PS) (Klein, 1946) and, ultimately, a "depressive" (D) mode of psychic experience (Klein, 1957), each with idiosyncratic (developmental) anxieties. The movement backwards and forwards between positions can be depicted as AC↔PS↔D.

At each level of development, the nature of the anxiety is related to "the experience of disconnectedness (disintegration) within that mode of experience" (Ogden, 1989, p. 138). In the autistic–contiguous position, this involves the disruption of the experience of "sensory cohesion" and "bounded-ness". In the paranoid–schizoid position, it involves the splitting of the self and the object. In the depressive position, it involves the challenge of integrating split feelings (of love and hate) towards the object and the negotiation of "Oedipal anxieties", that is, anxieties connected with the consequence of becoming aware of separateness and "otherness".

In the autistic–contiguous mode, it is the experience of sensation that creates psychological meaning and some basic experience of self. Ogden (1989) noted that the autistic–contiguous position is linked to a mode of attributing meaning to experience in which there are "Presymbolic connections between sensory impressions that come to constitute bounded surfaces. It is on these surfaces that the experience of self has its origins" (Ogden, 1989, p. 139).

He relates this to Freud's notion that "The ego [the 'I'] is first and foremost a bodily ego". The autistic–contiguous state is, thus, essentially an object-less psychic world wherein there is a predominantly psychosomatic sense of self. In the transference relationship, there is no sense of the analyst or therapist as an object.

In contrast, in the paranoid–schizoid position of psychic development, there is an attachment to an object, although the object has to be split in order for psychic balance to be maintained. In normal development, the split occurs in response to the dilemma that attachment to the object evokes *both* loving and hateful feelings, the latter because it is inevitably less than perfect in satisfying the demands of the baby.

In order to deal with this difficulty and the anxieties it generates, the baby splits off the good and bad parts of the object from himself and tries to control this state of affairs by omnipotent functioning. In this regard Klein (1946) noted that:

> The first object *is* being the mother's breast which for the child becomes split into a good (gratifying) and bad (frustrating) breast, which results in a severance of love and hate. [p. 2, my italics]

Crucial to a psychoanalytical understanding of psychopathic juvenile sex offenders is that when hate dominates the internal world, intense efforts are needed to obfuscate the need for others, which can lead, in extreme circumstances, to a detachment from others and a turning *to the self as the object* of attachment (malignant narcissism).

As a person relies less and less on splitting and projection, he can begin to bring together the different aspects of himself: the beginnings of a more integrated or whole self. Persons able to integrate hitherto split-off aspects of themselves can then begin to face the fact that they love and hate the same objects and that there are loving and hating aspects of themselves. In juvenile sex offending, split-off (unwanted) aspects of the self can be projected to the victim.

A capacity for integration is vital to mental health because it in turn enables others to be seen as separate. This is the point in psychic development when *separation and individuation* (developmental milestones most juvenile sex offenders do not achieve) can begin.

This stage of psychic development (in object relations theory terms, the "depressive position") is, however, not without its challenges, as the infant has to deal with the separateness of his objects, which involves an acknowledgement of their relationships (for example, his mother's) with others. This creates further psychological dilemmas and can result in powerful feelings of jealousy and of exclusion from other relationships. The experiences and anxieties associated with this awareness of "otherness" are referred to, in psychoanalytic theory, as "Oedipal anxieties". Resolution of these anxieties results in an increased ability to tolerate a triangular relationship, with its demands to be both included and excluded from the parental couple. This helps to develop a capacity to be aware of another's point of view and thus be able to see oneself from this vertex (Britton, 1989). Thus, it allows for a self-reflective capacity, or what Fonagy (2001) has referred to as "reflective functioning".

Attachment theory, a major lens through which we will view juvenile sex offenders, also emphasizes the relevance of internalized blueprints resulting from our experiences with our primary care-givers, but does so in a somewhat different way to object relations theory. Object relations theorists confer unconscious phantasy with a pre-eminent role in psychic life. In contrast, Bowlby (1969) de-emphasized its role (even though he subscribed to the concept of an unconscious mental life) and stressed the influence of external factors on psychic life.

To formulate attachment theory, Bowlby (1969, 1973) sourced ideas from ethology, the theory of evolution, control theory, and cognitive science. This resulted in a reformulation of psychoanalytic metapsychology in a manner that was more compatible with modern biology and psychology and conformed with the more usual criteria of natural science. Bowlby was criticized by psychoanalysts for emphasizing the role of external factors over internal psychic phantasies. As a theoretical framework, attachment theory was also criticized for not providing an adequate account of sexuality. This perhaps represents a lack of understanding, as Bowlby had made it clear that he saw sexual behaviour as a separate system to attachment behaviour.

Attachment theory, none the less, provided a language for many practitioners who felt uncomfortable with the lack of the usual criteria of natural science inherent in psychoanalytic, including object relations, approaches. Attachment theory consequently produced empirical proof for its theoretical tenets. Heralded by Bowlby's (1959, 1960, 1969) original theoretical ideas and developed by Ainsworth and colleagues (Ainsworth, 1979; Ainsworth, Blehar, Waters, & Wall, 1978), this empirical proof was derived from an experimental paradigm, which provided descriptions of "internal working models". These were descriptions resulting from experimental observations of infants exposed to separation from care-givers, subsequent exposure to strangers, and then reunions with their care-givers. Attachment theorists were able to describe a polarity of secure and insecure attachment in children and subsequently (through a different experimental paradigm) in adults. These internal working models were seen to be akin to the self and object representations described by object relations theory. Bowlby deliberately chose the description internal *working* model, a description he adopted from the philosopher Craik (1943), which implied dynamism and suggested that such working models are modifiable by experience.

Self and object representations in object relations theory are defined as mental structures with both cognitive and affective dimensions, which are influenced by unconscious phantasies and are also seen to develop "epigenetically", that is, with genetically determined potentials shaped by developmental experiences and associated successive differentiation. These cognitive–affective schemas of self and others are continuously developed over the life cycle, via the psychic mechanisms of introjection and projection under the *aegis of unconscious phantasy*. Such mental representations are, thus, seen to comprise conscious *and unconscious* cognitive, affective, and experiential components, which result from significant early interpersonal experiences. Blatt, Auerbach, and Levy (1997) have noted that these cognitive–affective schemas encompass what they refer to as "veridical representations of consensual reality" (p. 351). They are *idiosyncratic constructions* that often contain primitive and pathological distortions resulting in unique psychopathologies.

Whatever the differences between attachment theory and object relations theory in the way they describe the internal world, they can be seen to complement each other. Indeed, theorists such as Fonagy (2001) have explicated the relationship between psychoanalysis and attachment theory and have demonstrated how types of insecure attachment relate to particular configurations of object relations in a manner that makes the two more synchronous. I agree with this view, and consider that perhaps a key difference between attachment theory and object relations theory, in addition to the differences I have already mentioned, is the degree of specificity concerning internalized representations that each provides. The attachment status of an individual might point to the general topography of the internal world of an offender, but to fully understand an individual one needs to drill down into the rich soil of that individual's *unique* object relations. This can be achieved through an understanding of transference and countertransference experiences or, particularly relevant to the research discussed in this book, through the use of empirically based psychodiagnostic instruments such as the Rorschach test, which tap into the mental representations of self and other. In the forensic sphere, this permits a greater understanding of the significance of the victim to the offender and provides a unique means of estimating (psychodynamic) risk factors. Such factors can, together, uncover the "the total situation" of the internal world of an individual offender and its links to his relationships with his victims. These factors and their predictive potential are core themes of this book.

The internal world and the quality and nature of mental representations of juvenile sex offenders as a group are found to be varied and to reveal very different motivations for offending. As such, I propose that an assessment of the developmental quality, level, and uniqueness of the mental representations (object relations) of juvenile sex offenders can be of vital importance in understanding the likely risk and nature of reoffending. Such an approach might enrich current risk assessment strategies (Thornton, 2002), which conceptualize sex offenders as having difficulties in four areas of psychological functioning: self management and regulation, socio-emotional dysfunction, attitudes conducive to sex offending, and deviant sexual arousal.

As a concept, *psychopathy* can also provide a distal lens through which to appreciate the internal world of the juvenile sex offender. Psychopathy is, essentially, a diagnostic description of a set of behaviours and attitudes that are antithetical to a capacity to love and to be concerned for others, but which, in contrast, represents a malevolent view of others and a wish to be detached from them. It is a particularly useful forensic concept because it predicts recidivism and violent behaviour. As discussed in Chapter Five, when understood in terms of attachment theory, it can provide a view into the internal world, which I believe enables a rich forensic understanding of differential motivations for offending. In terms of its direct relevance to the internal world, psychopathy has been shown to be linked to malignant narcissism, which, as a psychic structure, represents a grandiose self without a need for relationship with the "other", apart from one involving manipulation, coercion, and force in order to gratify its own needs.

As concepts, attachment and psychopathy (and associated object relations) are, thus, proposed as good candidates to explain the maladjustment of juvenile sex offenders: a maladjustment that points to a dysfunction of their sense of self and ways of relating to others. These problems, associated with deficits in the "socio-emotional self", have specific neuro-biological underpinnings. Developmental disruption which leads to such difficulties can often occur very early during "critical periods" in development, especially during the rapid development of the right hemisphere of the brain in the first twenty-four months of life (Schore, 2005). This significantly affects the psychological and neurological integration necessary for the formation of the "agentive-self". Neural plasticity suggests the possible bi-directionality of the influence of experience and neurobiology, with significant implications for psychotherapeutic interventions that might focus on the modification of the psychic representation of self and relationships (Doidge, 2007).

Related to these findings, I advocate not only for a careful assessment of such deficits, but also for intensive psychoanalytically based interventions, particularly mentalization based therapy (MBT) for juvenile sex offenders who are at high risk of becoming recidivist adult sex offenders. This is because such treatments aim to develop mental representations of self and other (relationships) which are conducive to secure attachment, an increased capacity to form mature reciprocal relationships and a greater "agentive" or "socio-emotional" self. The implicit epigenetic view of mental representation sits well with the underpinning theory and philosophy of MBT, behind which is the accepted importance of an "agentive" or "psychological" self whereby "mental agency may be usefully seen as a developing or constructed capacity" (Fonagy, Gergely, Jurist, & Target, 2004, p. 4), rather than simply a genetic given.

The argument concerning the value of understanding the "internal world" of the juvenile sex offender is developed by a detailed consideration of the characteristics and underpinning psychodynamics of this group of offenders and their offences. I have organized our forensic investigation into four parts. In Part I, the forensic focus is identified and the juvenile sex offender and his clinical characteristics are examined.

In Chapter One, I describe the nature and extent of the problem of juvenile sex offending, pointing to its serious and pervasive nature and the early age at which juvenile sex offenders embark on their path of offending, as well as the extent of the pain and suffering which their offending causes. I also draw attention to the cost effectiveness of early and intensive interventions, given the long-term and costly sequelae of sexual assault.

Chapter Two subsequently reviews the personality and other characteristics of juvenile sex offenders. *They are shown to represent a heterogeneous group of offenders* who present as psychologically disturbed and maladjusted. I propose that these differences can be related to varying levels of insecure attachment and psychopathy (detachment).

In Part II of the book, I describe each lens through which the internal world of the juvenile sex offender can be viewed.

Chapter Three discusses juvenile sex offending in relation to attachment theory. In particular, the relevance of attachment theory to adolescent development is examined, along with the nature of the relationship between attachment and sexuality and sexual offending. In reviewing the research about the attachment status of sex offenders, I argue that a sub-set of juvenile sex offenders appears to manifest a contempt for attachment and attempts to obfuscate the need for it, while others seem to exhibit what has been described as an "attachment hunger".

In Chapter Four, I explore the relevance of the concept of psychopathy to the internal world of the juvenile sex offenders. Specifically, I argue a case for the assessment of psychopathy in juvenile sex offenders, as there is clear evidence of the existence of a sub-set of juvenile offenders (who are hostile towards others and deny their need for relationship) who offend against a background of other non-sexual offences.

Chapter Five examines the nature of the object relations driving psychopathy by linking it to the concept of malignant narcissism as a psychic structure or state of mind underpinning it. The relevance of malignant narcissism to the type of intervention and the clinical issues that need to be addressed in treatment is a particular focus of this chapter. A case vignette is presented to illustrate these ideas. Such psychopathology appears to be linked to the nature of the sexual perversion inherent in this type of offending. Consequently, the chapter concludes by examining the nature of sexual perversion and by providing a brief overview of the psychoanalytical conceptualizations of this pathology.

In Chapter Six, I consider the concept of "epigenetics" and provide an overview of the neurobiology of attachment and sexual behaviour. I describe how neurobiological (genetic) potential can be developmentally influenced. The concept of the social brain and the significance of the limbic system (and its biochemistry) to juvenile sex offending are considered. I also discuss findings concerning specific neurotransmitters/neurohormones underpinning sexual and attachment behaviour and draw some conclusions about their possible relevance to sub-groups of juvenile sex offenders that I identified in my own research. Some evidence concerning the potentially positive impact of psychological interventions on neurobiological functioning (and evidence of neuroplasticity) is also considered.

In Part III, I present the findings of my own research into this group of offenders using measures of psychopathology, capacity for attachment, interest in relationship (correlates of their internal world), and psychopathy.

Chapter Seven describes the nature and scope of the research and its key findings, and in Chapter Eight, I discuss how the findings highlight the nature of the attachment needs and levels of psychopathy among juvenile sex offenders and their link to offence type and the related differential motivations for offending. The findings suggest at least two sub-sets of juvenile sex offenders who can be identified on the basis of these indices.

Part IV considers the implication for practice, and the application of the understandings from the findings in the literature and from my own research about the internal world of juvenile sex offenders.

In Chapter Nine, I discuss the assessment of juvenile sex offenders. I review the issue of risk assessment and recommend a battery of psycho-diagnostic instruments that can address the attachment and psychopathy status of the offender. This battery is proposed as a means of differentiating juvenile sex offenders and assessing the risk of their reoffending. I also propose the concept of a "real time" risk assessment, which involves the assessment of *psycho*-dynamic risk factors. The issue of suitability for treatment is also addressed.

In Chapter Ten, I describe two case examples of juvenile sex offenders in order to illustrate the relevance of the internal world to their assessment and treatment. The cases highlight the differential nature of the underpinning object relations and related motivations, as discussed in Chapter Eight. In Chapter Eleven, I then examine the possible utility of MBT and other psychoanalytic treatments of juvenile sex offenders and consider the evidence and the case for the use of such interventions with juvenile sex offenders.

In the Epilogue, I consider the future directions for juvenile sex offender research and treatment. I underline the implications of the increased database concerning juvenile sex offenders, which highlight the underpinning motivations associated with different types of juvenile sex offending.

I hope the new conceptualization of the problem of juvenile sex offending presented in this book will improve the understanding and treatment of this very disturbed group of young people, many of whom are themselves victims of sexual and other abuse and help address this serious, costly, and distressing societal problem.

PART I
THE FORENSIC FOCUS

CHAPTER ONE

The nature of juvenile
sex offending

"Navigating quiet worlds inhabited by strangeness
Things no one identifies with"

(Murphy, 1996, p. 313)

Juvenile sex offending is an issue of major public concern, yet currently little is understood about its origins. In particular, there is a very limited understanding of the motivations and the internal world of the offender. The serious nature of juvenile sex offending has, however, led to a re-examination of previously held views and an urgency to know more about its causes and methods of prevention (Barbaree, Hudson, & Seto, 1993; Becker, Harris, & Sales, 1993; Lakey, 1992; Ryan, Miyoshi, Metzner, Krugman, & Fryer, 1996; Seto & Lalumière, 2010; Sickmund, Snyder, & Poe-Yamagata, 1997). Previously, the significance of juvenile sex offending has been minimized, with offenders often regarded as sexually curious, or engaged in sexual experimentation associated with their emergent sexuality (Davis & Leitenberg, 1987; Lakey, 1994; Quinn, 1992). The behaviour was often naïvely viewed as self-limiting with age and maturity (Barbaree, Hudson, & Seto, 1993; Finklehor, 1979), with offences committed by juveniles considered unlikely to be serious in nature (Becker & Able, 1985; Groth, 1977). Stereotyped social attitudes have also supported such perceptions (Anderson, Simpson-Taylor, & Herrmann, 2004). Subsequently, evidence has challenged these views and highlighted the simplicity of such accounts and the need for further research into the complex motivations of juvenile sex offenders (Anderson, Simpson-Taylor, & Herrmann, 2004; Davis & Leitenberg, 1987; Dolan, Holloway, Bailey, & Kroll, 1996; Kenny, Keogh, & Seidler, 2001; Kenny, Keogh, Seidler, & Blaszczynski, 2000; Seto & Lalumière, 2010; Snyder & Sickmund, 1995).

Pervading the research is confusion about the definition of juvenile sex offending internationally (Vizard, Monck, & Mirsch, 1995). There are also many variations in the nomenclature used to describe sub-groups of sex offenders. Sexual offending is usually defined as non-consensual sexual behaviour involving another person and encompassing force and/or manipulation (Ryan, Leversee, & Lane, 2010; Vizard, Monck, & Mirsch, 1995). It is often categorized according to the nature of the sexual activity (e.g., sodomy) and the degree of direct physical contact (e.g., molestation *vs.* rape) with a victim (Burton, Miller, & Shill, 2002). Sex offender behaviour frequently incorporates features of sexual disorders, especially paraphilias (Hilton & Mezey, 1996; Kenny, Keogh, Seidler & Blaszczynski, 2000). Different offence sub-types have been identified (Burton, Miller, & Shill, 2002; Graves, Openshaw, Ascione, & Ericksen, 1996; Herkov, Gynther, Thomas, & Myers, 1996; Kenny, Keogh, & Seidler, 2001; Knight & Prentky, 1993; Snyder & Sickmund, 1995) with a trend towards typologizing juvenile sex offenders. One of the most popular typologies is based on victim age and nature of the sexual behaviour involved in the offence (e.g., rapists with peer-aged or adult victims or child victims). Other authors (O'Brien & Bera, 1986; Sinourd, Hoge, Andrews, & Leschied, 1994) have utilized typologies based on the extent of previous offending (i.e., the extent of antisocial behaviour) and personality characteristics.

Notwithstanding these considerations, and despite indications that juvenile sex offenders are a heterogeneous group in terms of their clinical characteristics (Seto & Lalumière, 2010; Worling, 1995), much of the literature and many approaches to treatment regard them as a homogeneous group by not acknowledging apparent sub-group differences.

The extent and nature of juvenile sex offending

In the past fifteen to twenty years, the incidence and recidivism rates of juvenile sex offending has shown little sign of levelling or declining (Belanger & Earls, 1996; Brannon & Troyer, 1995; Dolan, Holloway, Bailey, & Kroll, 1996; Flatley, Kershaw, Smith, Chaplin, & Moon, 2010; Hagan, King, & Patros, 1994; Hunter, 2000; Långström & Grann, 2000; Ryan, 1997; Ryan, Leversee, & Lane, 2010; Sniffen, 2009; Snyder, Sickmund, & Poe-Yamagata, 1996; Tjaden & Thoennes, 2000). The National Violence Against Women Survey (Rosen, Fontaine, Gaskin-Lanlyan, Price, & Bachar, 2009) found that 13.5% of women and 5% of men in a US sample are sexually abused at some stage during their life. Eighty to ninety per cent of the victims are young women, a large proportion of these children (Lamont, 2011; Sniffen, 2009), with 83% of victims being less than twenty-four years of age. Juvenile sex offenders are responsible for up to half of all sex offences against children (Deisher, Wenet, Paperny, Clark, & Fehrenbach, 1982; Hunter & Figueredo, 2000; Sniffen, 2009) and 20% of all forcible rapes against peer aged or older victims (Snyder & Sickmund, 1995; Truscott, 1993).

Added to the serious and extensive nature of juvenile sex offending, there is a significant under-reporting of sexual assault, especially in cases of child sexual abuse (Groth, 1982; Sniffen, 2009). This might be due to fear and intimidation of victims. Also, despite the number of reports of sexual abuse of children, the actual conviction rates for such offences are still very low (Burton, Miller, & Shill, 2002; Finkelhor, 1979, 1984). This is important, as the majority of adult sex offenders begin offending sexually or demonstrating deviant sexual interest during adolescence and can continue in an unremitting way (Abel, Mittleman, & Becker, 1985; Långström & Grann, 2000; Valliant & Antonowicz, 1992). Thus, although adults commit many of these offences, juvenile sex offenders are responsible for a significant proportion of such offences, highlighting the significance and importance of identifying and treating the juvenile offenders appropriately.

Sex offending can also begin earlier than adolescence, with rates of child molestation by other children under the age of thirteen years accounting for between 13% and 18% of all childhood sexual abuse cases and 11% of all forcible rape charges (Butts & Snyder, 1997; Gray, Pithers, Busconi, & Houchens, 1999).

The impact of juvenile sex offending

Although sexual violation of children and adults (especially women) has occurred throughout history, the articulation of its impact is a more recent phenomenon (Clum, Calhoun, & Kimerly, 2000; Dallam et al., 2001; Ellis, 2002).

The significance of these rates of sexual abuse becomes apparent when the effect this abuse has on its victims is considered. Sexual abuse sequelae for women include somatic symptoms, medical problems, and psychiatric diagnoses (especially depression, anxiety, post traumatic stress disorder, and borderline personality disorder) (Asmussen, 2010; Dickinson, deGruy, Dickinson, & Candib, 1999; Rosen, Fontaine, Gaskin-Lanlyan, Price, & Bachar, 2009), as well as difficulties in performing the roles of wife, mother, and income earner (Finklehor, 1984). More than three out of four men and women who have been abused meet the criteria for a lifetime disorder of mood, anxiety, or substance abuse (Molnar, Bukar, & Kessler, 2001). For many victims of sexual abuse, the development of dysfunctional behaviour reduces their capacity to become part of the workforce. These data thus highlight the economic and emotional impact of sex offending.

Sexual abuse of children can have other, serious traumatic effects. For example, sexual abuse can result in raised levels of cortisol in the brains of children and infants, retarding the development of the brain and nervous system, which are still mylenating (Glaser, 2000; Meany, 2001). This might subsequently reduce the child's capacity for psychological adjustment (King, Mandansky, King, Fletcher, & Brewer, 2001).

Children who are sexually abused are also more likely to be subsequently arrested themselves for sexual assault. Specifically, they are five times more likely to sexually abuse a stranger and are eight times more likely to sexually abuse a family member (Dutton & Hart, 1992; Widom, 1989). Reports show that 40% of juvenile sex offenders have histories of being victims of sexual abuse (Cooper, Murphy, & Haynes, 1996; Hunter & Figuerado, 2000; Kenny, Keogh, Seidler, & Blaszczynski, 2000; Ryan, Miyoshi, Metzner, Krugman, & Fryer, 1996; Worling, 1995).

The costs associated with the incarceration and supervision of juvenile sex offenders are sobering (Lotke, 1996; Miller, Fisher, & Cohen, 2001). For example, the average cost of incarcerating an offender is approximately $US22,000 per year (excluding treatment costs), while the cost of community based supervision can be up to

$US15,000 per year. These costs do not include the costs of adjudication, which have been estimated to be as high as $US180,000 per offender (Marshall, 1996). The extent and nature of such costs prompt governments to develop strategies to prevent juvenile sex offending and to increase the sanctions and legal consequences of sexual abuse against others. These data vindicate the need to better understand juvenile sex offenders, given the seriousness and extensiveness of their offending, the misery that it causes their victims, and the costs of their offending to society.

Despite the increasing number of studies that describe juvenile sex offenders and their offences, until recently there has been scant understanding of the aetiology and the motivations underpinning juvenile sex offending (Cooper, Murphy, & Haynes, 1996; Kenny, Keogh, & Seidler, 2001). Overall, there have been few comparative studies which have identified the unique characteristics of such offenders or have incorporated a range of self-report, projective and collateral data (Keogh & Hayes, 2003). Research has been plagued with methodological problems, notably small clinical samples, which have hampered the development of an empirically based, aetiological framework from which to view juvenile sex offending.

Notwithstanding this, recent research and an emerging clinical profile of juvenile sex offenders indicate that some of these offenders show poor, yet variable, capacity for attachment and differential levels of psychopathy (Awad & Saunders, 1991; Cooper, Murphy, & Haynes, 1996; Goodrow & Lim, 1998; Kenny, Keogh, Seidler, & Blaszczynski, 2000; Kobayashi, Sales, Becker, & Figuerado, 1995; Marshall, Hudson, & Hodkinson, 1993). Specifically, significant numbers of these offenders offend following a history of antisocial behaviour, which suggests that psychopathy might be strongly linked to sex offending in a sub-group of offenders (e.g. Ford & Linney, 1995; Gregory, 1998). While psychopathy is usually associated with low levels of empathy and concern for victims, some juvenile sex offenders, in contrast, appear not to display such characteristics, but manifest other pathology, suggestive of difficulties negotiating relationships in a satisfactory way (Ward, Hudson, & Marshall, 1996).

Capacity for attachment and level of psychopathy seem to be potentially helpful constructs in understanding and differentiating sub-groups of juvenile sex offenders, as well as providing data concerning the likely nature of their internal (intrapsychic) worlds.

Psychopathy and capacity for attachment also appear to be related (Crittenden, 1997a) and might together contribute to understanding sub-groups of juvenile sex offenders who display unique personality characteristics (Gacono & Meloy, 1994; Kenny, Keogh, & Seidler, 2001).

Although there has previously been little or no research targeting attachment, scant research regarding the relevance of psychopathy, and no research examining an association between these factors in a juvenile sex offender population (Goodrow & Lim, 1998; Leguizamo, 2000; Loving & Russell, 2000; Marshall, 1993), new research suggests their connection and relevance (Keogh & Hayes, 2003).

There has been a limited amount of research that has identified the salience of attachment in the area of adult sex offending (Kear-Colwell & Sawle, 2001; Ward, Hudson, & Marshall, 1996). Taken together, these other reports further support important links among attachment, psychopathy, and juvenile sex offending, with an implication that these variables could be used to inform early intervention and prevention strategies and ensure that juvenile sex offenders are appropriately assessed, adjudicated, and treated.

To appreciate more fully the motivations and behaviour of juvenile sex offenders and their probable links to these constructs, it is important to look more closely at their characteristics and differences.

CHAPTER TWO

The characteristics and differences of juvenile sex offenders

"Knowledge becomes evil if the aim be not virtuous"

(Plato, 427 BC, cited in Wall, 2011, p. 247)

Juvenile sex offenders as a group have generally been shown to have significant psychopathology that is different from that of non-sexual offenders (Seto & Lalumière, 2010). They also appear to be different psychologically from other non-offending adolescents (Dolan, Holloway, Bailey, & Kroll, 1996; Kenny, Keogh, & Seidler, 2001; Kenny, Keogh, Seidler, & Blaszczynski 2000; Keogh & Hayes, 2003; van Wijk et al., 2006), although they may present as similar to other adolescents, often appearing like "the boy (or girl) next door" in many other respects. As a group, they also exhibit heterogeneity in terms of their psychopathology, which appears to account for differences in their sexual offence types.

Characteristics of juvenile sex offenders

Juvenile sex offenders have been found to be predominantly male, despite an increase in the number of female sex offenders (Burton,

Miller, & Shill, 2002), with the typical offender being fourteen years old and offending against children who are female and seven years of age (Dolan, Holloway, Bailey, & Kroll, 1996; Kenny, Keogh, Seidler, & Blaszczynski, 2000). Although Afro-American and Hispanic offenders are over-represented in US samples (Davis & Leitenberg, 1987; Hsu & Starzynski, 1990; Vinogradov, Dishotsky, Doty, & Tinklenberg, 1988), juvenile sex offenders in other western cultures, including the UK and Australia, have been found to be from Anglo-Celtic and European backgrounds (Dolan, Holloway, Bailey, & Kroll, 1996; Kenny, Keogh, Seidler, & Blaszczynski, 2000; Manocha & Mezey, 1998; van Wijk, van Horn, Bullens, Bijleveld, & Doreleijers, 2005).

Developmental difficulties are common among this group of offenders, with up to 30% of them having delayed developmental milestones (Dolan, Holloway, Bailey, & Kroll, 1996; Kenny, Keogh, Seidler, & Blaszczynski 2000). Their families typically exhibit dysfunction, especially extensive drug and alcohol abuse (Graves, Openshaw, Ascione, & Ericksen, 1996; Kenny, Keogh, Seidler, & Blaszczynski, 2000; Seidman, Marshall, Hudson, & Robertson, 1994), domestic violence, and frank sexual aggression (Epps, 2000; Kobayashi, Sales, Becker, & Figuerado, 1995; Ryan, Miyoshi, Metzner, Krugman, & Fryer, 1996; Zakireh, Ronis, & Knight, 2008). Such offenders have also been found to be commonly exposed to sexual coercion within their families (Seidman, Marshall, Hudson, & Robertson, 1994; Leguizamo, 2000; Zakireh, Ronis, & Knight, 2008; Zgourides, Monto, & Harris, 1997).

Many juvenile sex offenders often have had close relatives who are offenders and are consequently often exposed to sexually abusive attitudes and values demonstrated by family members, who themselves often exhibit a range of sexual deviance (Awad & Saunders, 1991; Daleiden, Kaufman, Hilliker, & O'Neil, 1998; Kahn & Lafond, 1988; Kobayashi, Sales, Becker, & Figuerado, 1995; Krauth, 1997). There is also an over-representation of adoptees among juvenile sex offenders (Ryan, 1997) and up to two-thirds of such offenders have spent time in care (Dolan, Holloway, Bailey, & Kroll, 1996; Keogh et al., 2004), experiences that are associated with disruption to attachment.

As a group, these offenders also under-achieve at school, with high rates of school behaviour and learning problems (Awad & Saunders, 1991; van Wijk, van Horn, Bullens, Bijleveld, & Doreleijers, 2005), which include significant deficits in reading, mathematics performance

(Lewis, Shanock, & Pincus, 1981), language and speech (Epps, 2000; Davis & Leitenberg, 1987; Fehrenbach, Smith, Monastersky, & Deisher, 1986; Ford & Linney, 1995; Kenny, Keogh, Seidler, & Blaszczynski, 2000; Lakey, 1994; Vizard, Monck, & Mirsch, 1995). Juvenile sex offenders have also been found to be arrested in their moral development and to resort to a preconventional level of moral reasoning to account for their offending behaviour (Ashkar & Kenny, 2006).

In terms of the developmental histories of these offenders, a number of authors have pointed to the prevalence of many serious developmental and family risk factors, many of which are known to contribute to impaired capacity for attachment (Atkinson & Zucker-mann, 1997; Kenny, Keogh, & Seidler, 2001; van Wijk, van Horn, Bullens, Bijleveld, & Doreleijers, 2005). Notwithstanding this, there is much variability in their experiences of sexual abuse, physical abuse, and neglect (Seto & Lalumière, 2010).

Although some research findings reveal that these offenders are not characterized by significant psychopathology or psychological adjustment difficulties (Dalton, 1996), most research finds clear evidence of such problems (Aljazireh, 1993; Kavoussi, Kaplan, & Becker, 1988; Lakey, 1992; Reid & Gacono, 2000; Seto & Lalumière, 2010; van Wijk, van Horn, Bullens, Bijleveld, & Doreleijers, 2005).

The documented psychopathology of juvenile sex offenders, however, represents an unlikely amalgam of features, which suggests that they are not all alike in terms of their personality and psycho-pathology (O'Callaghan & Print, 1995). Some profiling studies have revealed problematic peer-age interactions related to social anxiety, social withdrawal, social isolation (Awad & Saunders, 1991; Fehren-bach, Smith, Monastersky, & Deisher, 1986; Groth, 1977; Groth & Loredo, 1981; Miner & Dwyer, 1997), a preoccupation with self, and an obsessive self-absorption (Smith, Monastersky, & Deisher, 1987; Lakey, 1994; Kenny, Keogh, Seidler, & Blaszczynski, 2000).

Some of these offenders have also been shown to have neurotic concerns and to be self-belittling, display a weak self-image, and to have dependent, schizoid, and avoidant traits (Carpenter, Peed, & Eastman, 1995; Katz, 1990; van Wijk, Blokland, Duits, Vermeiren, & Harkink, 2007). Such offenders, when stressed, appear to retreat into comforting deviant sexual fantasies, which become substitutes for negotiating peer-aged relationships (Cortoni & Marshall, 1998; Groth & Loredo, 1981; Ryan, Leversee, & Lane, 2010). In contrast, other studies have revealed juvenile sex offenders to have fewer neurotic problems, but more antisocial behaviour and conduct disorders, such as reduced capacity for remorse or empathy compared with non-sex offenders (Bengis, 1997; Krauth, 1997; Lindsey, Carlozzi, & Ellis, 2001; Ness, 2001). Delinquent behaviour is common among a significant sub-group of juvenile sex offenders (Saunders, Awad, & White, 1986), with up to 50% having prior charges of other non-sexual offences (Becker, Cunningham-Rathner, & Kaplan, 1986; Becker, Kaplan, Cunningham-Rathner, & Kavoussi, 1986; Fehrenbach, Smith, Monastersky, & Deisher, 1986; Hanson & Bussière, 1998; Ness, 2001). Such conduct-disordered adolescents usually display a pseudo-confidence and self-esteem not evident in adolescents who have more neurotic concerns (Crittenden, 1997b).

Personality differences

Most comparisons of juvenile sex offenders have been made on the basis of their personality dimensions and find considerable psycho-pathology among them compared to other offenders, with the juvenile sex offenders also demonstrating considerable within-group personality trait differences (Herkov, Gynther, Thomas, & Myers, 1996; Smith, Gacono, & Kaufman, 1987; Valliant & Bergeron, 1997). A number of authors identified differences among juvenile sex offenders, noting in particular differences between those who have offended against children and those who had peer-aged or older victims (e.g., Awad & Saunders, 1991; Worling, 1995). Profiling studies identify within-group differences, depicting one group of juvenile sex offenders as being typified by social ineptness, isolation, and extensive psychopathology (Aljazireh, 1993; Kenny, Keogh, & Seidler, 2001; Seto & Lalumière, 2010), with another shown to offend against a background of antisocial behaviour (Dolan, Holloway, Bailey, & Kroll, 1996; Groth, 1977). Those who offended against children were much more likely to be socially isolated, immature, and to have awkward relationships with their peers (Awad & Saunders, 1991).

Overall, rapists and sodomists have been found to reveal more psychopathology when compared with child molesters (Herkov, Gynther, Thomas, & Myers, 1996), revealing the salience of conduct problems and delinquency among a significant number of these offenders

(Losada-Paisey, 1998). Other studies have found juvenile sex offenders overall to be more aggressive and impulsive than non-offending adolescents (Belcher, 1995; Csersevits, 2000; Leguizamo, 2000). Looked at more closely, however, those with peer-aged or older victims appear to be more antisocial and involved in more violent crimes than those with child victims (Cohan, 1998; Hughes, DeVille, Chalhoub, & Romboletti, 1992). When rapists are compared with child molesters, the former have been found to have peers who are aggressive and have characteristics similar to violent offenders (Ford & Linney, 1995; Hastings, Anderson, & Hemphill, 1997; Jacobs, Kennedy, & Mayer, 1997; Worling, 1995).

Overall, there are significant differences in the findings concerning the personality characteristics and psychological adjustment problems of juvenile sex offenders when sub-groups of these offenders are defined on the basis of the ages of their victims.

Alcohol and drug use

The fact that a significant number of these offenders manifest delinquent and antisocial problems suggests that they might also have alcohol and other drug use problems, since alcohol and drug abuse are strongly correlated with the development of antisocial behaviour and psychopathy (Hare, 1998a). This, in fact, turns out to be the case, with up to 33% of samples having problematic use of alcohol, cannabis, and solvents (Dolan, Holloway, Bailey, & Kroll, 1996; Kenny, Keogh, & Seidler, 2001; Langevin & Lang, 1990; van Wijk, Blokland, Duits, Vermeiren, & Harkink, 2007). Poly-drug use is involved in 23% of cases, alcohol alone in 18% of cases, and marijuana in 8% of juvenile sex offence cases (van Wijk, Blokland, Duits, Vermeiren, & Harkink, 2007; Vinogradov, Dishotsky, Doty, & Tinklenberg, 1988).

Among adolescents who rape adult or peer-aged victims, half have been shown to use alcohol and other drugs prior to committing the offences, while only a quarter of those offending against children do so (Kahn & Chambers, 1991; Miner, Siekert, & Ackland, 1997; Vinogradov, Dishotsky, Doty, & Tinklenberg, 1988). Moreover, in juvenile sex offenders who display coercive sexual behaviour, hyper-masculinity, and misogynist fantasy behaviour, alcohol abuse plays a key role in their offending (Johnson & Knight, 2000).

Such data not only suggest heterogeneity among the groups, but have indicated that the nature of the offences might link to different levels of psychopathy, since offenders whose problematic drug and alcohol use starts in adolescence often have developmental pathways that lead to antisocial personalities and psychopathy (Keogh, 2002). Other studies have implicated insecure attachment in the development of drug and alcohol problems (Sperling & Berman, 1994).

Corroborative research with adult sex offenders reveals that they are more likely than non-sexual adult violent offenders to abuse alcohol, although the proportion of adult sex offenders who meet the diagnostic criteria for substance abuse disorder is unclear (Abracen, Looman, & Anderson, 2000).

Experience of abuse among juvenile sex offenders

The extent of abuse in backgrounds might be of importance in understanding any heterogeneity among juvenile sex offenders, since abuse is not only disruptive to attachment, but also appears to lead to differential effects on capacity for attachment.

The rate of physical abuse and neglect is greater among juvenile sex offenders than non-violent offenders (Fehrenbach, Smith, Monastersky, & Deisher, 1986; Knight & Prentky, 1993). Overall, although the rate of physical abuse among these offenders as victims has been shown to exceed the base rate of child maltreatment in the general population, the rates of physical abuse do not distinguish them from violent juvenile offenders. Estimates of maltreatment rates in their backgrounds are also high, ranging from 40% to 90% (Aljazireh, 1993; Burton, Miller, & Shill, 2002; Caputo, Frick, & Brodsky, 1999; Jonson-Reid & Way, 2001; Ryan, 1997; Van Ness, 1984; Zakireh, Ronis, & Knight, 2008), although child molesters are not significantly different from other aggressive non-sexual offenders in this regard (Benoit & Kennedy, 1992). Aggression and antisocial behaviour, which have been shown to be linked with disorganized attachment and experiences of physical abuse in children (Lyons-Ruth, 1996), have also been shown to be more common among rapists (Goldberg, Gotowiec, & Simmons, 1995; Hubbs-Tait et al., 1996; Lyons-Ruth, 1996; Moss, Rousseau, Parent, St. Laurent, & Saintong, 1998; Richardson, Graham, Bhate, & Kelly, 1996; Shaw, Owens, Vondra, Keenan, & Winslow, 1996).

Research with adult sex offenders suggests that child molesters are more likely to have experienced physical abuse, with rapists more likely to have been victims of neglect (Knight & Prentky, 1993). Adult sex offenders frequently report psychological abuse and experience more sexual and physical abuse than violent offenders (Haapasalo & Kankkonen, 1997). Abuse, both physical and sexual, is highly disruptive to attachment and bonding, the impact being linked to the type of abuse, its chronicity, and timing (Fonagy, 2001).

Evidence concerning the sequelae of abuse among this group of offenders specifically implicates disrupted attachment, possibly related to sub-types of juvenile sex offending (Kenny, Keogh, & Seidler, 2001). The evidence concerning abuse also suggests the value of differentiating between child molesters and those offending against same- or older-aged victims.

A history of sexual abuse is one of the most salient distinguishing characteristics of juvenile sex offenders (Etherington, 1993; Hastings, Anderson, & Hemphill, 1997; Hunter, 2000; Murphy, Haynes, & Page, 1992; Veneziano, Veneziano, LeGrand, & Richards, 2004). Estimates of the rates of sexual abuse in their backgrounds vary from 23% to 81% (Becker, Kaplan, Cunningham-Rathner, & Kavoussi, 1986; Freidrich & Lueke, 1988; Zakireh, Ronis, & Knight, 2008). The prevalence of sexual abuse reported at the time of an initial assessment appears to be lower than when reported over a longer period in a therapeutic relationship (Burgess, Hartman, McCormack, & Grant, 1988; Finkelhor & Dziuba-Leatherman, 1994; Longo, 1982). These offenders seem to have difficulties acknowledging their abuse because they tend to normalize their abusive sexual experiences and behaviour (Ryan, Miyoshi, Metzner, Krugman, & Fryer, 1996).

Sixty per cent of child sex offenders and 30% of rapists who commence their offending in adolescence report having experienced sexual abuse as children (Katz, 1990; Knight & Prentky, 1993). In support of the importance of examining sub-groups of such offenders, data from adult sex offender research goes further and shows that adult paedophilic offenders report multiple sexual abuse experiences and experiences of physical abuse as children (Bagley, Wood, & Young, 1994). Adult child molesters charged with sexually coercive offences as adolescents are more likely to have been sexually abused only as children (Worling, 1995). A lower rate of sexual abuse has been found in the backgrounds of rapists compared to child molesters (Seghorn,

Prentky, & Boucher, 1987; Tingle, Barnard, Robbins, Newman, & Hutchinson, 1986). This once again suggests a significant difference in the nature of internalized representations of self and other.

Sexual abuse and paedophilia

Differences were found in the developmental backgrounds of juvenile sex offenders, highlighting that those offending against children were more likely to be victims of sexual abuse (Awad & Saunders, 1991).

A history of childhood sexual abuse thus seems linked with subsequent offending against children (Fehrenbach, Smith, Monastersky, & Deisher, 1986; Murphy, Haynes, & Page, 1994; Burton, Miller, & Shill, 2002; Leguizamo, 2000; Hunter & Figueredo, 2000; Zakireh, Ronis, & Knight, 2008), although it is not necessarily causal, given that the majority of children who are sexually abused (88%) do not become sexually abusive towards children (Skuse, et al., 1998). Sexual abuse is known to have an impact on attachment in unique ways, so these data suggest that child molesters might have their attachment disrupted in different ways to rapists.

Factors such as the age at which the victims experience their sexual abuse, the frequency with which the abuse occurs, the time delay prior to reporting it, and lower levels of perceived support from families contribute to the likelihood of future sexual perpetration by the victim (Hunter & Figueredo, 2000). The fact that a history of sexual victimization and subsequent sex offending by a victim are linked none the less adds weight to a developmental theory of sexual offending (Burton, 2000).

In summary, juvenile sex offenders report more experiences of various types of abuse than the general population and child molesters report greater sexual abuse experiences than rapists (Cooper, Murphy, & Haynes, 1996; Worling, 1995). Rapists report more experiences of neglect and maltreatment than of sexual abuse. Related to this, it appears that some child molesters experience disruption to attachment that results in them becoming ambivalent (and some fearful) about attachment, while rapists are more likely to report experiences which are conducive to the development of detachment and psychopathy.

The relevance of psychological differences among sex offenders

The findings concerning the heterogeneity of psychological character-istics among juvenile sex offenders support the idea expressed of the need to examine their sub-groups separately, especially on the basis of the age of their victims. The notion that there is a heterogeneity of offender characteristics, apparently related to the age of victims, has been noted for some time (e.g Worling, 1995), with data continuing to support this notion (Seto & Lalumière, 2010).

The review of the literature reveals that some of these offenders display characteristics that are commonly found in psychopathic offenders, while others present with sexual and social immaturity and inadequacy. For example, conduct problems, which predict later psychopathic behaviour, are common among juvenile sex offenders, especially in those with peer-aged or older victims, who exhibit a lack of empathy and interest in relationships (Christian, Frick, Hill, Tyler, & Frazer, 1997; Spaccarelli, Bowden, Coatsworth, & Klim, 1997). In contrast, other juvenile sex offenders are characterized as a group as being socially isolated loners; when within-group differences are examined, it is the child molesters who manifest these characteristics most strongly (Kenny, Keogh, & Seidler, 2001; Schram, Milloy, & Rowe, 1991). In fact, child molesters tend to be passive, socially imma-ture, and unusually dependent, as well as having difficulties in estab-lishing same-age peer relationships (Gal & Hoge, 1999; Worling, 1995). This group, however, is very interested in *relating* to their victims, and imagine a relationship with them. This suggests they have very differ-ent attachment needs to the more psychopathically orientated (detached) offenders.

With these understandings in mind, it appears that the constructs of attachment and psychopathy might account for much of the demonstrated heterogeneity of these offenders. As such, they warrant a more detailed exploration with a focus on their potential as a lens through which juvenile sex offending can be viewed.

PART II
THE LENS

CHAPTER THREE

Attachment and juvenile sex offending

"Because some of my ideas are alien to the theoretical traditions that have become established, and so have met with strong criticism, I have been at pains to show that most of them are by no means alien to what Freud himself thought and wrote"

(Bowlby, 1969, p. xv)

This chapter examines what is known about the connection between attachment and sex offending, specifically juvenile sex offending. Consistent with contemporary views and research findings in the broader field of enquiry into sexuality and attachment (Diamond, Blatt, & Lichtenberg, 2007), the research linking the two is underpinned by a view that attachment and sexuality are separate but strongly interconnected behavioural systems, such that secure attachment appears to strongly predict psycho-sexual maturity and adjustment.

Many definitions of attachment (Ainsworth, Blehar, Waters, & Wall, 1978; Bartholomew, 1990; Diamond, Blatt, & Lichtenberg, 2007; Fonagy, 2001; Main & Hess, 1990; Zeanah, 1993) have highlighted the fact that attachment involves the subjective perception of another person (initially the mother or primary care-giver) as a source of psychological safety and security (Widlocher, 2001). Attachment is, thus, antithetical to isolation and loneliness and is the vehicle through which human beings achieve the satisfying emotional exchanges necessary for psychological health and well-being.

Sperling and Berman (1994) have defined adult attachment as

> the stable tendency of an individual to make substantial efforts to seek and maintain proximity to and contact with one or a few specific individuals who provide the subjective potential for physical and psychological safety and security. It is normally mediated through *internal working models* (cognitive affective–emotional schema built up out of interpersonal experience). [p. 8]

This connects with what Bowlby (1988) originally observed when he noted, "The propensity to make strong emotional bonds to particular individuals [is] a basic component of human nature" (p. 3). Bowlby (1969) described attachment as "A lasting psychological connectedness between human beings" (p. 194). In describing it thus, Bowlby endorsed a fundamental psychoanalytic tenet: that early experiences in childhood have an important influence on development and behaviour later in life. He also saw that attachment had an evolutionary component, in particular that it enhances the chance of survival.

Bowlby identified four primary features of attachment which show that:

- it activates a need to maintain proximity to the attachment object;
- the attachment figure is seen to provide a safe haven when there is fear or threat;
- the attachment figure provides a secure base from which the child can explore the surrounding environment;
- distress occurs in the absence of the attachment figure.

He drew on data from ethology, evolution, and from psychoanalysis in theorizing that children build up internalized representations based on the basic style of their *actual* experiences in their relationships with primary care-givers, resulting in "internal working models" which become replicated in adult (couple) relationships. Subsequently, it was shown that these internal working models are built up by abstracting from interpersonal experience (Main, Kaplan, & Cassidy, 1985) and are consolidated during infancy, in particular the 9–18-month developmental period. This is the same period during which object permanence (i.e., a stable psychic image of others) crystallizes in the infant (Piaget, 1976). This emphasis is similar to that which object relations theory places on the importance of internalized experience, yet it differs in that it does not emphasize unconscious phantasy in the way that object relations theory does. None the less, the similarities between the two approaches appear to be greater than their differences.

Bowlby (1969) argued that security and attachment are prime motivators in humans. He saw *secure attachment as an important precursor to stable adult relations.* Bowlby's original ideas have subsequently been vindicated by substantial empirical data, which has shown how unsatisfactory attachment can lead to interpersonal maladjustment and destructive behaviour in oneself and towards others (Ainsworth, Blehar, Waters, & Wall, 1978; Lyons-Ruth, 1996; Main & Hess, 1990; Main & Solomon, 1990; Zeanah, 1993).

Bowlby first outlined his ideas about attachment in a series of three papers (Bowlby, 1958, 1959, 1960), beginning with a classic paper entitled "The nature of the child's tie to his mother". He theorized that children build up internalized representations based on the principal style of their relationships with their primary care-givers, resulting in internal working models that become templates to guide their future relationships.

He had envisioned giving psychoanalytic theory (in particular object relations theory) a scientific base in much the same way as Freud had envisioned in his *Project for a Scientific Psychology*. In deriving attachment theory, which became more fully developed in the 1960s, he realized something of this dream. Attachment theory drew on many sources of theory, but Bowlby was particularly inspired in developing his seminal ideas about attachment by ethology and, in particular, by the work of Konrad Lorenz. In his work on "filial imprinting", Lorenz (1935) had demonstrated how incubator-hatched geese would imprint on the first suitable moving stimulus they saw within what he called a "critical period" during the 13–16 hours shortly after hatching, most famously, the goslings imprinted on Lorenz himself (more specifically, on his wading boots). Like Lorenz, Bowlby also favoured naturalistic observation.

Attachment theory did not inspire Bowlby's psychoanalytic colleagues at the time, who felt his theory was simplistic and failed to privilege unconscious phantasy. Bowlby was upset by the lack of receptivity to his ideas by his psychoanalytic colleagues, since he felt he was attempting to make psychoanalytic ideas more accessible (Enfield, 2011). In recent decades, attachment theory and its empirical findings have been integrated with psychoanalytic theory, which it has been shown to complement (Fonagy, 2001; Holmes, 1993).

Ainsworth and empirically derived attachment styles in children

Mary Ainsworth, who was Bowlby's principle collaborator, was interested in testing Bowlby's ideas empirically (Ainsworth, 1967). Her thinking led to the development of a methodology to observe infant–mother attachment using the now famous Strange Situation Test (SST), which examined an infant's reaction to separations from a caregiver (Ainsworth, 1973). As a result, she derived a typology of children's attachment styles in which she described children as being secure, avoidant, or ambivalent in their attachment style (Ainsworth, Blehar, Waters, & Wall, 1978) (Table 1). Later research identified a "disorganized/disoriented" category of attachment style (Carlson, Ciccetti, Barnett, & Braunwald, 1989; Main & Hess, 1990; Main & Solomon, 1990).

Secure attachment in a child is characterized by:

- minimal distress when separated from care-givers;
- feeling secure and able to depend on adult care-givers;

Table 1.   Childhood attachment styles.

Secure	Avoidant
The child will express protest at the care-giver's departure, but is comforted by the care-giver's return (positive response upon return).	The child shows little or no distress when the care-giver leaves and displays little or no visible response upon the caregiver's return.

Ambivalent	Disorganized/disoriented
The child displays sadness when the care-giver leaves, but upon return is warm to the stranger while ambivalent and angry with the care-giver.	The child displays bizarre responses to the care-giver on return. Appears "stuck to the floor", or appears frozen. Lack of a coherent strategy

- feeling assured that care-giver will return;
- seeking comfort, when frightened, from care-givers and display-ing confidence that care-givers will provide comfort and reassur-ance;
- being comfortable seeking out care-givers when feeling needy.

Ambivalent attachment in a child is characterized by:

- an inability to be reassured or comforted by the return of the parent;
- a passive rejection of parents or care-givers and refusal of comfort from them;
- an open display of aggression toward parents or care-givers;
- clinginess and over-dependency.

Avoidant attachment in a child is characterized by:

- avoidance of parents and care-givers, especially after a period of absence;
- not seeking out comfort or contact;
- often showing no preference for a parent over a complete stranger.

Disorganized / disoriented attachment in a child is characterized by:

- having actions and responses to care-givers that reflect a mix of behaviours, including avoidance or resistance;
- displaying dazed behaviour, sometimes seeming either confused or apprehensive in the presence of a care-giver;
- showing a lack of clear attachment behaviour.

Care-giver/parenting styles associated with different attachment categories

Care-givers of children who are securely attached usually respond appropriately, consistently, and promptly to a child's or infant's needs. In contrast, the care-givers of children with avoidant attachment status often give little or no response to distress in their child and will discourage crying and encourage independence. Those with an ambivalent attachment style tend to display inconsistency in their responses to the child, giving variously appropriate and neglectful responses. Children who exhibit disorganized attachment usually have care-givers who are often frightening or intrusive or tend to withdraw from their children. There is also a high degree of maltreatment by care-takers in this group.

The development of internal working models is seen to become increasingly sophisticated with age and, in a securely attached child (and subsequently in an adult), to move from an enactive mode to more imagistic and lexical modes. Diamond and Blatt (1994) suggest that

> The securely attached six year old child's ready and cheerful acceptance and perusal of the family photograph of a separation, and the various disturbances of this pattern in insecurely attached children, illustrate how internal working models of attachment influence the development of representational processes *from nonverbal to imagistic and verbal (lexical) modes.* Finally, differences in the narratives of the adults rated as secure, preoccupied with attachment or dismissing of attachment on the Adult Attachment Interview, demonstrate both the potentially integrative and synthesizing power of lexical representation (in securely attached individuals, who move flexibly between generalizations about their attachment relationships and specific attachment memories and images) and the ways in which access to lexical representations *may be restricted in adults classified as dismissing or preoccupied with attachment.* [p. 91, my italics]

Empirically derived attachment styles in adults

As a result of subsequent developments in methodology, categories of adult attachment status were also developed (Bartholomew & Horowitz, 1991). Most significant among these was a series of empirical studies based on the Adult Attachment Interview (AAI) methodology (George, Kaplan, & Main, 1984; Main, Kaplan, & Cassidy, 1985), which used verbatim texts of interviews where a subject had been asked to give adjectives to describe their experiences of their primary care-givers. These interviews, once transcribed, were rated for theory coherence. Securely attached adults were found to have more easy access to memories of these experiences and to be able to integrate positive and negative memories.

As distinct from childhood attachment, which is primarily a description of patterns of behaviour, adult attachment is based on a mental representation of childhood attachment experience such that the earlier working models of attachment become re-enacted in subsequent relationships. Similar to the object relations conceptualization, it becomes the means of seeing oneself and others and is, therefore, predictive of certain behaviours in adult relationships.

Four types of adult attachment were identified:

1. Secure;
2. Preoccupied/anxious;
3. Dismissive/avoidant;
4. Fearful/avoidant. (Table 2.)

Secure attachment in adults

Adults who endorse statements such as, "It is relatively easy for me to become emotionally close to others. I am comfortable depending on others and having others depend on me. I don't worry about being alone or having others not accept me" are usually considered to be securely attached.

Such individuals tend to report a history of warm and responsive interactions with relationship partners. They tend to have positive views of themselves and their partners and of their relationships.

Table 2.   Features of adult attachment styles.

Secure (autonomous)	Preoccupied/anxious
Positive view of self/partners of their relationships.	Positive view of others/negative view of self.
Comfortable with intimacy and independence—able to balance these in relationships.	Overly dependent style. Intense feelings of unworthiness/excessive need for approval.
Dismissive/avoidant	*Fearful/avoidant*
Compulsive self-reliance/positive self-image. Minimizing of importance of intimate relationships.	Believe they are unlovable/perceive others as uncaring and unavailable. Avoid intimacy/have difficulty trusting others.

They are individuals who also feel comfortable both with intimacy and with independence and are able to balance these in their relationships.

The anxious/preoccupied adult

In contrast to securely attached adults, anxious–preoccupied individuals usually report experiences such as, "I want to be completely emotionally intimate with others, but I often find that others are reluctant to get as close as I would like." In addition, they might report, "I am uncomfortable being without close relationships, but I sometimes worry that others don't value me as much as I value them."

In such individuals, there is a focus on seeking approval, intimacy, and responsiveness from their partners. The focus on intimacy can lead to them being seen as "clingy". Consequently, they also tend to have less positive views about themselves and doubt their worth as partners. They are also inclined not to trust in people's good intentions and can exhibit high levels of emotional expressiveness, worry, and impulsiveness in their relationships.

The dismissive/avoidant adult

The dismissive–avoidant adult will often endorse statements such as, "I am comfortable without close emotional relationships. It is very important to me to feel independent and self-sufficient and I prefer not to depend on others or have others depend on me." They are often overly independent and desire independence, seemingly as an attempt to avoid attachment altogether.

Such individuals see themselves as self-sufficient and invulnerable to feelings associated with being closely attached to others. As such, they will frequently deny the need for close relationships. Some of these individuals might even view close relationships as relatively unimportant. They also tend to suppress and hide their feelings.

Adults who exhibit an avoidant attachment will usually endorse statements such as, "I am somewhat uncomfortable getting close to others. I want emotionally close relationships, but I find it difficult to trust others completely or to depend on them." And, "I sometimes worry that I will be hurt if I allow myself to become too close to others."

Some adults are ambivalent about relationships, variously desiring to have emotionally close relationships but feeling uncomfortable when emotional closeness comes. They often mistrust the intentions of their partners and at the same time feel unworthy of responsiveness from their partners.

The fearful/avoidant adult

The fearful/avoidant adult has low self-esteem and has a level of mistrust about interpersonal relationships that influences their perception of others. They typically feel that most people do not like them.

They will tend to endorse statements such as, "I sometimes worry that that I will get hurt if I allow myself to get too close to someone." Such individuals want closeness with others but fear it. They find it difficult to trust others completely or to depend on them.

They are, thus, generally very uncomfortable with the idea of getting close to others. Such people often have difficulty getting along with others and often suffer from jealousy and are anxious in social situations. They tend to see themselves and others negatively.

Adult attachment categories can be seen to refer to two axes:

1. Positive to negative views about self;
2. Positive to negative views about the other.

Secure attachment suggests positive self and other, preoccupied as negative self–positive other, dismissive as positive self–negative other, and fearful as negative self and negative other (Table 3).

As Sperling and Berman (1994) note,

Attachment theory and research on the internal working models have contributed significantly to an understanding of the representational

Table 3.   Four styles of adult attachment/view of self and other (after Bartholomew, 1990).

Model self–other	Positive (self)	Negative (self)
Positive (other)	Secure	Preoccupied
Negative (other)	Dismissing	Fearful

world. Most notably, observation from attachment research on aspects of internal working models have enabled us to appreciate how representational structures follow an epigenetic developmental sequence *from the enactive to imagistic to lexical modalities* as they are transformed from pre-operational, habitual motor patterns into symbolic, cohesive representations of self, other and their interaction. [pp. 90–91]

Secure attachment has been shown to predict adaptive behaviours (Rothbard & Shaver, 1991) and to be linked to normal cognitive and social cognitive development as well as social competence (Sroufe, Egeland, & Kreutzer, 1990). Secure attachment facilitates coping and competence in dealing with stressors by reducing emotional arousal and restoring a sense of calm (Parkes & Stevenson-Hinde, 1982; West & Sheldon-Keller, 1994).

Insecure attachment patterns are seen to represent forms of unresolved mourning of the longed for, but never experienced, tender care-giving relationship with the parent. These feelings result in the renunciation of authentic relatedness with others in favour of detachment from emotions, which cause these individuals to adopt one of a number of defensive styles (West & Sheldon-Keller, 1994). In terms of offending, a significant body of evidence links disrupted attachment to criminal behaviour. General criminality appears associated with dilemmas about attachment, while serious violent crime is linked with detachment (Fonagy, Target, Steele, & Steele 1997; Fonagy et al., 1997).

Bowlby (1980) noted that there were three psychological states associated with disruption to attachment, which seem to be particularly apposite to the clinical characteristics of juvenile sex offenders. These are:

1. Detachment characterized by the infant being apathetic, with an intensification of interest in physical objects;
2. Self-absorption;
3. Superficial sociability.

The mechanisms by which attachment difficulties affect behaviour are still poorly understood, yet it is clear that they are cognitively mediated. In this regard, Fonagy (2001) argues that disruption to attachment leads to a "failure to mentalize" about experience, and that this lack of a self-reflective ability results in a need to physically deal with psychological distress.

Early attachment patterns have a temporal stability, which predicts psychological adjustment and also attachment styles in individuals as they develop from infancy to childhood to adolescence, and thence to adulthood (Greenberg, 1999; Grossman & Grossman, 1991). Securely attached children are later rated as more confident, self-assured, and competent, while insecurely attached children are found to be more dependent on adults (Elicker, Englund, & Sroufe, 1992). Children who are originally defined as avoidant have the lowest levels of interpersonal understanding and sensitivity. There is also an association between an avoidant attachment pattern and later pre-school aggression (Egeland & Sroufe, 1981).

Attachment, adolescence, and sexuality

In adolescence, secure attachment is associated with an ability to cope with the developmental challenges of relinquishing childhood dependency, establishing peer group attachments, maintaining friendships, and developing a capacity for intimacy as a basis for a mature romantic relationship (Batgos & Leadbeater, 1994; Sperling & Berman, 1994). In contrast, insecurely attached adolescents (such as juvenile sex offenders) use sex as a means of dealing with conflicts about impaired capacity for intimacy, which they generally avoid or about which they are seriously ambivalent (Crittenden, 1997a). Insecurely attached adolescents, regardless of any sexual satisfaction derived, remain emotionally isolated, despite sexual contact with others.

This links with research into adult sexuality that shows adult attachment style and internal working models are linked with actual sexual behaviour (Ferreira, Carvalho, Santos, Peralta, & Carvalho, 2008). This research reveals that adults with dismissing attachment style report more short-term relationships and more sexual partners while *those with preoccupied or fearful attachment styles reported higher levels of sexual compulsivity.*

Research in the past ten to fifteen years shows that poor capacity for attachment is associated with the development of a range of psychopathology (Boris, Wheeler, Heller, & Zeanah, 2000; del Carmen & Huffman, 1996), depression, and aggression (Carlson & Sroufe, 1995; Cummings & Cicchetti, 1990; Lyons-Ruth, 1996). Adolescents who have a dismissive attachment organization (akin to the childhood avoidant category) rely on an attachment strategy that minimizes distressing thoughts and affects associated with rejection by the attachment figure (Rosenstein & Horowitz, 1996). Where such disruption of attachment occurs, the deviation from normal developmental pathways creates sensitivity to other risk factors that can have an adverse impact on personality development (Cowan, Cohn, Pape, Cowan, & Pearson, 1996). Adolescents with dismissive attachment patterns are more likely to self-report antisocial personality traits (Fonagy, 2001).

In line with Bowlby's view, research suggests that sexuality and attachment are separate systems that are, none the less, strongly correlated. Secure attachment, for example, has been found to strongly predict the capacity for monogamous relationships, with many studies demonstrating how attachment history affects the capacity to negotiate intimacy and achieve relationship permanence (Collins & Read, 1999; Feeney & Noller, 1990; Hazan & Shaver, 1987; Hindy, Schwartz, & Brodsky, 1989). Consonant with the observation that monkeys deprived of emotional comfort and contact manifested later disordered sexual behaviour (Novak & Harlow, 1975), evidence now suggests that insecure attachment status in humans also predicts sexual disorder (Marshall, 1989) and, in particular, that poor paternal attachments are linked to sexually coercive behaviour (Smallbone & Dadds, 1998).

The evidence suggests that the more disturbed the attachment process, especially when it is disturbed by abuse, the more likely one is to find later manifestations of this in violent behaviour (Fonagy et al., 1996). These findings are reinforced by studies which show that abuse experiences can also produce biochemical abnormalities, particularly with the functioning of the hormones oxytocin and vasopressin, which can act as neurotransmitters in those areas of the limbic system which influence attachment-seeking behaviour (Young, 2002). (See Chapter Six.)

Attachment theory, like object relations theory, also acknowledges the influence of relationships with significant others on the formation of a sexual self and on the way in which one attempts to satisfy one's attachments needs in the arena of intimate and sexual adult relationships. Within the attachment theory framework, sexuality, as mentioned above, is considered to be a separate system to the attachment activation system which, like that system, can be activated by external events that threaten basic safety and security or contribute to its maintenance. As such, adolescent and adult sexuality reflects the level of attachment security in an individual.

Object relations theorists posit that at the core of adolescent sexuality there is an internalized representation of intimacy, derived from the earliest intimacies of the mother and baby interaction. Consider, for example, the mother who is uncomfortable with her baby seeking physical comfort and associated sensual experiences or, in an extreme instance, expressing repulsion of her male infant's erection. Object relations theorists also suggest that it is from such early mother–infant interactions, that the infant develops his future expectations about adult relationships in particular expectations of pleasure, anticipation, and satisfaction of desire.

It is also the arena in which the infant has its first experience of what Kernberg (1995) refers to as "love containing hate". The ability of the mother (and father) to help the baby contain his feelings of aggression becomes the basis of an adult sexual relationship, wherein the necessary level of aggression to provide passion and excitement is contained by concern and love for the object.

Such a positive, foundational infant–mother experience requires what has been referred to as an adequate level of "maternal containment" (Winnicott, 1958) (see Chapter Five). Failures with maternal containment are seen by many psychoanalytic theorists to be at the base of many psychological disorders. The concept is consonant with what attachment and other infant theorists have referred to as "mis-attunement" in the mother–baby dyad, which leads to insecure attachment.

In terms of maternal containment of the infant's psychic experience, receptivity by the mother (care-taker) to manifestations of infantile sexual experience, as suggested above, is of particular importance. Where there is a psychological difficulty in the mother and these expressions are denied or ignored, it can lead to a difficulty in integrating one's sexuality as a part of oneself (Fonagy, Gergely, Jurist, & Target, 2004). In mature sexuality, through the processes of projection and introjection, it becomes possible to find oneself in "the other" in a way that provides the basis for satisfaction of sexual desire. Where the sexual self is felt to not be part of oneself (an "alien self"), this becomes impossible. These considerations highlight the fact that in such circumstances separation and individuation would not be achieved.

These observations also underline the fact that a mature, reciprocal, and satisfying adult sexual relationship rests on the capacity to
experience *intersubjectivity*. In turn, this implies the achievement of a
psychological separation and individuation. Sexual satisfaction in the
context of secure attachment requires a complex psychic manoeuvring
which encompasses an ability to have a sense of merger with another,
while retaining a sense of one's own separateness.

In a situation where psychological separation and individuation
have not been achieved, there can be a sense of danger about engag-
ing in intimacy and sexual intercourse, which is linked to a fear of
losing one's identity and, in more extreme cases, a risk of psychological fusion with the other. Primitive annihilation fantasies can be activated and, in extreme cases, these can result in ("affective" or "self-
preservatory") violent reactions (Ruszczynski, 2010a). Such primitive
reactions are linked to primitive anxieties associated with a failure to
develop a sense of self at the level of skin and bodily boundaries. This
can result in the fear of losing oneself in another. Ogden (1989) described these anxieties as related to a level of psychic development,
which he termed "autistic–contiguous". These anxieties represent the
earliest level of developmental anxieties and can manifest in psychotherapy as an undifferentiated experience with the therapist (that is,
no transference to the therapist as an object).

Problems relating sexually, thus, emerge in the absence of adequate maternal containment, the associated unintegration of one's
sexual self, and the failure to achieve separation and individuation. In
attachment terms, such individuals might be anxious/preoccupied or
avoidant/dismissive, and might employ their sexuality as a means of
addressing their attachment deficits.

In the case of individuals with a preoccupied attachment style,
there is an experience of affects that can hyperactivate the attachment
system. This is what might also be described as "attachment hunger".
In contrast, the individual with a dismissive attachment style tends to
obfuscate the need for attachment, that is, to "detach" or deactivate
the attachment system (Cassidy & Kobak, 1988).

Mikulincer and Shaver (2007) have suggested that the sexual psychopathology in the dismissively attached adult involves a defensive
strategy whereby intimacy is replaced by a desire for power and
domination, with sexual aggression liberated to varying degrees. That
is, attachment is achieved through control and power, or, in extreme

cases, through aggression and violence. In terms of sex offending, the rapist whose sexual behaviour might also encompass sadism and cruelty is representative of such dynamics.

In contrast to individuals with an underpinning psychic structure of malignant narcissism (an extreme variant of narcissism which involves the manipulation and coercion of others) (see Chapter Five), there are other individuals who might reflect what Britton (2004) has referred to as "adherent narcissism" (narcissism which involves an imitative quality), which might underlie their sexual behaviour. These individuals are likely to have a preoccupied attachment style whose fundamental driver is an "attachment hunger". This is linked to an unconscious fear of rejection and abandonment and a strong need for reassurance and love. In these individuals, there is often a basic insecurity about the self and gender identity.

The developmental achievement in adolescence, which is the prerequisite for negotiating adult intimacy, is a transition from a childlike dependence on parental figures to secure self-reliance and self-agency with an associated independence. Securely attached adolescents are more able to make this transition (Kroger, 1989).

The emergence of sexuality in adolescence appears to interact with attachment style in a variety of ways. For example, isolated adolescents who might normally be uncomfortable with intimacy find that promiscuity eases their loneliness, while other, more securely attached adolescents can sublimate their sexual feelings into sporting or academic excellence (Crittenden, 1997a). In some cases, superficial sexual bravado and promiscuity belie difficulties with intimacy (Crittenden, 1997b). Much of the internalized template about expectations of intimate relationships is acted out and powerfully reinforced by sexual satisfaction.

Relevant to the expression of sexuality, it appears that secure children learn to use both cognitive and affective data in balance in responding to others (Crittenden, 1997b). Alternatively, children whose affective expressions meet with punitive responses tend to rely only on their cognition. Where the response to affect is inconsistent, children do not orientate their behaviour in an effective way to either affect or cognition, and instead become distressed at their inability to comfort themselves.

Insecure children have a fundamental difficulty in coping with the relationship demands placed on them. In particular, they have difficulty developing "meta-models of relationships", which allow for appropriate differentiation of relationships (Crittenden, 1997b). In adulthood, such difficulties can lead to inappropriate sexual relationships with children, as sexual incompetence overrides the normal protective relationship with a child (Fonagy, 2001).

Poor capacity for attachment leaves an individual ill-prepared to meet the challenge of negotiating intimacy and establishing relationship permanence in adolescence (Fonagy & Target, 1997). It is also associated with difficulties in regulating emotions, controlling impulses, and poor self-image. The manifestations of incapacity for attachment vary. For example, some individuals can become isolated and ambivalent about relationships and poorly equipped in terms of interpersonal skills, while others can become dismissive of attachment needs and organize their emotional needs narcissistically.

Attachment and sex offending

There has been little research that has directly addressed the capacity for attachment of juvenile sex offenders. However, research conducted with adult sex offenders has provided support for the hypothesis that juvenile sex offenders could have an impaired capacity for attachment (Sawle & Kear-Colwell, 2001; Smallbone & Dadds, 2000, 2001; Stirpe, Abracen, Stermac, & Wilson, 2006). Adult sex offenders have been shown to have attachment difficulties that appear to be connected with their offending, with different types of adult attachment patterns associated with different offence types. For example, sex offenders with preoccupied attachment want to have more emotional involvement with their victims than those with dismissive attachment styles, the latter of whom are more coercive and controlling with their victims (Smallbone & Dadds, 1998). It is, however, still unclear to what extent and exactly how incapacity for attachment relates *to the development of* sexual offending (Ward, Hudson, & Marshall, 1996).

The attachment problems of adult sex offenders appear to be related to their developmental experiences and their clinical characteristics (Burk & Burkhart, 2003). They report less secure childhood and adult attachment than non-offenders and non-sex offenders (Cortoni & Marshall, 1998; Gal & Hoge, 1999; Sawle & Kear-Colwell, 2001; Smallbone & Dadds, 1998) and as a group they are poorly identified with their parents, with the fathers of rapists tending to be alcoholic and physically abusive (Langevin, Paitich, & Russon, 1985). Adult sex offenders who are either rapists or child molesters have been found to have parental relationships that are disrupted and chaotic (Tingle, Barnard, Robbins, Newman, & Hutchinson, 1986), with child molesters often having suffered physical abuse and abandonment. As a group, adult sex offenders have also reported low rates of affectional bonds, with over three-quarters of both child molesters and rapists indicating no close friends in childhood (Marshall, 1997). Adult rapists haven been shown to have dismissive attachment styles and child molesters preoccupied attachment styles in which there is an active, but highly anxious and ambivalent interest in relationship (Stirpe, Abracen, Stermac, & Wilson, 2006; Ward, Hudson, & Marshall, 1996).

A theoretical framework integrating attachment theory findings with intimacy deficits has been used to explain sex offence type among adult sex offenders (Hudson & Ward, 1997; Marshall, 1989; Ward, Hudson, Marshall, & Seigert, 1995). Specifically, some adult sex offenders are seen to seek intimacy but also avoid it, because of their fears of rejection, while others appear to neither fear nor desire intimacy. Data support three categories of insecure attachment, which might account for differences in adult sex offenders (Ward, Hudson, & Marshall, 1996). These are: (1) anxious/ambivalent, (2) avoidant I, and (3) avoidant II. Category 1 describes overly dependent individuals who are likely to offend against children; Category 2 includes those who are fearful of adults and seek non-rejecting partners; Category 3 incorporates those who are hostile and not relationship-seeking. Individuals in all three categories have intimacy deficits. In terms of the links between these categories and the adult attachment styles depicted in Table 2, Category 1 equates to preoccupied attachment style, Category 2 to the fearful/avoidant attachment style, and Category 3 to the dismissing/avoidant attachment style.

Psychopathic individuals appear to be the most impaired with respect to capacity for attachment. When non-sexually offending psychopaths, sexual homicide perpetrators, and non-violent paedophiles are compared, non-sexual psychopaths have the lowest level of interest in relationships and attachment to others (Bridges, Wilson, & Gacono, 1998; Gacono, Meloy, & Bridges, 2000). Psychopaths appear to have developmental antecedents, which relate to their coercive emotional style. Their incapacity to use affect in decision making makes psychopaths uniquely vulnerable to inverting logic and unable to deal with discrepant reality in a way which allows them to appropriately modify their behaviour (Crittenden, 1997b).

When the attachment style of adult paedophiles is compared with non-offenders and non-offending sexual abuse victims, the paedophiles are found to avoid or to be ambivalent about close and intimate relationships (Sawle & Kear-Colwell, 2001; Ward, Hudson, Marshall, & Seigert, 1995). Such offenders are vulnerable to seeking sexual interactions that minimize intimacy and are particularly prone to choosing children as partners. Closer analysis of the interest in attachment of paedophilic adult sex offenders reveals a sub-group (with preoccupied attachment status) who exhibit "attachment hunger" (i.e., a compulsive need for attachment) and another which shows less interest in (and has a fearful) attachment status (Gacono & Meloy, 1994).

A correlation between attachment pattern and sex offending behaviour, therefore, has been demonstrated among adult sex offenders, along with a correlation between attachment style and offence type. Rapists are generally found to spend only as much time as necessary to perpetrate the sexual/violent acts with victims, while child molesters tend to groom victims and engage in perverse forms of courtship (Smallbone & Dadds, 1998). Intra-familial child molesters report that one motivation in their offending against children is a felt need for affection (Ward, Hudson, & France, 1993).

Adult sex offenders are not only an insecurely attached group, but are also insecurely orientated to intimate adult relationships (Smallbone & Dadds, 1998). Familial child molesters have histories of particularly problematic relationships with their mothers. In contrast, rapists seem to have more problematic relationships with their fathers and perceive them as abusive and uncaring toward them (Smallbone & Dadds, 2000). The extent of abusive relationships with fathers in this group is consistent with the development of a dismissive attachment style, which could predict psychopathic behaviour.

In summary, secure attachment is clearly linked to the development of stable adult relationships and the capacity to develop intimacy. Not surprisingly, insecure attachment is associated with adult sex offending and, presumably, juvenile sex offending, with different types of sex offending linked to different attachment difficulties as represented in Table 4.

Table 4.   Adult attachment styles and adult sex offender type.

Secure attachment/non-offender	Preoccupied attachment/propensity for child molestation
Normal attachment needs associated with positive view of self and others.	Attachment hunger associated with negative view of self and positive yet insecure view of others.
Dismissive attachment/ propensity for rape (adult victims)	*Fearful attachment/propensity for sexual offending (child victims)*
Hostile view of attachment associated with positive view of self and negative view of others.	Minimizes importance of attachment associated with negative view of self and others.

Juvenile sex offenders and attachment

There is little reported research about attachment and juvenile sex offending. Notwithstanding this, it appears that attachment styles of children can help to explain the development of juvenile sex offending. For example, the categories developed by Ainsorth (1979) and further articulated and renamed by Crittenden (1997a) to apply to older children, identified basic patterns of individual attachment, which Crittenden referred to as Type B (secure–balanced), Type A (defended) and Type C (coercive). In this schema Type A individuals are seen to omit feelings from cognitive processing and behave in accordance with expected consequences. Type C individuals do the opposite and act in accordance with their feelings with little attention to the consequences. Type A and Type C individuals tend to overestimate the probability of danger and act in an unnecessarily self-protective manner. Type B individuals make use of both sources of information such that they have a balanced assessment of emotional situations and respond adaptively. Crittenden and Claussen (2000) later added a further category (A/C), which includes obsessive and compulsive strategies. Together, these categories help to explain some of the likely variations of attachment style among juvenile sex offenders and how these might account for, for example, the difference between a more compulsive, sexualized form of offending and a more coercive and violently sexualized one.

Crittenden's categories explain how individuals who operate on the assumption that all information is potentially false and threatening can have difficulty with their sexuality. They blend false affect with false cognition, which results in a distorted sense of reality. In response, they feel a need to be coercive and controlling. Consequently, such individuals are characterized by aggression and being (malignantly) narcissistic and omnipotently controlling of others as a means of denying the importance of attachment. The ablation of affect in a psychopathic individual to which Crittenden (1995) alludes is resonant with historic definitions of psychopathy such as those of Pinel (1801), who referred to the psychopath's lack of affect to be "as if the faculties of affect alone had suffered injury" (p. 9).

In contrast, as in the case of the compulsive paedophilic juvenile sex offender, one sees the inability to deal with overwhelming affect in the preoccupation with the victim (object) who arouses the erotic desire. The grooming and masturbatory fantasies often serve to heighten emotional intensity. There appears to be a desire to identify and merge with the object (victim). Experiences of childhood sexual abuse might then become re-enacted with the victim. In such re-enactments, perpetrators appear to be attempting to meet their attachment needs (pathologically) as well as triumph in their sexual fantasy, which is driven behaviourally by their conflicts surrounding separation and individuation and their early failures of maternal containment (Stoller, 1975).

These differences appear in both cases to relate to deficits in mentalizing which involve, variously, an over- and under-reliance on cognitive and/or affective strategies in social perception and appraisal. (This is discussed more fully in Chapter Eleven.)

Despite the lack of empirical evidence concerning attachment status among juvenile sex offenders (Goodrow & Lim, 1998), research involving path analysis has suggested a possible aetiological link between juvenile sexual recidivism and developmental experiences likely to be disruptive of secure attachment (Kenny, Keogh, & Seidler, 2001) (Figure 1).

This is consistent with findings that experiences disruptive to secure attachment can have an impact on self-reflective functioning, self-organization, morality, and the development of the capacity for empathy (Fonagy, Gergely, Jurist, & Target, 2004).

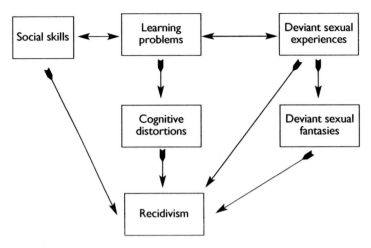

Figure 1.   Proximal factors in juvenile sex offender recidivism (Kenny, Keogh, & Seidler, 2001).

While it appears that social isolation, loneliness, and ineptness with interpersonal relationships characterize those juvenile sex offenders who choose children as their victims and contribute to recidivism (Aljazireh, 1993; Kenny, Keogh, & Seidler, 2001), those who target peer-aged or older victims are characterized by a more conduct-disordered and antisocial set of personality characteristics. Moreover, all juvenile sex offenders appear to have difficulties which have an impact on their ability to form satisfying relationships and achieve intimacy, suggestive of attachment incapacity. In particular, it is likely that they are a heterogeneous group in terms of their attachment difficulties, with some being ambivalent and some being avoidant (either as a result of fear or as means of rejecting the need for others).

In conclusion, attachment research and emergent data concerning adult sex offenders support the assertion that the level of interest in relationship and capacity for attachment are strongly associated with juvenile sex offending and might explain many juvenile sex offender characteristics and account for offender sub-types.

Having reviewed the likely linkages of attachment to juvenile sex offending, it is also worth considering how detachment (psychopathy) might also contribute to its aetiology.

CHAPTER FOUR

Psychopathy and juvenile sex offending

"The determination at all costs not to risk again the disappointment and resulting rages and longings which wanting someone very much and not getting them involves"

(Bowlby, 1944, cited in Holmes, 1993, p. 87)

Psychopathy is synonymous with an obfuscation of the need for attachment. Bowlby (1944) described psychopaths as "detached". Psychopathy can, therefore, be seen as representing psychopathology, which involves the most extreme incapacity for attachment. There is considerable evidence that implicates psychopathy in juvenile sex offending.

The nature of psychopathy

Psychopathy is regarded as a personality disorder. Drawing heavily on Cleckly's (1941) work, Hare describes psychopathy as consisting of a characteristic pattern of interpersonal, affective, and behavioural symptoms so that, on an interpersonal level, psychopaths are shown to be grandiose, egocentric, manipulative, forceful, and cold-hearted. In terms of their affect, they display shallow and labile emotions and are unable to form long-lasting bonds to people, principles, and goals. They experience little anxiety, genuine guilt, or remorse. Behaviourally, psychopaths are impulsive and sensation seeking, and they readily violate social norms. The most obvious expressions of these predispositions "involve criminality, substance abuse, and a failure to fulfill social obligations and responsibilities" (Hare, 1991, p. 3).

Violent psychopaths demonstrate a behavioural pathway to increasingly aggressive behaviour, usually manifesting in escalating violent crime for which there is little, if any, remorse. Violence is, however, not a feature of all psychopaths, with notable exceptions being the so-called corporate psychopath and the fraudster or "conman". Violence, when perpetrated by a psychopath, is typified by being cold, calculating, and callous rather than reactive and hotheaded, as in the case of the paranoid personality disorder (Felthous & Sass, 2010; Hervé & Yuille, 2007).

Violent psychopathy, often encompassing sadistic behaviour, is associated with the development of a trajectory of increasingly antisocial behaviour commencing in childhood, the development of drug and alcohol problems, and an increase in violent behaviour during adolescence (Christian, Frick, Hill, Tyler, & Frazer, 1997; Hare, 1999; Holt, Meloy, & Strack, 1999; Knop, Jensen, & Mortensen, 2003; Myers, Burket, & Harris, 1995). The set of traits associated with psychopathy is relatively stable into adulthood (Olweus, 1979). Psychopathy accounts for the difference between what Meloy (1997) refers to as "predatory" and "affective" violence. Although both are seen in the context of a distorted desire to engage in emotionally significant interchanges, in the case of the predator the action is usually designed to seek proximity with destructive intent. With an affectively violent person, there is a desire to be close to others, but this proximity produces an intensely violent defensive reaction (Ruszczynski, 2010a). These differences are consistent with findings in the literature that some juvenile sex offenders are motivated by desires for (albeit a perverse form of) closeness. In contrast, psychopathy, with its associated extreme attachment difficulties, leads to attachment being dismissed or, in severe cases, denied.

The construct of the psychopath, defined operationally by the Hare Psychopathy Checklist-Revised (PCL-R), is one largely derived from

Cleckly's concept of psychopathy outlined in his book, *The Mask of Sanity* (1941). Psychopathy emerges as one of the most important constructs in the field of criminology and forensic psychology of the past two decades (Arrigo & Shipley, 2001; Felthous & Sass, 2010; Hervé & Yuille, 2007; Millon, Simonsen, Birket-Smith, & Davis, 2003). In particular, as a construct operationalized in the form of the PCL-R, it predicts recidivism and violence and is pivotal as a construct in the identification of the most serious offenders. The PCL-R has two factors compromising a number of traits (Table 5).

Factor 1 has been labeled by Hare as "selfish, callous and remorseless use of others", while Factor 2 is labelled as a "chronically unstable, antisocial and socially deviant lifestyle". Factor 1 is generally seen to represent the core personality traits of psychopathy.

Much has been written about the concept of psychopathy (Cleckly, 1941; Doren, 1987; Felthous & Sass, 2010; Hare, 1996, 1998a,b,c; Hervé & Yuille, 2007; Millon, Simonsen, Birket-Smith, & Davis, 2003; Weiss, 1985). Historically, it has been discussed under a variety of terms, including sociopathy, moral insanity, and antisocial personality: terms all used to describe the same or aspects of the same concept, which have created significant confusion concerning definitions of psychopathy in the literature. Psychopathy has a well-defined developmental pathway, an early onset, and tends to be long-term and persistent.

Table 5.   The traits comprising the two factors of the PCL-R.

Factor 1	Factor 2
Glibness/superficial charm	Need for stimulation/proneness to boredom
Grandiose sense of self-worth	Parasitic lifestyle
Pathological lying	Poor behavioral control
Cunning/manipulative	Promiscuous sexual behaviour
Lack of remorse or guilt	Lack of realistic long-term goals
Shallow affect	Impulsivity
Callous/lack of empathy	Irresponsibility
Failure to accept responsibility for own actions	Juvenile delinquency
	Early behaviour problems
	Revocation of conditional release

Psychopathy is characterized by an impaired emotional function-ing which is not conducive to reciprocal relationships, is inversely related to depression, and can predict violence and recidivism (Herpetz & Sass, 2000; Lovelace & Gannon, 1999). These are among the most clinically and forensically useful findings concerning psychopathy (Furr, 1994).

As emotional deficiency can predispose the psychopath to vio-lence, it is important to understand its role in the behaviour of the psychopath. Emotional deficiency predisposes an individual to vio-lence in three ways (Herpetz & Sass, 2000). First, the deficiency is asso-ciated with a general level of under-arousal, which causes these individuals to seek stimulation and sensation and can be associated with, for example, drug use and sexual promiscuity. Second, individ-uals with emotional deficiency do not engage in consequential think-ing. This, in turn, leads to a failure to be able to consider the poten-tially harmful consequences of one's behaviour, with the individual therefore not appropriately avoiding dangerous or risky situations. It appears that there is no "signal anxiety". Finally, emotional deficiency includes emotional detachment, which prevents the person from expe-riencing feelings such as empathy, which might otherwise inhibit the acting out of violent impulses (Herpetz & Sass, 2000).

Many researchers and theoreticians stress a biological basis for psychopathy. However, most research data describe biological corre-lates, rather than causes of psychopathy. In terms of genetic evidence (Laakso et al., 2001), there are some consistent findings, derived from twin studies and adoption studies, of a genetic loading to psychopa-thy (Chandler & Moran, 1990) and some evidence that neuro-anatom-ical irregularities underpin some psychopathic behaviour (Bernstein, Newman, Wallace, & Luh, 2000; Kiehl et al., 2001). For example, psychopaths show abnormal levels of fronto-temporal lobe activation during a word task involving emotional and non-emotional stimuli. Linked to this, they also exhibit dysfunction in the amygdala and ventromedial prefrontal cortex, which contributes to poor processing of emotional experience and low tolerance of frustration (Blair, 2008, 2010). In a review of neuro-imaging studies, Pridmore, Chambers, and McArthur (2005) provided evidence of dysfunction of particular frontal and temporal lobe structures in psychopathy. In particular, they noted evidence of decreased prefrontal grey matter and pos-terior hippocampal volume, some evidence of reduced metabolism in the frontal cortex (associated with aggression in psychopathy), and dysfunction of the right anterior temporal gyrus. Overall, the authors concluded that the research about brain dysfunction in psychopaths was inconclusive and they noted that "Should further studies substantiate that psychopathy is associated with abnormal brain activity, caution will be required and many questions will remain. It is important to avoid an excessively reductionist approach" (p. 864).

Psychopathy has also been shown to be associated with attenuated autonomic activity related to fearlessness. Psychopaths reveal an absence of a "startle response" to aversive stimuli, which normally includes a blink of the eye (Patrick, Cuthbert, & Lang, 1993). These data also link to a theory of general physiological under-arousal in psychopathy (Gacono & Meloy, 1994), which is seen to account for the feelings of boredom and need for stimulation in psychopaths, which have been linked to neuroendocrine abnormalities (discussed in Chapter Six). This response is also absent in groups of sex offenders who achieve high scores on Factor 1 of the Hare Psychopathy Checklist. Factor 1 measures the extent of the selfish, callous, and remorseless use of others and represents a constellation of the interpersonal and affective characteristics fundamental to the construct of psychopathy (Hare, 1991).

In terms of neuropsychological factors, one of the main findings has been that psychopaths are relatively lacking in their ability to process and utilize contextual cues that are peripheral to their dominant response set, which suggests their vulnerability to social dysfunction (Newman, Schmitt, & Voss, 1997; Vitale & Newman, 2001). Irregularities in hormonal functioning have also been cited with psychopaths, with testosterone levels implicated as a biological marker for psychopathy and alcoholism (Aromaeki, Lindman, & Eriksson, 2002; Stalenheim, Eriksson, von Knorring, & Wide, 1998).

Further, there is strong evidence of genetic loading to psychopathy, a relationship between aggression and testosterone, and a link between aggression and neurotransmitter dysfunction (Meloy, 1997; Giotakos, Markianos, Vaidakis, & Christodoulou, 2004). (This is discussed further in Chapter Six.) More generally, psychopathic behaviour has been found to be associated with lower levels of overall activity of serotonin, lower rates of turnover of dopamine, and higher levels of testosterone (Minzenberg & Siever, 2007).

In summary, however, when neuro-anatomical, genetic, hormonal, and neuro-behavioural data are considered together, it appears that a biological causation of psychopathy is not well established and developmental factors appear to play an equally important role in the aetiology of psychopathy. These findings highlight the potential importance of epigenetic factors (discussed in Chapter Six).

Developmental factors and psychopathy

There are also a number of studies identifying developmental precursors to psychopathy in childhood (Marshall & Cooke, 1999). Developmental theorists have argued that psychopathy is an endpoint of a behavioural pathway commencing in early childhood, with the development of psychopathy subject to similar factors stressed by attachment theorists in their explanations of other psychopathology. Psychopathy initially manifests in early hyperactivity and impulsivity in early childhood, followed by the development of pronounced oppositional defiant symptomatology and conduct disorder. This can later develop into antisocial personality disorder and ultimately in psychopathy. Such aberrations are linked to a variety of developmental factors, of which attachment appears to be the most significant (Keogh, 2002).

In the Cambridge Study of delinquent development, Farrington (2000) reported that there is a temporal stability of anti-social traits, confirming the previous view of Olweus (1979). Antisocial males measured at the age of eighteen years remain the most antisocial at the age of thirty-two years. In this study, Farrington demonstrated that it is possible to predict antisocial behaviour. In particular, two-thirds of boys aged eight years who are described with factors thought to be predictive of antisocial behaviour are confirmed as antisocial by age eighteen years.

The most significant psychosocial predictors in Farrington's study were large family size, convicted parent(s), low intelligence or attainment on the part of the child, and inconsistent child-rearing practices. Many of these factors can be related to the quality of attachment and the level of abuse, neglect, and maltreatment that these individuals experience in their childhood. Psychopathy is also associated with, and predictive of, recidivism, offending versatility, a tendency to violent offences, and rehabilitation resistance and failure (Blackburn, 1993). Rorschach findings show that psychopathy is correlated with borderline and narcissistic personality dimensions and that psychopaths show less attachment and less anxiety than non-psychopaths, factors that appear to facilitate their remorseless violence (Gacono & Meloy, 1994).

In summary, evidence concerning psychopathy suggests that, while there may be a biological substrate to the propensity to psychopathy, developmental experiences appear to play key roles in its aetiology.

Links between psychopathy and sex offending

Following the establishment of the PCL-R as a means of operationally defining and measuring psychopathy, the construct has become well established as valid and useful and rests on substantial research literature (Cooke, Forth, & Hare, 1998; Forth, Hart, & Hare, 1990; Hare, 1996; Hervé & Yuille, 2007; Millon, Simonsen, Birket-Smith, & Davis, 2003).

As the following selected review of literature demonstrates, psychopathy is an important construct in considering the motivations of juvenile sex offenders and the aetiology of their behaviour.

First, studies have shown that psychopathy can predict general recidivism (Hanson & Bussière, 1998; Ponder, 1999), violent recidivism (Bartol, 2001; Dolan & Doyle, 2000; Edens, Skeem, Cruise, & Cauffman, 2001) and, in interaction with sexual deviance, sexual recidivism among adult sex offenders (Serin, Mailoux, & Malcolm, 2001). Although psychopathy has been associated with juvenile sex offending (Långström & Lindblad, 2000; Myers & Monaco, 2000), it has not been shown to differentiate sub-groups of juvenile sex offenders, or to predict juvenile sexual recidivism, but is specifically associated with violent behaviour among sex offenders (Auslander, 1999).

In contrast, comparative studies that explore within-group differences among adult sex offenders reveal a sub-group of sex offenders who feature psychopathic behaviours (Barbaree, Seto, Serin, Amos, & Preston, 1994; Brown & Forth, 1997; Dorr, 1998; Furr, 1994; Gretton, McBride, Hare, O'Shaughnessy, & Kumka, 2001). There are also studies that have shown correlations among psychopathy, the PCL-R, recidivism, and sub-types of sex offending (Serin, Mailoux, & Malcolm, 2001). Adult sex offenders with the most elevated PCL-R scores were found to be the most likely to reoffend after release (Seto & Barbaree, 1998). Psychopathy *interacting with* sexual deviance, along with prior offending and the inclusion of male and stranger/nonrelative victims, strongly predicts adult sex offender sexual recidivism (Hanson & Bussière, 1998; Harris & Forth, 1998; Harris & Rice, 1996).

Among the adult offenders, rapists are found to reoffend nonsexually more than child molesters, indirectly indicating that child molesters are generally less antisocial. Sexual recidivism in adult sex offenders, however, has been reported to be unrelated to sexual abuse history in childhood, substance abuse, or general psychological problems (Hanson & Bussière, 1998).

There is also no direct correlation between the apparent level of distress adult sex offenders experience and recidivism, although they react deviantly when distressed, owing to their poor coping ability (Cortoni & Marshall, 1998). Rapists are at higher risk than child molesters for sexually reoffending, with a ten-year follow-up study identifying rapists to be more psychopathic than other adult sex offenders (McCoy, 1998). These sub-group differences in recidivism appear to be indicative of variations in the levels of psychopathy in sex offender sub-groups. Offenders have been found to be less likely to reoffend if they offend against children to whom they are related, suggesting the possible mitigating effect of attachment (Hanson & Bussière, 1998).

Compared with incest offenders, adult sex offenders who commit homicide have significantly higher levels of psychopathy and antisocial history, as measured by the PCL-R, and are usually charged or convicted more frequently with violent and non-violent non-sexual offences (Firestone, Bradford, Greenberg, Larose, & Curry, 1998). Research has revealed that adult offenders who reoffend during a seven-year follow-up period are characterized by their level of psychopathy and sexual deviance. In the same research, prediction of recidivism was based on offence type and level of psychopathy, with Factor 2 scores on the PCL-R discriminating general recidivists from non-recidivists (Serin, Mailoux, & Malcolm, 2001).

Mixed rapist and child molesters in the adult offender group have been found to be more psychopathic than child molesters. Sex offenders with the highest levels of psychopathy were motivated by "thrill seeking", which was directed at a diverse range of sexual victims. This stresses the importance of psychopathy in understanding sexual violence (Porter et al., 2000). Such data have suggested that psychopathy, recidivism, and sub-types of sex offending are likely to be interrelated among juvenile sex offenders.

In summary, research about psychopathy suggests its relevance to understanding the motivations of some juvenile sex offenders, as well as its importance in predicting sexual recidivism. As it is such a central forensic concept, the psychoanalytically orientated clinician needs to understand the psychodynamics of such pathology as well as how it might link to sexual perversion.

CHAPTER FIVE

Malignant narcissism, psychopathy, and perversion

"The human mind needs to relate to the other in order to develop"

(Ferro, 2005, p. 15)

I have previously noted how, as a result of disruptions to attachment and emotional development, some juvenile sex offenders *relate* to others through either sexualized or violently sexualized means. Indeed, what characterizes the psychopathic offender is his desire to hurt and coerce others. In this chapter, I explicate how narcissism, when it becomes "malignant", links to the behaviours and attitudes which constitute what is described as psychopathy and to consider its connection to sexual perversion.

Malignant narcissism, as a term, has evolved over time. Eric Fromm (1964) in his book, *The Heart of Man*, described it as: "The most severe pathology and the root of the most vicious destructiveness and inhumanity" (p. 33).

Akhtar (2009) points to Weigert's (1967) view of malignant narcissism as involving a regressive state, encompassing denial and a distortion of reality and coexisting with a benign narcissism, which she saw as a type of enhanced self-esteem linked to having survived adversity. Ahtkar notes that Weigert also felt that "there was no sharp division between the two forms of narcissism" (Akhtar, 2009, p. 163).

Rosenfeld (1971) gave the concept greater specificity in describing it as a psychic state of grandiosity founded on aggression and wherein cruel and destructive aspects of the self become idealized. This provided a basis for Kernberg's (1984, 2004) subsequent, more forensically applicable view of it as a narcissistic personality disorder, encompassing antisocial behaviour and a deeply paranoid view of the world which is used to justify their behaviour and ego-syntonic sadism (Meloy, 1997). The relevance of malignant narcissism as a concept to psychopathy becomes clearer when the nature of the internal world it connotes is appreciated. Meloy (1997), drawing on Kernberg's (1984) elaboration of the concept of malignant narcissism, suggests that "Psychopathy is a process: a continuous interplay of factors and operations that are implicitly progressing and regressing toward a particular end point, *a fundamental dis-identification with humanity*" (p. 21).

In defining psychopathy, Meloy (1997) highlighted its links to malignant narcissism. This notion of malignant narcissism as a psychic structure underlying psychopathy is a view vindicated by empirical research (including my own), which demonstrates the centrality of a severe form of narcissism in psychopathy: one which involves an obfuscation of the need for relationship and a desire to coerce and control others (Meloy, 1997).

Narcissism, viewed as part of the psychic structure (a set of object relations) underpinning various forms of psychopathology, is best seen as a continuum, with the more extreme end of the spectrum representing an inner world where the self is taken as the object and where the need for others is replaced by a ruthless manipulation and use of it. In extreme malignant narcissism (associated with psychopathy scores of 30-plus on the Hare Psychopathy Checklist (PCL-R)), there is a *complete* denial of the need for others. The differentiation (or malignancy of the narcissism) seen in this way is, thus, the degree to which others are also de-humanized. Not surprisingly, Factor 1 of the PCL-R (see Chapter Four), which captures the personality traits of the psychopath, is seen to tap into "aggressive narcissism", which characterizes a person who sees others as a means of reinforcing his megalomaniacal state of mind (Meloy, 1992, 1997).

As noted in Chapter Two, juvenile sex offenders appear to represent a heterogeneous group, with a sub-set of them strongly endorsing psychopathic (especially aggressive narcissistic) traits. It is this sub-group that can be seen to be positioned at the extreme end of the (*malignantly*) *narcissistic spectrum*. Identifying such a sub-group is crucial, as its members represent one of the biggest challenges in terms of their treatment and suitability for treatment.

Psychoanalysis, crime, and narcissism

Psychoanalytic writers and researchers have long identified the relevance of narcissism to serious crime. While Freud did not write extensively on psychopathy, he observed that some offenders, because of their narcissism and aggression, had ego disturbances which made them incapable of being honest and therefore unsuitable for treatment (Freud, 1928b). Meloy and Shiva (2010) have highlighted that the psychopath's personality is still defined essentially in the way Freud defined it in 1928, with emphasis on the offender's pathological narcissism and his cruel aggression, what they note Freud referred to as "boundless egoism and a strong destructive urge" (p. 335).

Following Freud, many analysts defined psychopathy in a similar manner, retaining the reference to narcissism and aggression. For example, Aichorn (1925), in his book *Wayward Youth*, also delineated his own prescient view of crime based on the idea that a psychopath's difficulty was linked to narcissism. The treatment and advice to the magistracy, provided by the psychoanalytically based Psychopathic Clinic, London (established in 1931 and later to become known as the Portman Clinic), was tied to such theories of psychopathy. Other analysts, such as Reich (1945), further emphasized the importance of narcissism (and aggression) in the psychopathic character type he described. Anna Freud (1949) highlighted the failure of the transition from primary narcissism to object love in the development of aggression towards others. The relevance of narcissism to psychopathy in infants and children was also underlined by Levy (1951).

Object relations theorists, in particular, have teased out the relevance of narcissism to psychopathy, highlighting that psychopathy entailed a perverse grandiosity. Klein only made two direct statements about narcissism (Segal, 1983), but her seminal theoretical ideas on object relations had heuristic value to explanations of serious crime. Klein's (1957) ideas about envy contributed important understandings about the sub-processes of narcissism, which can drive cruel behaviour. The grandiose self in narcissism deals with envy by believing that it contains all that is wanted, otherwise attempting to destroy what is envied. Truman Capote's (2000) description of the murderous crime in his novel *In Cold Blood*, based on a true story, illustrates this dynamic in the senseless slaying of a family that was related to the envy of their happiness.

Post-Kleinian ideas about narcissism/malignant narcissism were developed by Rosenfeld (1971, 1987). As noted, Rosenfeld (1971) used the term "malignant narcissism" in a particular way. His 1971 paper, which explicated his use of the term malignant narcissism, also introduced the notion of the "mafia gang" to describe how destructive aspects of the personality are seen to corrupt the self. In outlining the destructive aspects of narcissism, he described what he referred to as "narcissistic omnipotent object relations", which represent a means of defending against separateness and which entail an "omnipotent mad self" (Rosenfeld, 1987). This explanation was invaluable in the development of thinking about how a malignant narcissism develops (Kernberg, 1984), which fosters perverse and destructive grandiosity. In this regard Rosenfeld (1971) noted, "The strength and persistence of omnipotent narcissistic object relations is closely related to the strength of the *envious* destructive impulses" (p. 172, my italics).

Hyatt-Williams (1998) also applied and extended the thinking of Klein (1957) and Bion (1962, 1967) and showed how lack of separation and individuation could also help explain psychopathy and the grandiosity of narcissism and its sequalae: cruelty, sadism, and murder. More recently, the work of Kernberg (1984) and Meloy (1997) has done much to elaborate the link between narcissism and psychopathy. Kernberg (1984), in addition to describing the link between malignant narcissism and antisocial behaviour and grandiosity, also detailed the unfolding of malignant narcissism in the transference relationship in psychopathically disturbed patients.

Subsequently, Meloy (1997) has usefully articulated how psychopathic offenders come to idealize the self as they turn away from "the other". He proposed that psychopathic individuals come to identify with what he calls the *stranger self-object*. He saw this identification with the stranger self-object as resulting from actual abuse and/or other serious failures of emotional (maternal) containment. Meloy (1997) introduces the concept of the stranger self-object (based on the ideas of Grotstein (1982) and Mahler, Pine, & Bergman (1975)) to explain malignant narcissism. He noted that this self-object is one that, in normal development, helps the infant deal with or anticipate the presence of a predator. As the stranger self-object is a self object, the anticipated predator is experienced as both external and internal. When the infant is not assisted in its difficulties with such a threat by adequate emotional containment (and/or perceives malevolence in the primary care-giver), he comes instead to *identify with* this self-object (predator). Meloy (1997) notes that psychopathy, at the (internal world) level of mental representation, involves

> a precocious separation from the primary parent during the symbiotic phase of maturation; failures of internalization that begin with an organismic distrust of the sensory–perceptual environment; a predominate archetypal identification with the stranger self-object that is central to conceptual self and object fusions within the grandiose self structure during of separation–individuation . . . [p. 59]

and that what results is *"A primary narcissistic state of attachment* to the grandiose self and states of relatedness that are aggressively and sadomasochistically pursued with actual objects" (p. 59, my italics).

Meloy (1997) regards the identification with others in malignant narcissism as quite different from that of the borderline or the narcissist. In the borderline, the object is identified with (and internalized) as a persecutory object. Within the narcissistic personality, it is more benign and less aggressive. Gacono and Meloy (1994) note that, in malignant narcissism, a complete obfuscation of the need for the other is achieved by a psychic appropriation of all that is good and desired into themselves, which is accompanied by a ruthless and, at times, violent control of the object. Here, the role of *envy* is strongly emphasized.

These psychoanalytically based clinical and theoretical contributions have all stressed the consequences of earlier disruption to *separation and individuation* and its links to the development of a potentially destructive narcissism with its "corrupting" effect on the self and others. Related to this, psychoanalytic theorists have warned of therapist enactments and difficult countertransference reactions (often associated with the repulsive nature of the crimes of some offenders) when treating such patients. McWilliams (1994), for example, notes how the treatments offered need, as far as possible, to be incorruptible. This is linked to the need to challenge the omnipotence associated with malignant narcissism. She notes that, with such patients, the incorruptibility of "the therapist, the frame, and the conditions [are what] makes therapy possible" (p. 161). She illustrates the psychopath's talent for corruption by reference to the manipulation of the detective by the psychopathic character in the film *Silence of the Lambs*.

Developmental theorists argue that psychopathy is an endpoint of a behavioural pathway commencing in early childhood, with the development of psychopathy subject to similar factors stressed by attachment theorists in their explanations of other psychopathology (Keogh, 2002). The lack of relatedness found in psychopaths appears to be associated with the cumulative effect of interpersonal developmental experiences (Sperling & Berman, 1994), where sexual and other forms of abuse contribute to the development of mistrust and poor levels of relatedness and impede normal reciprocal modes of relating. These are all factors that facilitate the identification with the sadistic stranger self-object. McWilliams (1994) has noted that, in the histories of the more destructive and criminal psychopaths, "one can find virtually no consistent, loving, adequately protective influences" (pp. 155–156). Bowlby (1944) pointed out that such criminals usually displayed evidence of being devoid of attachment. There is also evidence, however, that in more moderately psychopathic (malignantly narcissistic) individuals (who would *not* achieve the cut-off score for psychopathy on the PCL-R), the parenting provided has stressed material rather than emotional support and has conveyed that dependency and vulnerability are weaknesses, yet has still facilitated some level of attachment. This is the group for whom analysis or analytic therapy, particularly at younger ages, might offer some hope.

Linked to the issue of developmental disruption and failed maternal containment and the consequent development of destructive (and malignant) narcissism, Fonagy and Bateman (2008) have noted that psychopathic offenders show no capacity for "reflective functioning" (i.e., capacity for self-monitoring and awareness of the states of mind of others), which they link to a failure to establish a sense of self or to become "individuated". That is, they lack the capacity to be able to think about their emotional states. Consequently, such offenders have no other resort than to act out criminally as a means of unburdening themselves of psychic tension. This is what has been referred to as the "evacuation" of indigestible psychic experience (Symington & Symington, 1996, p. 15). The acting out of aggression, which is a central feature of conduct disorder (and a precursor to psychopathic behaviour), Fonagy (2001) proposes, is a consequence of a lack of this reflective functioning or mentalizing. He comments,

> Negative affectivity appears to point to the absence of a core capacity to properly regulate negative emotions in interpersonal relations . . . Because [such] children cannot inhibit negative arousal or suppress the negative reactivity, they cannot plan effective coping responses or control their attention to reduce exposure to disturbing stimuli [and as a consequence] . . . they will inevitably experience considerable difficulty in social relationships and [will have difficulty with] their capacity to establish affective attachment relationships. [p. 42]

In terms of the violent behaviour, research reveals a difference between what Meloy (1997) refers to as "predatory" rather than "affective" violence, the latter being a similar idea to the concept of self-preservative violence (Ruszczynski, 2010b). Predatory violence reveals the least interest in relationship and incapacity for attachment.

Research about the internal world of the psychopath and its links to malignant narcissism

Research concerning the internal world of the psychopath using Rorschach indices has confirmed that it is associated with malignant narcissism and that psychopaths show less attachment and less anxiety than non-psychopaths: factors that appear to facilitate their remorseless (and predatory) violence (Gacono & Meloy, 1991). Such variables also discriminate adult psychopaths from non-psychopaths when the Hare Psychopathy Checklist (PCL-R) is used as an independent measure (Loving & Russell, 2000). Other data have revealed that psychopathic adolescents are more egocentric, have impaired capacity for attachment and are less anxious than non-psychopathic adolescents (Smith, Gacono, & Kaufman, 1997).

In my own research (see Chapter Eight), I found that measures of narcissism and capacity for attachment also reliably discriminated groups of adolescents with low, medium, and high psychopathy scores (Keogh, 2004). Such studies have, thus, shown that psycho-pathic individuals represent a severe and pathologically detached variant of narcissistic personality disorder, perhaps simply, the most malignantly narcissistic group. They suggest that psychopathic offenders have psychic representations of violent symbiosis, narcissistic mirroring, and boundary disturbance reflected, such that there is "a malevolent and destructive internalized object world characterized by intense and violent intra-psychic conflict, surrounding attachment and separation" (Gacono, Meloy, & Berg, 1992, p. 46).

In these individuals, empirical evidence has confirmed clinical impressions that there is a symbiotic merging, as well as narcissistic mirroring, related to an impossible pathological wish which cannot be fulfilled, that is, to join and achieve a perfect reflection with their primary "object" (Gacono & Meloy, 1991). In this regard, it is interesting to note the triggers of violent psychopathic behaviour. Consider, for example, the serial killer, the famous "Son of Sam", whose murders of young women began after he was forced to face the reality that that his mother, whom he idolized in fantasy, was promiscuous (Abrahamsen, 1985).

Malignant narcissism and the psycho-dynamics of psychopathic offending

The theoretical views and studies to which I have referred highlight the importance of pathological narcissism in understanding psychopathic offending. This represents a contemporary focus in the psychoanalytic understanding of psychopathy, as exemplified by the research and theory of Kernberg (1984) and Meloy (1997), whose theories can be seen to link its development with the consequences of failures of maternal containment. Meloy (1997) links this failure directly to the identification with the stranger self-object (predator). The work of these theorists can be seen as an elaboration and application of earlier object relations formulations of failed containment (e.g. Hyatt-Williams, 1998) and narcissism (Britton, 2004; Rosenfeld, 1964, 1971, 1987) and other developments (particularly at the Portman Clinic) in forensic psychoanalysis. Hyatt-Williams (1998) articulated the importance of a number of psychoanalytic factors in the emergence of anti-social behaviour and psychopathy. Among these was *failed maternal containment* (Winnicott,

1956, 1958), which is seen to foster the retardation of the growth of a sense of separateness and the failure to recognize "otherness".

Hyatt-Williams (1998) used Bion's concepts to explain how a mother's failure to receive her baby's projective identifications leaves the baby in a state of psychic indigestion. He sees maternal containment as assisting the development of a capacity to tolerate frustration or psychic pain. He also noted,

> The importance of the developmental intolerance of psychic pain cannot be over-emphasized because it decreases the likelihood of distortion in reality testing and leads inevitably to maladaption, especially from the point of view of attacks on life. [pp. 8–9]

He also explained the significance of the processes of splitting and projection to explain victimology and how unwanted aspects of oneself are projected and seen to reside in another which has to be attacked or destroyed (or, in cases of homicide, murdered). Building on this, Hyatt-Williams (1998), along with other psychoanalytic theorists and researchers such as Campbell (2010) and Welldon (1992, 1994), have contributed to an understanding of explosive murderous attacks such as high street massacres, emphasizing how encapsulated, split-off, murderous aspects of the self can become released under conditions of psychic pain that cannot be tolerated. Such accounts can help to explain why, for example, in such individuals, events, such as being fired from a job, can trigger murderous rage. Such dynamics may have been in play in the recent murders perpetuated by Raoul Moat in the UK. These theorists focused on projective and introjective intrapsychic processes, notably splitting and projection, which are ways of dealing with the developmental anxieties associated with the paranoid–schizoid level of psychic development.

Narcissism and psychological development

The above-mentioned research and theory have pointed to the importance of the self-object relationships underpinning psychopathy. To more fully appreciate such relationships, we need to consider how the self develops as a result of its experiences with a significant other, moving from a state of psychic merger with its object to a gradual differentiation from it, resulting in a relatively autonomous self capable of seeing others as separate from oneself.

At the earliest stages of psychic development, there is a massive defence against separateness. This is the core feature of narcissism. Narcissism seen in this way represents a basic resistance to acknowledging difference and the need for an object on which to depend. As Rosenfeld (1964, 1971) has pointed out, the self instead attempts to omnipotently control its objects in a mad way as a defence against anxieties associated with separation. Britton's (2004) clarification of the clinical manifestations of narcissism in the transference has also helped us to understand the resistance to separateness and need for the other inherent in the narcissistic defence.

In malignant narcissism in particular, as I have indicated, there is a denial of the need for *the other* which is replaced by a ruthless control and manipulation of it. This also involves self-idealization. This idealization has two aspects: the overvaluing of the self, so that the self, by attempting to incorporate the object, becomes convinced that he possesses all that it is good and desirable (and, thus, defends against envy), and an idealization of the omnipotent, destructive (predatory) parts of the self. This latter aspect accounts for the perverse sadomasochistic excitement involved in inflicting suffering in sadistic acts (De Masi, 2003) and, in the therapy situation, the phenomena of trying to corrupt ("con") the therapist while camouflaging the true needy and impoverished self (Keogh, Howard, Chappell, & Hooke, 2010; McWilliams, 1994). The refinement of this understanding by Meloy (1997), especially in identifying the *differential* role of the stranger self-object as an idealized self, has been particularly useful.

In this regard Kernberg (1980) has also noted that the greater the level of internalization of satisfactory reciprocal human relationship, the less need there is for omnipotent control and grandiosity to be reflected in fantasy, as in the case with malignant narcissism and extreme psychopathy. In my own research (see Chapter Eight), I found only rudimentary or no psychic representation of human interaction in the severely psychopathic offenders.

Kernberg (1980) argued that, in individuals with more internalized reciprocal relationships, there is more protection from violent and destructive impulses afforded to the "object" and via projection to potential victims. Related to this, the effect of maternal (and paternal) containment in the de-escalation of perverse sadomasochistic excitement has been reported in infant–child observation studies, especially in the relationships with siblings by Magagna (2011). She highlights that, with maternal containment, that the love and hate towards to the object can become more integrated. Kernberg (1995), in his exploration of such issues in his book, *Love Relations*, shows how such integration can allow for aggression to be contained by love, for intercourse to be passionate, rather than violent and cruel. This is, in turn, linked to the fact that genuine relatedness is predicated on the achievement of a sense of self that is separate from others, a self with the capacity for reflective thought and a capacity to appreciate the mental states of others.

Blos (1967) also highlighted the relevance of separateness and in-dividuation to psychopathic violence in adolescents. He saw that when separation and individuation, which are reflected in internal-ized psychic representations of relatedness, are not achieved, condi-tions of stress can trigger responses that are characterized by rage and hostility directed towards the self or others. These theoretical ideas, now substantiated by empirical findings, show the importance of understanding the core object relations in the psychopathic offender. The fundamental resistance to allowing the "other" to exist and to be relied upon results in identification with the cruel, sadistic, stranger self-object.

As a consequence, such an individual enters a dangerous world of distorted reality, one in which he feels forced to create, in order to maintain a precarious psychic equilibrium. This, in turn, explains how the actions of the perpetrator and the selection of his victim(s) can be understood in terms of specific aspects of an individual's develop-ment and experience, especially his identifications with the victim.

Consider the following vignette, which I believe illustrates the general and psychoanalytic characteristics that I have described, along with the relevance of the crime and its victims to the developmental history.

The case of Mario

Mario was an eighteen-year-old man who had been incarcerated as a result of a brutal sexual attack that was carried out in the context of a home invasion, with children present who witnessed violence perpetrated by the invaders (of whom he was one). He talked of this crime coldly, showing no identification with the victims' suffering, but rather revealing his feeling of power in controlling the situation.

He had a history of violence at school, often bullying younger and more vulnerable children, for which he was finally expelled. This began when his mother allowed strangers (her casual partners) into the house. Some of these partners became violent towards him and his mother. He had also been a truant.

When he started bullying during primary school, he was found to have learning and attention difficulties. By the time he was a teenager, he had started abusing alcohol and gradually started using cannabis. He was a poly-drug user by the time he was fifteen years old and had become part of a deviant peer group who were involved in car break-ins and petty theft, as well as "rolling" people for money. He displayed little remorse for the injuries he had caused others, although he gradually acknowledged that it would have caused some of them "some hassle" and, in one instance, that it was probably upsetting for a child to witness the injury of her mother. In his early adolescence, he had a number of police cautions related to his aggressive behaviour.

Mario's background told the story of a childhood of failed maternal containment and an environment which gradually taught him to trust no one and rely on nobody. His home environment was one in which dependency and vulnerability were seen as weaknesses, as were any displays of feelings. There was also no sense of protection, but an atmosphere of fear and unpredictability. He was the eldest of three children, all born of different fathers. His mother was an intravenous drug user who gradually rehabilitated herself as he grew older, but was largely emotionally unavailable to him as an infant. He had been placed in foster care a couple of times before reaching the age of five. His mother's partners (*his* home invaders) were also drug users and, as I have said, abused his mother and him. He was physically abused by at least two of them as a latency age child. There was also some uncertainty about sexual abuse. One can see how his identification with the cruel, sadistic "stranger self-object" began to take shape.

His reaction to therapy sessions with me was initially to view the sessions as a means of getting time out from other unwanted activities. None the less, he seemed to like coming to his weekly sessions. During these sessions, it was very important to him that he was in control. He needed to impress me about his importance in the unit in which he was placed. I was often made to feel, however, as if I had nothing to offer. This was his way of dealing with his envy. Very early in our contact, I also felt that anything I said that was different to how he saw things was experienced by him as a threat to his sense of self.

Over time, I encouraged Mario to tell me about his life experiences and he seemed to enjoy this. I would make links between some of the things he told me he had done between sessions with me and how he had been feeling at the time. This seemed to help him begin, as Fonagy (2001) would say, to mentalize about his experience. He also seemed to develop some minimal awareness of me as being separate to him. As this happened, he started to become somewhat paranoid that I was probably "doing this to find out more stuff about him". This break-down of a psychopathic transference to a paranoid one has been well documented (Kernberg, 1984).

The work with him was slow and painstaking and there seemed, especially at first, nothing to report other than feeling conned and controlled by him for a long period of time. The work with him also involved many uncomfortable countertransference feelings, includ-ing, at times, feeling repulsed by him and, at other times, variously fearful and intimidated. Occasionally, I even experienced cruel feel-ings towards him and at moments, as result of what Ruszczynski (2010b) describes an "identification with the neglector", a feeling *that I had failed him*.

As therapy progressed, he tried to corrupt it by attempting to bend the frame (e.g., asking that I send a message to someone or whether I might get him help with some privilege) or, in more subtle ways, by attempting to con me that he was being honest when he was not, or by giving me pat responses, such as saying how sorry he was when he felt his review was due and he thought I might influence it.

His assessment records showed he was typical of subjects involved in my research who were classified as psychopathic. In particular, he showed a score on the Hare Psychopathy Checklist as being moder-ately psychopathic and a score on the MPPI-A that showed an extreme elevation of the psychopathic deviate score, typical of severely conduct-disordered adolescents.

Work with him also highlighted the idealization of the bad self or, in Meloy's (1997) terms, the "stranger self-object" and the way in which he projected his victim self and the personal relevance of his victims and his actions with them. It further revealed his inability to tolerate frustration and (until he was able to reflect on his feelings more) the inevitability of his acting out. This underlined the need to be able to accept his projective identifications and to gradually feed these back to him in a more digestible form. The containment afforded to me by my body of psychoanalytic knowledge, my *psychoanalytic third*, also helped me to deal with pressures against separateness and, thus, enactment. Containment was also afforded by clinical supervision and through my own analysis, which were invaluable to me in the work with him.

In the case of Mario, one can see how his offending behaviour is in the service of preserving his primitive internal world of grandiosity through destructiveness and cruelty associated with his malignant narcissism. In such an individual, violence becomes the means of attachment necessitated by the underlying narcissistic vulnerability. Violence, thus, becomes the means of psychic repair. The dilemma of the adolescent with malignant narcissism is his inability to respond to the main psychological challenge of adolescence: the achievement of separation and individuation in order to achieve a secure identity.

In the case of such an individual, there was never any real separation and individuation achieved, let alone a second chance to consolidate it. Instead, there was an ongoing precarious psychic state of grandiosity and omnipotence. The inability to separate from the object (usually the maternal object) and, through the process of mourning, develop a sense of otherness and a capacity to mentalize and understand states of mind of the other, has to be replaced by a massive denial of a need for attachment and an identification with grandiose, aggressive objects and taking himself as the object. These identifications serve the purpose of shielding the individual from emotional vulnerability, especially underlying feelings of shame (Campbell, 2010). This, in turn, provides a rationale for ruthless and remorseless behaviour towards other people. Psuedo-autonomy conceals a huge dependence on idealized objects.

Mario's background and the development of his psychopathology anticipates many of the research findings about a sub-group of juvenile sex offenders which I discovered in my own research.

The psychopathic sex offending described in this case vignette can be regarded as encompassing *a sexual perversion wherein the main motivator is a desire to experience an excitement associated with violence and destructiveness*. This perversion was worked through in the vicissitudes of the transference–countertransference (Ogden, 1996).

Psychoanalysis and sexual perversion

"Perversion" is a concept that has been in psychological use since the nineteenth century when Krafft-Ebing (1886) elaborated the concept in his landmark study of sexuality and sexual aberration, *Psychopathia Sexualis*. Krafft-Ebing (who was one of the first writers to acknowledge that sex offending represented psychopathology) characterized sexual perversion by reference to the build-up of excitability culminating in ecstatic orgasm. Perversity, as a term, has also been used to refer to the extent to which behaviour is seen to depart from the normal and conventional. It is, thus, a subjective term that is also linked with the term "paraphilia", which refers to sexual arousal that involves either a non-human object, the infliction of pain to oneself or another, or where children or non-consenting adults are the objects of the sexual arousal and behaviour.

Rape and child molestation are, thus, both regarded as sexual perversions and paraphilias in that they represent serious departures from normal sexual behaviour and involve behaviours which produce sexual arousal in individuals in unconventional ways. With offences involving children, the non-normative nature of the child as the object required for sexual arousal, as well as the non-normative mode of sexual stimulation achieved through the offending, characterizes the perversion and the paraphilia that it represents. In the case of the adult rapist, the perversion and paraphilic nature of the behaviour is characterized by the nature of the sexual object (e.g., a non-consenting and or an elderly or frail individual) and the sexually sadistic behaviour.

In so far as I have noted that juvenile sex offenders might be better seen as a heterogeneous group in terms of their motivations for offending, it might also be the case that no single psychoanalytic account of sexual perversion easily accounts for the range of sexually perverse behaviour found among juvenile sex offenders. For example, the perversion inherent in certain forms of paedophilia seems better accounted for by theories which emphasize the repair of trauma and the defensive and relational meaning of perverse behaviour. Other theories, which emphasize the lack of relational meaning the victim has to the offender and focus on the excitement inherent in destructiveness, might better account for the sexually perverse behaviour to be found in the forceful and brutal rape of adult (and occasionally child) victims.

De Masi (2003), in presenting a new theoretical view of the sadomasochistic perversion, rejected Freud's original *Sexualtheorie* (a theory of psychopathology based on a disruption to the normal psychosexual stages of development). In particular, he disagreed with Freud's view that sexual perversion could be explained simply as an admixture of aggression and sexuality. Sexual perversions have been explained by a number of theorists who followed a tradition of describing perversion on the basis of drive theory and psychosexual stages of development (Chasseguet-Smirgel, 1983; Freud, 1905d, 1924c; Gillespie, 1956). De Masi refers to these as "first paradigm theories". Gillespie (1956) is representative of such theoretical views about perversion. In quoting Freud's seminal contribution to understanding perversion, contained in his *Three Essays on the Theory of Sexuality* (Freud, 1905d), he noted,

> I think the essence of the book may be expressed by saying that perversion represents the persistence into adult life of elements of infantile ('polymorph-perverse') sexual activity at the expense of adult genitality, these infantile strivings having failed to undergo the normal transformations of puberty, and having failed also to succumb to the defence mechanisms that would have converted them into neurotic symptoms. [p. 396]

De Masi felt that other psychoanalytic accounts of perversion also failed to account for sadomasochistic perversion and, therefore, were not adequate theories of perversion. These included those theories he referred to as "second paradigm" (trauma and relational) post-Kohutian and post-Winnicottian theories, which focus on perversion as a means of repairing or defending against trauma (e.g., Kohut, 1977; McDougall, 1995; Winnicott, 1945), and by "third paradigm" (post-Kleinian) theories, which regard perversion as the sexualization of power and cruelty, a split self, in which a perverse self dominates (Klein, 1932; Meltzer, 1966, 1973; Rosenfeld, 1987). De Masi regards Stoller's (1975) traumatist view of perversion, which depicts sexual perversion as an "erotic form of hatred" (where, in the sexual fantasy, there is an adult triumph over a childhood trauma) as not easily linked to any of the three major psychoanalytical paradigms that he articulates.

While De Masi (2003) eschewed all these views, regarding them as inadequate accounts of the clinical phenomena of especially the sado-masochistic perversion, he did have some sympathy with the relation-ist and traumatist (second paradigm) approaches, which he saw as able to account for "certain episodic perversions and pathologies char-acterized by problems of aggression or anti-social behaviour [which are] directly connected with very early narcissistic wounds" (p. 39).

He described a structured sexual perversion, as distinct from perverse acting out, as involving "a flight and withdrawal that begins in early infancy through the production of sexualised mental states" (p. 85). And he argues that this gives rise to "a closed world that prevents any development towards other types of love relationship . . . a destructive defence that does constant damage to the psyche . . ." (p. 87).

He regards the sadomasochistic perversion, in particular, as rep-resenting *excitation resulting from being destructive* (and, I would add, of what is desired). He regards it as destructive to, and in no way reparative of, the ego. De Masi's theoretical view is, thus, in contrast to earlier theories, as the excitation in the sadomasochistic perversion is seen to directly relate to a sexualization of primary destructiveness. He sees that it is a *non-object*-related, purely destructive orgasmic pleasure. In terms of it being a non-object-related phenomenon, he introduces the concept of "the sadomasochistic monad" "to describe the fusional and masturbatory combined figure that appropriates the pleasure of both partners. The sadomasochistic monad has the subject's own body as its locus and *has no need of the other*" (p. 82, my italics).

I see these ideas as being *consistent with the type of perverse, sadistic behaviour inherent in psychopathic sexual offending and with the concept of malignant narcissism.* Supporting my view, De Masi notes,

It is easy to show that the driving force behind pleasure in this dimen-sion (sadomasochism) is precisely narcissism, in one of its purest and most extreme forms. I am referring here to narcissism not as an expe-rience of confirmation or idealization of the self, but rather as pleasure in the control and subordination of the other, *the absolute triumph of the self.* [p. 90, my italics]

De Masi also emphasizes that it is a sexualization of a state of mind that is involved in sexual perversion, a view to which I subscribe. He notes, "Sexualization is a withdrawal of the mind into a private world based on the sexualized distortion of perceptions that underlies *all forms of perversion*" (p. 85, my italics).

De Masi's scholarly and extensive review of the literature on sexual perversion leads him to a paradigmatic shift to explain the sadomasochistic perversion. As the above-mentioned quotation implies, some of his ideas apply to all forms of sexual perversion. Further, while his description of sadomasochistic perversion does not set out to explain criminal sexual behaviour, he does note that sadomasochistically perverse phantasies can result in criminal behaviour and that, in some sexual crimes, it is pure destructiveness that causes the sexual excitement. As such, his depiction of behaviours associated with sadomasochistic perversion appears to be resonant with the perverse behaviour inherent in psychopathic (sadistic) sexual offences.

In contrast, the sexually perverse behaviour found in certain forms of paedophila, which reveal more capacity for attachment and relatedness in the perpetrator, do not seem to be as well explained by such a theory and indeed might be better accounted for by some of the "second paradigm" theories. Of these, I find McDougall's (1995) theory to have utility in explaining sexually perverse behaviour, wherein an unindividuated self uses others as self-objects in order to maintain a sense of self, such that something other than destructiveness gives rise to arousal.

McDougall (1995) regarded perversion

> as a label for acts in which an individual (1) imposes personal wishes and conditions on someone who does not wish to be included in the perverse individual's sexual scenario (as in the case of rape, voyeurism and exhibitionism); or (2) seduces a non responsible individual (such as a child or the mentally disturbed adult). [p. 177]

She noted that

> Perhaps in the last resort *only relationships can actually be termed perverse*; this label would then apply to sexual exchanges in which the perverse individual is *totally indifferent to* the needs and desires of the other. [p. 177, my italics]

Although her definition refers to the perverse individual being "totally indifferent to the needs and desires of the other", it does not make a distinction between the real, as distinct from the perceived or *cognitively distorted view* of the needs of the other, as often found in the paedophile who believes he is "helping" the victim.

McDougall's views regarding the perverse sexualities (such as sadomasochism and exhibitionism) suggest an aetiology that is linked to a poorly integrated self. She describes psychological development that becomes stuck at the level of a psychosomatic self that is dependent on the object for its sense of integrity. The absence of a further development to a lexical self, with associated capacities for self-soothing, is used to explain the reliance on the object (of perversion) *as well as the compulsive quality of the sexual perversion*. As such McDougall explains *perversion as involving something more than domination, control and destructiveness in the perverse excitation*. Her view of sexual perversion does not imply a "no-object" relating.

Like De Masi, however, McDougall's description of the dynamics of the neo-sexual inventor (her optional term for the pervert) *implies a sexualization of a state of mind* (Meltzer, 1973) *in the place of a mature sexual and loving relationship*.

In summary, De Masi's ideas concerning the sadomasochistic perversion could be applied to understanding the perverse sexual behaviour inherent in the more sadistic psychopathic sexual offending, while ideas such as McDougall's could be applied to sexual perversions which involve a sensation-dominated (non-lexical) self, as seen in the attachment hungry paedophile, who engages in compulsive, sexualized behavior with an object that is used to maintain his sense of self.

Interestingly, what these theories have in common is an implicit reference to narcissism. For De Masi, it is a malignant narcissism in which the self is taken as the object, the need for others denied, and destructiveness valued. McDougall, on the other hand, stresses a self that is impaired and underdeveloped and needs and uses (projects aspects of himself into) others as self-objects in order to help maintain a sense of self.

These ideas link to the fact that, in the case of (some) child molesters and rapists, there is a manifestly different emotional significance and meaning of the victim to the perpetrator. These are illustrated further in the cases presented in Chapter Ten.

In conclusion, the sexual perversions inherent in juvenile sexual offending appear to be at least as varied as the attachment styles of juvenile sex offenders and are accounted for by different object relation constellations. What they have in common, perhaps, is the way and extent to which the sense of self has developed (the level of narcissism or malignant narcissism) and its *need or lack of need for others.* These ideas are also consonant with the conclusion of the meta-analytic review of the majority of studies conducted on this group of offenders, which suggests that the range of the psychopathology their offending represents cannot easily be accounted for by a unitary theory (Seto & Lalumière, 2010).

Moreover, it can be seen that if a sub-set of juvenile sex offenders who are characterized by psychopathic traits underpinned by maliganant narcissism can be identified, it is likely that their motivations and *the nature of the sexual perversion inherent in their offending will be qualitatively different* to that of other offenders. This needs to be carefully assessed, as the failure to recognize it has significant implications.

CHAPTER SIX

Epigenetics and aspects of the neurobiology of attachment and sexual behaviour

> "The phrase 'nature and nurture' is a convenient jingle of words, for it separates under two distinct heads the innumerable elements of which personality is composed. Nature is all that a man brings with himself into the world; nurture is every influence without that affects him after his birth."
>
> (Sir Francis Galton, 1874)

The view into the internal world of the juvenile sex offender can be enhanced by a brief overview of some of the key aspects of the neurobiology of both attachment and sexual behaviour and their interaction with developmental factors. In this chapter, therefore, I explain the relevance of epigenetics to the development of the "social brain" and provide something of a helicopter view of the brain's limbic system, its neurochemistry, and its relevance to understanding juvenile sex offending.

Epigenetic factors and their relevance to attachment and sex offending

The human genome experiment and the associated genetic (chromosomal) mapping onto human diseases and characteristics have had wide ranging implications. These include a refocus on the biology of human behaviour and the rise of biological psychiatry. Importantly, the field of epigenetics has also evolved as a consequence of advancing knowledge of the human biological system. Epigenetics identifies mechanisms that influence the phenotypic expression of genetic potential and gives equal and reciprocal primacy to both nature and nurture, that is, to gene–environment interactions.

Epigenetic factors are important regulatory mechanisms in the field of neurobiology, in particular, the neurobiology of attachment and sexual behaviour. For example, and relevant to the backgrounds of some juvenile sex offenders, there is evidence that enhanced maternal care can positively affect the biological underpinnings of emotional regulation (Meany, 2001; Weaver et al., 2004). Specifically, it has been shown that enhanced maternal care can lead to an increase in the genetic expression (throughout the lifespan) of the glucocorticoid receptor (GRII). This is a neural receptor that reduces (via a negative feedback loop) the blood levels of circulating cortisol. Cortisol is a stress related hormone released from the adrenal gland via the so called hypothalamic-pituitary-adrenal axis. By helping to reduce cortisol levels the glucocorticoid receptors (GRIIs) lead to reduced activation of the amygdala leading to an increased capacity for emotional regulation (Liu et al., 1997; Weaver et al., 2004). Moreover, and pertinent to our consideration of attachment and sex offending, there is also evidence of an epigenetic effect in this system, whereby insecure attachment has been shown to result in elevated levels of the corticotrophin releasing hormone (CRH) (Korosi & Baram, 2008). The secretion of cortisol from the adrenal glands is mediated initially by the secretion of CRH from the hypothalamus. The CRH then travels the short distance in the brain to the pituitary gland, where it stimulates the release of corticotrophin, a pituitary hormone which then travels the much larger distance from the brain to the adrenal glands, causing secretion of the stress hormone, cortisol.

One of the many effects of stress (including the associated elevated levels of cortisol) is the tendency to premature and, thus, abnormal neuronal dendrite pruning in childhood (Helmeke et al., 2009) which, when added to normal neuronal dendrite pruning in adolescence, can result in significantly impaired limbic system functioning in adulthood (Heim et al., 2000; Meany, 2001).

Epigenetics, thus, has brought back into fashion the importance of gene–environment interactions, previously referred to as the nature–nurture argument. The emergence of this field of interest has been accompanied by a new lexicon of terms including "environmental (re)programming".

Mental representations as epigenetic factors

Epigenetics also points to some important implications concerning mental representations and their influence on the expression of sexual and attachment behaviour among juvenile sex offenders. In particular it underlines the probable importance of mental representations (the internal world) in influencing the expression of biology. As Crittenden (2002) suggests,

> Recognizing that behavior results from the process of mental representation helps to explain why individuals exposed to similar dangers can have different outcomes and why genetically identical individuals exposed to different threats have different outcomes. The representational process, rather than genes or experience directly, organizes individuals' behavior. This suggests the need to differentiate between contributing, necessary, and sufficient conditions for psychopathology. There is little evidence that genes alone are sufficient to cause mental illness, nor is it evident that they are an essential condition. To the contrary, genetic influence more often functions as a contributing factor. Neither, however, does experience determine outcomes. Attachment theory, through its emphasis on individual representation of events, suggests a process by which similar circumstances could yield different outcomes. [p. 75]

Such biology–environment interactions are, thus, important to consider when attempting to understand how certain attachment and sexual behaviours (especially those associated with sex offending) come to be established and maintained. In this regard, it is interesting to consider how mental representations might mediate both cognition and perception and influence the consolidation of hormonal and neurotransmitter dysfunction. It is also worth considering how non-pharmacological treatments, such as psychotherapeutic interventions, might potentially influence or normalize neurobiological dysfunction.

For example, while, as we have seen, there is evidence showing that abuse and trauma can impact on the hypothalamic–pituitary–adrenal (HPA) axis, leading to the overproduction of corticosteroids which, in turn, can have an adverse impact on the neuro-chemicals which mediate attachment and sexual behaviour (Carter, 1998; Heim et al., 2002), there is also evidence that this might not be a unidirectional influence. Recent data concerning brain plasticity, especially those concerning "the social brain", whose development was thought to be fixed, suggest a potential reversibility of effect, such that psychotherapy treatments might have a positive impact in helping to readjust such underpinning biological mechanisms (and their neuro-chemistry) in the service of healthy psychological development (Doidge, 2007).

Research into the neurobiological effects of psychotherapy could also challenge the notion that neurobiological dysfunction can only be ameliorated by psychopharmacology. For example, Kjaer and colleagues (2002) have produced evidence of increased dopamine tone during meditation-induced changes of consciousness. There is also some evidence suggesting that psychotherapy enhances 5-HT_{1A} receptor functioning in patients with major depressive disorders (Karlsson et al., 2010). Such mechanisms are still only incompletely understood, yet there is mounting evidence which suggests that interventions that have an impact on the mind (change mental representations) in a psychotherapeutic context can produce changes at the brain level, impact which could result in possible changes in the underpinning neurochemical functioning, which might mediate attachment and sexual behaviour (Kumari, 2006).

The social brain

The neurobiology and neurochemistry that is of particular interest in terms of juvenile sex offending is that which has an impact on the so-called "social brain": those neurological structures and neurochemical systems which affect both the capacity to self-regulate emotions and impulses and the ability to eventually psychologically separate and individuate. (The psychodynamics of this phase of development and its impact are discussed in Chapters Nine and Ten.)

As Frith (2007) has noted,

> The notion that there is a 'social brain' in humans specialized for social interactions has received considerable support from brain imaging and, to a lesser extent, from lesion studies. Specific roles for the various components of the social brain are beginning to emerge. For example, the amygdala attaches emotional value to faces, enabling us to recognize expressions such as fear and trustworthiness, while the posterior superior temporal sulcus predicts the end point of the complex trajectories created when agents act upon the world. It has proved more difficult to assign a role to medial prefrontal cortex, which is consistently activated when people think about mental states. [p. 26]

In terms of the relevance of the social brain to agentive behaviour, he continues,

> I suggest that this region may *have a special role in the second-order representations needed for communicative acts when we have to represent someone else's representation of our own mental state.* These cognitive processes are not specifically social, since they can be applied in other domains. However, these cognitive processes have been driven to ever higher levels of sophistication by the complexities of social interaction". [p. 26, my italics]

The discovery of the social brain and related findings concerning the automaticity of higher mental processes has caused a Galilean-like revolution in the view of human thinking (Bargh & Ferguson, 2000). In particular, the centrality of the conscious mind in thinking and action has been challenged and the importance of unconscious processes (and I would add, internalized representations) highlighted. For example, Bargh and Ferguson (2000) have noted how "Research has revealed that social interaction, evaluation and judgment, and the operation of *internal* goal structures can all proceed without the intervention of conscious acts of will and guidance of the process" (p. 925, my italics).

This complexity of human thinking is related to the way in which the brain has developed. The human brain is characterized by the presence of an extensive cortex, which, in conjunction with other sub-cortical structures, allows humans to behave as rational beings, capable of intentional behaviour. In turn, epigenetics explains how development can influence genetic expression. From this perspective, it can be argued that secure attachment might be a necessary perquisite for the fullest expression of human potential. This point of view sits comfortably with the evidence that, in evolutionary terms, secure attachment confers an advantage in terms of adaptation and survival of the species (Crittenden, 2002). Despite the evidence supporting polyvagal theory, which suggests that, in humans, the more primitive (sub-cortical) structures in the brain still have a primary influence in terms of attachment and self-regulation (Mac-Lean, 1990; Porges, 2003), there is evidence that higher cortical structures (in particular, areas of the right hemisphere, and especially structures such as the orbito-frontal cortex (OFC)), which assist in the development of an "agentive self", operate in conjunction with these structures.

As suggested previously, early adverse attachment experiences can cause dysfunction in the secretion of neurohormones and neurotransmitters, which, in turn, can have an impact on these brain structures so that the desire and need for attachment can be disrupted (Hertsgaard, Gunnar, Erickson, & Nachmias, 1995). As a consequence, the neurochemical pathways, which in secure attachment would normally facilitate bonding and attachment in adult life through loving relationships, appear to dysfunction (Meany, 2001). In the case of disrupted attachment, the need to attach might instead become expressed through sexualized or aggressively sexualized behaviour, depending on the particular type of attachment insecurity that ensues (van IJzendoorn, Schuengel, & Bakermans-Kranenburg, 1999).

The relevance of the limbic system

To more fully appreciate the neurobiology of attachment and the "socio-emotional" and sexual self, we need to understand something about the limbic system, or "reptilian brain", in man. The limbic system, which was originally described by the French neurologist Broca (Jay, 2002), is the part of the brain which is involved in regulating emotions and feelings, such as rage, fright, passion, love, hate, joy, and sadness. It is also involved in the regulation of sexual behaviour, hormone production, the functioning of the autonomic nervous system, and with regulating hunger, thirst, sleep, body temperature, motivation, and a sense of smell. This structure also has a role in the sense of personal identity. It accommodates the pleasure centres in the brain and has some functions related to memory. It is a part of the brain that was much larger and had a greater influence in the functioning of pre-mammalian brains (MacLean, 1990) (Figure 2).

The limbic system essentially consists of cortical and sub-cortical structures as well as other structures that are linked to it, significantly the orbito-pre-frontal cortex and the hypothalamus. The cortical structures are the para-hippocampal gyrus and the cingulate gyrus, while the sub-cortical structures are the hippocampal formation amygdala and septal nuclei. It is, thus, a complex system, incorporating a number of sub-structures in the brain. The limbic structures that can be regarded as biological substrates of attachment behaviour include: the

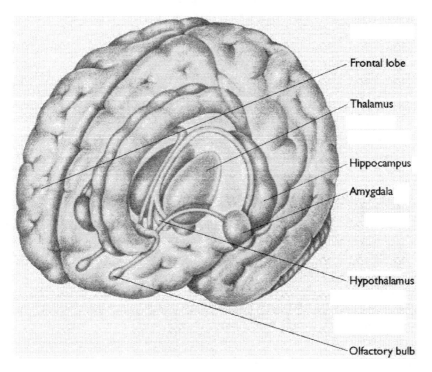

Figure 2.   The limbic system (Helena Karnolz-Langdon, 2011).

cingulate gyrus, the hypothalamus, the septum, and, importantly and uniquely in humans, the pre-frontal cortex (Lorberbaum et al., 2002).

The limbic system and sex offending

A landmark finding implicating the limbic system with sexually aberrant behaviour relevant to sex offending was the discovery of hypersexuality associated with a constellation of symptoms that together are known as the Kluver–Bucy syndrome. This syndrome is caused by lesions (damage) to the amygdala (and hippocampal horns) and can cause sufferers to (among other symptoms) seek sexual satisfaction from inappropriate objects, including children (Poeck, 1985).

Moreover, the structure and functioning of the limbic system has been linked to psychiatric syndromes, and used to explain them, some of which might be relevant to understanding juvenile sex offending. For example, Mega, Cummings, Salloway, and Malloy (1997) have argued that there are two major divisions within the limbic system, which can account for specific functions. The structures referred to from a phylogenetic perspective are an older, so-called "paleocortical" division, with the amygdala and orbito-pre-frontal cortex at its centre, and a newer "archicortical" division featuring the hippocampus and cingulate cortex. The former is considered by these authors to be involved in affect, drive, and object association, while the newer division is involved in sensory process encoding and attentional control. The two are seen to work together in a way that integrates thought, feeling, and action. This has immediate relevance to the differential difficulties related to affect regulation and impulse control with which juvenile sex offenders often present with.

On the basis of these considerations, it has been suggested that depressive disorders could be accounted for broadly by a decreased activity in the limbic system, obsessive–compulsive symptomatology by an increased activity, and psychosis by other dysfunction in the system. The notion that there are (differential) psychiatric disturbances linked with limbic system dysfunction also raises speculation about their role in juvenile sex offending, especially given that the early development of such offenders are often marked by abuse and trauma, which could damage such structures and lead to different behavioural consequences (Carter, 1998; Heim et al., 2002).

In addition to the anatomy of the limbic system, the neurochemistry of this system also informs our understanding of the sexual and attachment behaviour of juvenile sex offenders.

Limbic system neurochemistry and attachment

In order to understand something of the neurochemical basis of attachment and sexual behaviour, it is important to examine some of the key neurotransmitters and neuro-hormones in the limbic system and their interactions. While the whole field of the neurochemistry of social and sexual behaviour is in its infancy, such an insight helps in understanding the complexity involved in producing change in sexual and attachment behaviour.

Two neuro-hormones (which can act as neurotransmitters) that are critically implicated in the activation of attachment behaviour are oxytocin and arginine vasopressin (also known as vasopressin) (Keverne & Curley, 2004). Discovered by du Vigneaud (du Vigneaud et al., 1953), who was awarded the Nobel Prize in Chemistry for his efforts, oxytocin and vasopressin are closely linked and both have an impact on social behaviour. Recent findings concerning the effects of these neuro-hormones have also significantly enhanced our understanding of attachment behaviour (and its dysfunctions) (Insel & Winslow, 2004) and their likely role in adult sex offending (Beech & Mitchell, 2005).

Oxytocin is secreted during orgasm in both sexes and facilitates social recognition, bonding, trust, and empathy (Rodrigues, Saslow, Garcia, John, & Keltner, 2009). Oxytocin has been associated, through a variety of animal and human studies, with the establishment and maintenance of infant and mother attachment and bonding. In animal studies, it has been shown that the release of oxytocin leads to a notable increase in nurturing behaviour (e.g., Insel & Young, 2001). In humans, oxytocin has been found to be released during breast-feeding and to be associated with increased maternal behaviour, which facilitates attachment (Sjögren, Widström, Edman, & Uvnäs-Moberg, 2000). While oxytocin has been found to play a significant role in mother–infant bonding, vasopressin has been found to increase mate protection behaviour in animal studies (Insel & Winslow, 1998).

What is particularly important in terms of understanding the role of insecure attachment and its possible link to deviant sexual behaviour is the disruption of the chemical basis to secure attachment and bonding that can result from abuse experiences (common in the backgrounds of juvenile sex offenders), especially when they occur early in the development of the brain. In this regard, it has been shown that oxytocin and vasopressin concentrations are inversely related to corticosteroid levels. Increased levels of corticosteroids might reduce the attachment and bonding effects of oxytocin and vasopressin (Chaouloff, 2000). This can result in the establishment of a disrupted trajectory of associated emotional development (Meany, 2001). Oxytocin and vasopressin are also linked with serotonin/5-HT (serotonin) receptor functioning, which, in turn, can exert a regulatory effect on them (Insel & Winslow, 1998).

In summary, the current state of knowledge concerning oxytocin and vasopressin suggest that they are at the neurobiological heart of the attachment system (Winslow & Insel, 1993, 2002).

Neurotransmitters and sexual behaviour

Neurotransmitters such as serotonin and dopamine are neurochemicals which facilitate the transmission of signals from one neuron to another via electrical impulses generated at points between neurons called "synapses". In terms of sexual arousal, and impulsive and compulsive sexual behaviour, dopamine and serotonin are of particular interest. Hull, Muschamp, and Sato (2004) have provided one of the most comprehensive reviews of the impact of dopamine and serotonin on male sexual behaviour. Such data have added substantially to our understanding of the persistence of impulsive and compulsive sexual behaviour and excitement and how this may be reinforced neurochemically. They have also helped to shed light on other factors such as boredom and the need for stimulation in the physiologically underaroused psychopathic offender and how these might relate to his offending (Dolan, 1994).

Serotonin and 5-HT (5 hydroxy-tryptamine) receptors

Serotonin is one of the major neurotransmitters in the human brain and is influential in the regulation of arousal and mood, as well as attention. Serotonin is also critical to early neural development and helps to regulate the development of serotonergic neurons as well as neural tissue in areas of the brain such as the hippocampus and the cerebral cortex (Whitaker-Azmitia, 2001).

5-HT (5 hydroxy-tryptamine) receptors, which are essentially serotonin receptors, can have excitory and/or inhibitory effects on the nervous system. When stimulated, these receptors modulate the release of a range of neurotransmitters, as well as hormones including oxytocin and vasopressin (Insel & Winslow, 1998). As a consequence, these receptors have been found to have an impact on a variety of behaviours, including aggression and anxiety (Dolan & Anderson, 2003). In addition, and as mentioned above, it is now known that 5-HT has an inverse relationship with corticosteroids, so that when they are elevated, 5-HT works to suppress the action of oxytocin and vasopressin. Serotonin also regulates dopamine in such a way that dopamine is adversely affected by impaired 5-HT functioning (e.g., Chaouloff, 2000; Lorrain, Riolo, Matuszewich, & Hull, 1999).

Pertinent to juvenile sex offending is the discovery that decreased levels of 5-HT are associated with increased sexual and sexually violent behaviour (Lorrain, Riolo, Matuszewich, & Hull, 1999). In violent sex offenders whose psychopathy was measured (and confirmed) with the PCL-R, outwardly directed aggression was associated with low serotonin levels (Soderstrom, Blennow, Sjodin, & Forsman, 2003). This links to previous (meta-analytic) research (Dolan, 1994; Dolan, Anderson, & Deakin, 2001), which found that reduced activity of serotonin (5-HT) was correlated with both the behavioural and affective states of psychopathy. It also confirmed a frequently found association between aggression and low serotonin (5-HT) functioning.

Selective serotonin re-uptake inhibitors (SSRIs) (antidepressant drugs which modulate serotonin levels) have been trialled with adult sex offenders in the hope of inhibiting sexually deviant behaviour. The results of such studies indicate that there is some impact of these drugs on sexual behaviour, but, interestingly, this is largely on the compulsive behaviour that is usually found in the paedophilic group (Beech & Mitchell, 2005). This effect is associated with the known antiobsessional action of the drug that is related to its down-regulating effect on dopamine (Bradford, 1999). SSRIs, thus, do not seem to be indicated for the under-aroused psychopathic offenders with, presumably, low levels of oxytocin and dopamine deficiencies (Blair, 2008).

None the less, as serotonin mediates the action of dopamine (Kruger, Hartman, & Schedlowski, 2005; Lorrain, Riolo, Matuszewich, & Hull, 1999), the interrelationships between the two neurotransmitters (particularly the down-regulating effect of adequate levels of serotonin and the optimal functioning of 5-HT) and the roles they play in the establishment and maintenance of deviant sexual behaviour, are important to our understanding of juvenile sex offending.

Dopamine

Dopamine is a neurotransmitter of interest in its own right, due to its capacity to powerfully reinforce sexual behaviour by exciting the pleasure centres in the brain. It is a catecholamine neurotransmitter, which is a precursor of norepinephrine (noradrenalin), a stress hormone involved in mediating attention, motivation, pleasure, and reward. Noradrenalin also has interactive effects with serotonin and dopamine in affecting mood and anxiety.

Dopamine has a number of receptor sites and is modulated differently within cortical and sub-cortical structures. It also has three main pathways of action: the mesolimbic, mesocortical, and the nigrostriatal pathways. Evidence suggests that it is the mesolimbic pathway that is involved in the rewards (motivation), emotions, and reinforcement of behaviour. Therefore, it is this system that is of key interest when thinking about juvenile sex offending behaviours (Meck, 2006).

While the action and effects of dopamine are complex and involve interactions with other neurotransmitters (particularly serotonin and norepinephrine), generally speaking, a deficit in dopamine has been shown to be related to an inability to love as well as to addictive and antisocial behaviour and a lack of remorse about personal behaviour. An excess of dopamine, on the other hand, has been found to be associated with sexual compulsivity, addictiveness, and unhealthy risk taking (Pickering & Gray, 2001). An experimental paradigm to study the activity of dopamine in clinical populations is the "amphetamine challenge". This experimental intervention has been used to investigate the role of dopamine in psychopathy, focusing on the mesolimbic dopamine reward system. It has been found that when psychopaths are investigated in this way, they reveal a *hypersensitivity* in this dopamine reward system, showing a release of dopamine in response to the amphetamine challenge that is four times greater than in normal control subjects (Buckholtz et al., 2010). Despite such findings, which reinforce the physiological under-arousal hypothesis of psychopathy (which, in turn, explains the psychopath's proneness to boredom and a need for stimulation), knowledge about dopamine and its actions, like serotonin, is still emerging and overly simplistic statements about its actions and effects are unwise.

Dopamine and sex offending

Recent research (Pai, Huang, Chen, Yang, & Zhang, 2006) has investigated the hypothesis that central nervous system dopamine could play a role in the susceptibility to sexually *violent* behaviours. This study implicated three functional genetic markers suggesting the role of dopamine in sexually violent behaviour. Supporting these data is a consistent finding of an interrelationship among serotonin, dopamine, and aggression (Pridmore, Chambers, & McArthur, 2005). The relationship between prolactin and dopamine has also been investigated in sex offenders. While dopamine regulates the pleasurable emotions and is released during sexual arousal, prolactin (a hormone that is released after orgasm) reduces sexual arousal. The suggestion of a possible role for prolactin in regulating sexual drive has, however, not been found to account for the heightened sexual drive in sex offenders (Kruger, Hartmann, & Schedlowski, 2005). Such research was, however, useful in that it established that there was no difference between sex offenders and controls in their baseline endocrine levels, nor in their neuroendocrine response to sexual arousal and orgasm. In highlighting once again the inadvisability about generalizations concerning the neurobiology of sex offenders, the authors concluded that "Altered psychosexual states in sex offenders are probably not due to simple changes in hypothalamic dopamine" (p. 136).

Notwithstanding such cautions, some general observations can be made about the likely relationships between dopamine and subgroups of juvenile sex offenders. First, in the case of the psychopathic offender, a deficiency in the level of dopamine and a hypersensitivity in the dopamine reward system might be linked to an inadequate stimulation of the pleasure centres in the brain, along with a certain level of dysphoria and a need for excitement that are key motivational factors in their offending behaviour (Pickering & Gray, 2001). Second, excessive dopamine levels are linked with compulsive sexual behaviours and help to explain the neurobiological underpinnings of the clinical characteristics of attachment-hungry juvenile sex offenders who display features of preoccupied attachment status.

Moreover, dopamine clearly has a central role in powerfully reinforcing sexual behaviour and consolidating connections between sexual excitement and the object of sexual excitement. This could be a fantasy object or a real (but non-normative) sexual object, including a child. It might also explain why sexual behaviours that are powerfully reinforced by this neurotransmitter are among the hardest to change. Not only might this neurotransmitter facilitate sexual attraction to an inappropriate object, but it might also link together different aims, such as violence and sex.

Although excessive dopamine cannot be simplistically linked as the cause of sexual offending, on the basis of current knowledge it can be considered "a chemical conspirator" in consolidating associations between sexual pleasure and admixtures of feelings, including sadism, as well as links to fantasy and perverse sexual objects. As such, it facilitates a broadening of what might be referred to as the "sexualized pleasure map" in the brain. This might, thus, help to account for the perverse excitement in the period leading up to the commission of a sexual offence against a child. For example, in those paedophilic offences which involve extensive masturbatory fantasies about a child and a planning of sexual activity with that child, such thoughts and fantasies become associated with dopamine release, helping to create part of a "pleasure–reward chain", ultimately building to what becomes an inevitable sexual event which finally reduces the tension involved in the build up of sexual arousal.

Such mechanisms might also be relevant in those who access internet pornography. From the moment they start thinking about the sites they can access, they can enter into a chain of dopamine release that leads to the inevitability of orgasm, which then powerfully rewards the behaviour. This also relates to the fact that, with chronic overstimulation, dopamine receptor sites can become desensitized, so that more of the dopamine-related behaviour is required to produce the same effect, as in drug addiction.

In summary, the interplay of serotonin and dopamine (and norepinephrine), along with androgens, appear to be at the neurochemical centre of the sexual/attraction system (Bartels & Zeki, 2004).

Sex hormones, adolescent brain development,
and juvenile sex offending

At puberty, the above-mentioned neurochemical functioning is also affected by the production of sexual hormones (which constitute the sexual drive). Adequate blood levels of androgens are required in both sexes to produce sexual feelings. In this regard, it has been found that men who have engaged in rape behaviour have (on average) more elevated levels of testosterone (Giotakis, Markianos, Vaidakis, & Christodoulou, 2004). Estrogen and progesterone (antiandrogens) have been used to reduce compulsive behaviour in sex offenders (Berner, Brownstone, & Sluga, 1983).

In addition to the hormonal changes in adolescence and natural dendritic (neuron dendrite) pruning processes, there are also powerful psychological factors, which come into play during this period of development (discussed in more detail in Chapter Ten). Added to this are the effects of the differential rate of development of the frontal lobes during adolescence, which result in a reduced regulatory capacity with respect to emotional impulses and arousal due to a lag in development of planning and other "executive", cognitive functioning. This can result in more risk taking and impulsive behaviour during adolescence (Steinberg, 2005), behaviours that are common among juvenile sex offenders. All of this, when it builds on prior behavioural and neurobiological dysfunction, can give rise to differential behavioural (sexual) outcomes. The outcome in the case of the paedophilic offender is a form of behaviour which has a compulsive characteristic, while in the case of the psychopathic offender, it is often behaviour which is impulsive and which is characterized as cold, calculating, aggressive, and even sadistic.

Implications for juvenile sex offending

Many of the neurobiological research findings reviewed above fit comfortably with the other findings concerning both the clinical characteristics of juvenile sex offenders and their developmental precursors. They also link with the categorization of sub-groups of juvenile sex offenders whose developmental experiences have resulted in different forms of insecure attachment, associated with different types of sexual offending. The neurobiological findings can, thus, help to explain the consequences of early abuse experiences and other disruptions to attachment, which set in train an adverse trajectory of socioemotional development linked to juvenile sex offending. These might encompass sexual abuse and/or premature exposure to pornography, which might directly foster sexual deviance, which is, in turn, a predictor of sexual recidivism. The findings reviewed in this chapter show how deviant sexual behaviours that develop in response to developmental disruptions can subsequently become powerfully reinforced by neurotransmitters, in particular dopamine. Further, these findings link to others that have described how adverse developmental experiences have an impact on limbic system neurophysiology and contribute to insecure attachment patterns that, in turn, make sexual maladjustment more likely.

Moreover, while the neurobiology of attachment, sexual, and social behaviour is still an emerging field, there are many convergences in the findings which support an attachment theory informed psychodynamic view of juvenile sex offending. In particular, the general finding that excess cortisol reduces levels of oxytocin and impairs the functioning of 5-HT clearly shows the link between adverse development experiences and disrupted attachment (common in the backgrounds of juvenile sex offenders) at the neurobiological level.

Notwithstanding this, there are still some apparently contradictory findings and a fully integrated neurobiological theory remains elusive. One example of this is the fact 5-HT function does not appear to correlate with psychopathy as a uni-dimensional phenomenon. In fact, the impulsive–antisocial component of psychopathy (measured by the PCL-R) is found to correlate negatively with 5-HT function, while the arrogant–deceitful component correlates positively with 5-HT (Dolan & Anderson, 2003). Further, while the impact of early and significant trauma in contributing to insecure attachment is relatively clear, the differential neurobiological effects underpinning particular types of insecure attachment are less clear. In terms of juvenile sex offending, is less clear *how* these result in compulsive sexuality and hyper-arousal of attachment in some cases, while in others they result in under-arousal and boredom and a chronic need for stimulation. That is, it is not clear why, in some instances, developmental stressors might act to increase dopamine and oxytocin production, thus establishing and maintaining compulsive sexual behaviour, while in others it might decrease it with very different behavioural correlates.

Regardless of this, it is clear that oxytocin and vasopressin play a central role in the neurobiology of attachment, while serotonin, dopamine, and norepinephrine are pivotal to understanding hypersexual behaviour, along with the need for stimulation that drives psychopathic behaviour. Further, it is also clear that dopamine can have an extremely important role in motivating and rewarding sexual behaviours (albeit in different ways) in sub-groups of juvenile sex offenders, and that there is a significant association between low levels of serotonin and aggressive sexual behavior in psychopathic juvenile sex offenders.

Conclusions

A consideration of epigenetics and the neurobiology and neurochemistry underpinning both attachment and sexual behaviour appear to be broadly relevant to our understanding of juvenile sexual offending from a number of points of view.

1. Juvenile sex offenders, as a group, reveal a psychological profile suggestive of insecure attachment status and often experience significant physical abuse and/or sexual abuse. Severe abuse (resulting in dismissing or fearful attachment) can cause the release of the stress related neurochemicals (corticosteroids), leading to the reduction of hormones that modulate attachment and bonding behaviour. This can result in various neurochemical dysfunctions and deficits (e.g., those involving dopamine), which are associated with antisocial behaviour, an inability to form secure attachments, and a lack of remorse about personal behaviour. This most closely describes a psychopathic sub-group of offenders.

2. In contrast, in the case of those juvenile sex offenders described as "attachment hungry" (associated with preoccupied attachment), the underpinning neurochemistry of their compulsive behaviour appears to be linked to an excess of dopamine, which is, in turn, linked to dysfunctional serotonin modulation of dopamine. This group of sex offenders appears to benefit from

SSRIs, which "down-regulate" their dopamine levels. In terms of treatment, if pharmacological treatments were indicated in treating juvenile sex offenders, it would seem that their role should be as part of a wider bio-psycho-social intervention.

3.   While still an incomplete picture, the findings support the view that the neurobiological underpinnings of the motivations of the paedophilic *vs.* the psychopathic offender are quite different and have important implications for their assessment and treatment.

4.   The evidence reviewed regarding attachment and sexual behaviour, along with that concerning the impact of psychological interventions on neurobiology, raises the interesting possibility that psychotherapeutic interventions could exert an epigenetic effect, and, hence, that they could normalize neurochemical dysfunction.

PART III

MAGNIFYING THE LENS:
RESEARCH FINDINGS

CHAPTER SEVEN

The study and its findings

C linical descriptions of juvenile sex offenders suggest that they may be a heterogeneous group with varied attachment styles and different levels of psychopathy. This profile is supported by the more prolific research with adult sex offenders (Marshall, Geris, & Cortoni, 2000; Marshall, Hudson, & Hodkinson, 1993).

Psychopathy in combination with sexual deviance has also been found to predict recidivism. It also predicts offence types among adult sex offenders. Adult rapists appear to have much higher levels of psychopathy than child molesters, with the latter group appearing to have other types of personal difficulties associated with social isolation and immaturity (Marshall, 1989; Marshall, Cripps, Anderson, & Cortoni, 1999). It is important to note that this does not preclude a group of psychopathic offenders (whose intent is primarily to hurt) who also target children.

Juvenile sex offenders have been found to reveal different levels of antisocialness which appeared to be linked with their offence type (Worling, 1995). Types of offending and victim choice also seem to link with different personality characteristics, which, in turn, appear to have some correlation with antisocialness (see Chapter Two). Related to this, adult sex offenders who molest children are less likely to be antisocial or to offend non-sexually. Their personality characteristics seem to be related to their inability to relate to adults in a mature, reciprocal, and emotionally meaningful way (Ward & Siegert, 2002).

These types of findings link with the fact that 33% of juvenile sex offenders have been found to perceive sexual behaviour with children as a way to demonstrate "love" or "care" (Ryan, Miyoshi, Metzner, Krugman, & Fryer, 1996). Those with higher levels of antisocial personality (psychopathy) seem to have less interest in relationships and attachment. Capacity for attachment might, therefore, explain why some of these offenders spend a longer time with their victims. In terms of the style of their offending, those who spend less time with their victims are usually more violent and coercive, rather than obsessed and involved compulsively with masturbatory fantasies about them.

Such findings are the basis for the central hypothesis of this book, which is that psychopathy, capacity for attachment, and level of relatedness to others are key determinants of juvenile sex offence type and of the clinical characteristics of sub-groups of these offenders, whose *internal worlds are likely to be structured relative to the predominance of such factors.*

The study

In the study I conducted, the personality profile and psychopathology of a group of juvenile sex offenders was compared with a group non-offending adolescents. The study also compared a sub-group (child molesters) who offended solely against children with a sub-group who offended against peer-aged or older victims. Overall, the study explored the central question of whether the level of psychopathy and the capacity for attachment differentiated juvenile sex offenders from non-offenders and predicted within (sex offender) group differences that are reflected in their offence type. It also examined the implications of these issues to the aetiology, assessment, and treatment of such offenders.

Broadly, the findings of the study demonstrated that juvenile sex offenders and their sub-groups were identifiable by their scores on a number of selected variables. These were indices of their capacity for attachment, level of relatedness, psychopathy, and psychopathology. The findings also showed that a juvenile sex offender's capacity for attachment and his level of relatedness to others was linked to the age of his victim and the nature of his sex offending.

The design of the study is schematically presented in Figure 3.

Measuring the differences

The study used instruments with a known sensitivity to the clinical characteristics of juvenile sex offenders. Three types of test instruments were used to assess the personality characteristics of juvenile sex offenders in comparison with a non-offending group of adolescents. These instruments were the Minnesota Multiphasic Personality Inventory for Adolescents (MMPI-A), the Hare Psychopathy Checklist-Revised (PCL-R), and the Rorschach. The MMPI-A, a self-report instrument, was selected to assess patterns of personality factors associated with juvenile sex offending. In addition to the general

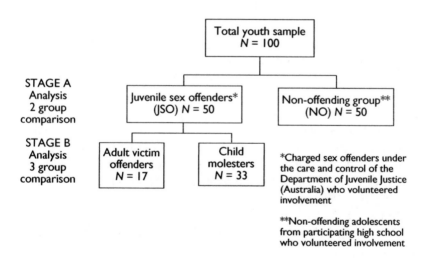

TARGETED MEASURES
1. Hare Psychopathy Checklist Revised (PCL-R) Total factor, Factor 1 & Factor 2
2. MMPI-A: Validity and clinical scales, PSY-5 scales and item analysis
3. Rorschach: Texture response and human experience variable (HEV)

Figure 3. Design of the study.

clinical and validity scales, the psychopathology five (PSY-5) scales were utilized. These provide data on introversion, extroversion, constraint, psychoticism, and aggression. A projective instrument, the Rorschach, was used to provide indicators of capacity for attachment and interest in relationship. In particular, the "texture" determinant (as a measure of capacity for attachment) and the "human experience variable" (HEV) (as a measure of interest in relationship or "human relatedness") were isolated and the groups compared on these variables. Finally, a rating scale, the Hare Psychopathy Checklist (PCL-R), was used to assess psychopathy (level of detachment).

A more detailed description of these instruments and the above-mentioned variables and a consideration of the controversy surrounding the validity and reliability of the Rorschach can be found in Chapter Nine.

Research participants

Fifty convicted juvenile sex offenders under the care and control of an Australian State Department of Juvenile Justice were included in the study (prior to commencing any treatment). Only offenders who had committed a sex offence involving actual physical contact with a victim were included in the study. Of these fifty offenders, thirty-three had committed offences against children at least three years younger than themselves. The average age of the offenders who had offended against children was 15.7 years and the average age of their victims was seven years. The other seventeen participants had offended against adult or peer-aged victims. No mixed offenders were included. Specifically, those who had offended against both adult and child victims (usually against the backdrop of conduct disorder) were excluded.

All the participants gave their voluntary and informed consent to being involved in the study. Those participants who were offenders were either remanded in the community or in custody. Juvenile offenders are usually remanded in the community prior to their sentencing and disposition if they have had no prior convictions. A small number of offenders were, therefore, interviewed after their disposition when they were already in custody (owing to the seriousness of their convictions), although they had not started treatment. Fifty non-offending comparison group participants were also included in the study (see Figure 3) and completed the same assessment battery. These participants were recruited from an inner-city secondary school. They volunteered following a brief lecture explaining the research, which also asked for interested participants to become involved. The high-school population was derived from a low socio-economic geographic area and reflected a range of ethnicity similar to that of the offending group. The comparison group participants were, thus, closely matched to the experimental participants in terms of age and socio-economic profile.

Assessing the participants

The offenders were given a brief interview to gain the information required to complete the collateral form of the PCL-R, with most of the data gathered by file examination and through discussions with department staff handling the cases. Each participant was then administered the MMPI-A, followed by the Rorschach, which was administered in accordance with the standardized instructions of the comprehensive system (CS) (Exner, 2003). The period of testing also allowed for collection of observational data and other material, which contributed to the scoring of the PCL-R.

The Rorschach was administered using the standard ten cards, asking first for the basic response to each card, followed by the enquiry. The test was introduced by the standard instructions, as a personality test, with no right or wrong answers. The Rorschach was administered in its entirety, but only the human experience variable (HEV), a composite variable derived from human content (H) responses, and the texture response were targeted in the current research. A number of related variables, however, were examined *post hoc* to determine if they provided any corroborative evidence for the main thesis or any incremental validity to the targeted variables.

The results of the assessments were then analysed and the offender, non-offender, and sub-groups of offenders were then compared on the indices measured.

Results concerning differences between offenders and non-offenders

All of the offenders in the study were adolescent males. Of the offender sample, 66% had offended against children (defined as individuals who were at least three years younger than the offenders). The remainder of the sample had offended against peer-aged or adult victims. Of the total group, 26% were recidivists, with two or more adjudicated offences. The best estimates that could be made indicated that 63% of the victims of the child molester sub-group were female, whereas for the adult-victim offender sub-group all victims were female. All of the offenders in the study had been charged with contact sexual offences, that is, offences where there had been physical contact with a victim. In the adult victim sub-group, all of the offences involved penetration or partial penetration, whereas in the child molester sub-group the offences predominantly had involved molestation (87%), with a lesser number of offences (13%) involving penetration.

Results of the study

Capacity for attachment

The results indicated a significant difference between the offender and non-offender groups in terms of their capacity for attachment. The offender group revealed few texture responses, while most of the non-offenders revealed a normative number of texture responses. Similarly, when the texture response rate was analysed as a categorical variable, the difference between the observed and the expected texture response values revealed the same significant difference between the two groups. (The over-production of texture responses has been shown to be an indicator of psychopathology associated with dependency and a strong need for affection (Gacono & Meloy, 1997).)

The overall finding was an impaired capacity for attachment in the offender group.

Interest in relationship

The total HEV score is a composite of the sum of good (non-distorted) human (H) responses compared to poor human (H) responses on the

Rorschach (see Chapter Nine). Negative scores represent the highest level of "human relatedness". The results (compared to the Burns and Viglione (1996) norms for this variable) showed a significantly higher level of interest in human relationships in the non-offender group than in the offender group.

Typically, the results of the non-offenders revealed frequent responses involving (psychic representation of) human figures, usually paired and often engaged in co-operative action, such as dancing together. In comparison, the offender group contained many responses that were completely devoid of human content and tended to consist primarily of animal or inorganic content responses. In addition, instead of co-operative responses, aggressive responses and special scores indicative of abnormal constructions of reality and flawed judgement were evident. *The offender group, thus, revealed an internal world with poorer psychic representation of reciprocal human relationship compared to the non-offending adolescents. They also revealed less interest in human relationships.*

Differences in psychopathology

The offender group revealed clinically significant levels of psychopathology on both the validity and clinical scales on the MMPI-A (see Chapter Nine for more details of the MMPI-A). The validity scale results revealed that the L (Lie) scale and the true response inconsistency (TRIN) scale scores were higher in the offender group. The clinically significantly Lie scale scores described individuals who showed evidence of favourable impression management as having little awareness of the consequences of their behaviour on others and little or no insight into their motivations and behaviour. People who have such scores are usually inflexible in their problem-solving skills, might be defensive (usually employing denial and repression as defence mechanisms), and tend to over-evaluate their own worth. The TRIN score, which measures true response inconsistency responding, revealed a clinically significant high score in the offender group and indicated a non-acquiescent approach through indiscriminate responses with false answers. Overall, the results suggested a considerable *variation of scores within the group.*

On the clinical scales, Scale 4 (psychopathic–deviate), the results for the offender group, represented moderately high and clinically significant scores, indicating the likely presence of clinical behaviours and symptoms associated with Scale 4. This scale is the only MMPI scale to reliably predict delinquency among adolescents and is associated with acting out and delinquency as well as resentment of authority, poor school adjustment, and academic problems. In addition, clinically significant scores on Scale 4 describe individuals who are likely to have drug and alcohol problems and who are prone to being impulsive and aggressive (Ben-Porath, Graham, Hall, Hirschamn, & Zaragoza, 1995).

The Scale 2 (depression) score for the offender group also represented a moderately high and clinically significant score, which predicted the likely presence of some of the symptoms related to this scale. Clinically significant scores on Scale 2 indicate a propensity to depression, associated guilt and suicidal ideation, poor levels of self-confidence, and poor school performance.

Overall, the offender group revealed more antisocial and depressed features than the non-offender group, but with the standard deviation scores *suggesting considerable within-group variation*, which might explain the seemingly contradictory nature of the psychopathology (e.g., evidence of psychopathy *and* guilt) in this group. The non-offenders' clinical scales scores were, in contrast, unremarkable, suggesting this group was predominantly a well-adjusted group, consistent with reports of this group's academic progress, good conduct, lack of serious disciplinary problems, and generally sociable and co-operative behaviour with other students.

In terms of the MMPI-A psychopathology five (PSY-5) scales, there were also important and significant differences. The PSY-5 scales reflect a dimensional approach to personality and psychopathology, which can be used in tandem with the categorical approaches. On these scales, there were significant differences on the constraint scale, with the offender group revealing less capacity for constraint than the non-offending group. Also, when the offenders were compared to the non-offenders on the positive emotion/extroversion scale, the offenders were revealed to be significantly less able to experience positive affect than the non-offender group. Compared to the non-offending adolescents, juvenile sex offenders were characterized on the PSY-5 scales by a lower capacity for restraint and less ability to experience positive affect, consistent with clinical profile descriptions of juvenile sex offenders.

In summary, the results revealed the offender group to have a mixed picture of significant psychopathology compared to the non-offending group. Their antisocial features, depressive characteristics, problems with constraint, and inability to experience positive emotion described the group, in line with results of previous studies, as having problems with self-regulation, particularly affect regulation and impulse control.

Psychopathy

The Hare Psychopathy Checklist (PCL-R) was used as the measure of psychopathy. The PCL-R provides a total psychopathy (T) score, while Factor 1 measures the level of callous disposition towards others and Factor 2 the extent of chronic antisocial lifestyle features. On all scales, the offender group had significantly higher psychopathy scores. Nevertheless, the group mean for the sex offenders as a whole (T=21) was below the cut-off score for taxon psychopathy (T= or >30). This result was not surprising, however, as the cut-off score for taxon psychopathy is based on a sample of 229 adult inmates (Hare, 1991).

The results did not describe the offender group *overall* as a highly psychopathic group in terms of the cut-off scores for psychopathy given by Hare (1991). Furthermore, the results showed the offender group had lower scores on the PCL-R scales than those of a group of generally conduct-disordered delinquents (Loving & Russell, 2000). Once again, however, there was *an indication of considerable within group variability*, which suggested there might be sub-types of juvenile sex offenders who could be distinguished on the extent of their psychopathy.

Intra-group differences

The differences among the non-offender group, the offenders who molested children, and the offenders who raped peer-aged or older victims were examined and compared.

Capacity for attachment

The child molester sub-group, adult-victim offender sub-group, and non-offender group were compared in terms of their capacity for attachment. The adult-victim offender sub-group revealed the lowest

capacity for attachment. In contrast, there was a statistically significant elevation of texture responses found in the child molester sub-
group as compared to the adult victim offender group. This indicates
that, on the basis of published research concerning this variable
(Gacono & Meloy, 1994; Gacono, Meloy, & Berg, 1992; Gacono, Meloy,
& Heaven, 1991), the child molester sub-group appears to have significantly more need for attachment (albeit expressed pathologically)
than the adult-victim offender sub-group.

Interestingly, there was also a difference in the type of texture
responses given by the offender sub-groups and the adult victim
offender group, where texture was reported, producing what can be
characterized as "hard" rather than "soft" texture. Hard texture is
considered developmentally to be more impoverished than soft
texture, which is more normative (Meloy, 1997).

Human relatedness

There were significant differences among all groups in their "human-
relatedness" (HEV) scores, with the non-offending group having the
highest HEV score. The results also showed a significant difference
between the peer/adult-victim offender sub-group and the child
molester sub-group, with the latter having the higher HEV score. This
finding was consistent with the texture results and indirectly supported the finding that this sub-group revealed the most antisocial
traits and the highest level of psychopathy. These results point to
significant within sex offender sub-group differences in the level of
interest in human relationships ("human relatedness") and particularly show the adult-victim offender sub-group to have the lowest
levels of "human relatedness" as measured by the (composite) HEV
Rorschach variable.

Personality differences

There were also significant differences in psychopathology among the
non-offender and offender sub-groups. On the F (fake) scale, the
adult-victim offender sub-group had a significantly higher score. The
score suggests a tendency for members of this sub-group to deliberately misrepresent themselves on the items. The F scale (originally
developed to tap atypical or deviant responding) is considered a
reliable indicator of overall psychopathology. Comrey (1958) identifies

nine content dimensions of the scale, which include antisocial attitudes and behaviour, hostility, and paranoid thinking. The adult-victim offender sub-group TRIN scores were also significant. In particular, this suggested that they answered items falsely and in an indiscriminate manner.

When the validity scale scores were taken together, they painted a picture of the adult/peer-aged victim offender sub-group as attempting to misrepresent themselves more and to have more psychopathology than the other groups. This was consistent with an emerging profile of them as displaying more antisocial traits and the most psychopathology.

The results on the clinical scales also revealed important differences between the groups. In particular, the adult-victim offenders showed significantly higher scores on both Scale 4 (psychopathic–deviate) and on Scale 6 (paranoia) than either of the other groups. Even though Scale 4 (psychopathic–deviate) was significantly elevated in the child molester sub-group compared to the non-offender group, it was neither clinically significant nor close to the level of the adult-victim offender sub-group. Further, the adult-victim offender sub-group scale scores on the depression, mania, psychaesthenia, and schizophrenia scales suggested that they have difficulties with emotional regulation and impulse control. Their profile is quite similar to the profile that has been reported with delinquents, with higher scores typically found on Scales 2, 4, and 9 (Ben-Porath, Graham, Hall, Hirschamn, and Zaragoza, 1994). In this sense, this sub-group of sex offenders has a similar profile to delinquents, with the additional features of Scales 7 and 9, that is, more psychopathological trends.

The child-molester sub-group, though more pathological than the non-offender group, displayed significantly lower levels and extent of psychopathology compared to those with peer-aged or adult victims. The child-molester group still appeared to be maladjusted, yet their maladjustment was characterized more by depression and social introversion than antisocial behaviour and paranoia.

Other intra-offender group personality differences

The adult-victim offender sub-group evidenced significantly different scores on the PSY-5 scales compared with the child-molester subgroup, consistent with other measured differences.

The initial analysis of the offender and non-offender groups' aggressiveness scale scores revealed no significant differences. However, when the offender sub-groups and the non-offender group were compared, significant differences among the three groups on the PSY-5 scales were found. In particular, these differences revealed that the adult-victim offender sub-group was significantly more aggressive than the child-molester sub-group and also more aggressive than the non-offender group. The child molester sub-group was also found to be more aggressive than the non-offender group, although their scores were closer to the non-offender group than to those of the adult-victim offender sub-group.

In conclusion, while the offender group as a whole is not characterized as aggressive, when those who commit offences against peer-aged or older victims were compared to the child molester sub-group, the adult-victim offender sub-group was significantly more aggressive. It maight be that manipulation and subtle forms of coercion are not necessarily captured by this measure of aggression.

The psychoticism scale scores revealed a further significant difference between the adult-victim offender and the child molester sub-groups and between the adult-victim offender sub-group and the non-offender group. In particular, the adult-victim offender sub-group showed significantly higher scores on the psychoticism scale. This is consistent with the findings of the clinical scale comparisons between these two groups, which showed the child molester sub-group to have less psychotic symptomatology. The adult-victim offender sub-group scores were also clinically significant.

The two sub-groups of sex offenders also displayed significant differences in their mean scores on the constraint scale. Specifically, the adult-victim offender sub-group showed the least constraint out of the three-group comparison, and displayed a significantly lower score than that of the child molester sub-group. In fact, the child molester sub-group score was not significantly different to that of the non-offender group. These results, thus, provided further evidence of a profile of more antisocial (psychopathic) traits within the adult-victim offender sub-group. Moreover, when the two groups of sex offenders were compared to the non-offender group with respect to the positive emotion/extroversion scale scores, both sub-groups of sex offenders revealed less capacity to experience positive affects compared to non-offending adolescents. There was no significant difference between the two sex offender sub-groups on these scores.

In summary, the adult-victim offender sub-group revealed the most psychopathology as measured by the MMPI-A/PSY-5 Scales. Specifically, they had significantly higher scores on the aggression and psychoticism scales, and their scale scores suggested that the adult-victim offender sub-group is the least constrained and has the least capacity for positive affect. These findings are consistent with an anti-social personality profile. The child molester sub-group, by contrast, more closely resembled the non-offender group, yet appeared to have significantly more psychopathological tendencies than this group.

Intra-offender group differences in relation to psychopathy

The child molester sub-group revealed lower total PCL-R, Factor 1, and Factor 2 scores than the adult-victim offender sub-group, but higher scores than those of the non-offender group. The adult-victim offender sub-group had the highest Total Factor, Factor 1, and Factor 2 scores. The Factor 2 scores were also higher than the Factor 1 scores in this sub-group.

The child molester sub-group had the next highest Factor 1 score, while the non-offender group had scores comparable with normative scores for this age group. The Total Factor mean score for the adult-victim offender sub-group placed this sub-group in the high category in terms of dimensional psychopathy (T score = 24–30 or greater). Approximately 18% of the adult-victim offender sub-group members met the criteria for taxonomic psychopathy (T score = 30 or greater). In the sex offender sub-groups, the total mean T scores were either in the low or moderate clinically significant range. As predicted, the non-offender group had negligible scores on all psychopathy scales.

Other Rorschach findings

Lambda (regarded as a measure of defensiveness) revealed the offender group to be significantly more defensive than the non-offender group. Further, there was a significant difference between the adult-victim offender sub-group and the non-offender group, with the former having the higher scores.

Rorschach content and special scores

While the adult-victim offender group had the lowest co-operative human movement (or COP) responses, the offender group overall had a significantly lower co-operative response rate when compared with the non-offender group. The adult-victim offender sub-group also registered significantly more aggressive responses than the other groups, consistent with, and supportive of, other results, which suggested that it is the most psychopathic group. The child molester sub-group, however, produced significantly more aggressive responses than the non-offender group. The adult-victim offender sub-group had a substantially higher mean number of aggressive responses, which paralleled the findings on the MMPI-A/PSY-5 aggression scale. The results have an internal consistency with other findings that described them as the most psychopathic, aggressive, and psychopathological group.

The lack of human (psychic representation) form (H) responses in the adult-victim offender sub-group relative to the other groups is consistent with the texture and psychopathy findings, and supports the HEV data that suggest *it has the poorest level of internalized schema of reciprocal relationship*. The non-offender group had a mean pure-H response score similar to the normative score, while the child molester sub-group mean score is the same as that found in a mixed offence group of juvenile sex offenders (Csersevits, 2000). The juvenile sex offender group as a whole also had a significantly lower human response rate than the non-offender group.

The reflection (Rfr) response scores (a measure of narcissism) also differentiated the three groups. Specifically, the adult-victim offender sub-group had the highest rate of reflection responses, followed by the child molester sub-group. There was no significant difference between the child molester and non-offender group on this score. The results for the sex offender group as a whole are similar but slightly lower than that found in other samples (Csersevits, 2000) and those found in a conduct-disordered sample (Gacono & Meloy, 1994). Participants with higher levels of reflection responses were also those with the highest psychopathy scores.

The reflection response has been found to be a reliable indicator of the presence of narcissism (Gacono & Meloy, 1994) and, when it occurs with other indicators of antisocial personality, is also shown to be predictive of psychopathy. There is, however, a debate in the literature about the reliability of this variable (e.g. Lilienfeld, Wood, & Howard, 2000). This is discussed further in Chapter Nine.

Taken overall, the Rorschach findings corroborated and were consistent with data derived from other measures used in the research. Where there were inconsistencies in the results, these were related to Rorschach variables with relatively weak reliability coefficients.

Capacity for attachment was related to psychopathy among juvenile sex offenders

A central question in the research was whether the capacity for attachment could be demonstrated to be associated with the level of psychopathy. A bi-variate correlation calculation revealed a strong relationship between texture and the PCL-R Total score (r -0.61, $p<$ 0.01). Further, a Receiver Operator Characteristics (ROC) curve analysis showed that texture predicted psychopathy when the two variables were plotted together. When this analysis was performed, 91% of (predicted) cases were found under the curve. Texture also accurately predicted membership of the offender category, as did the psychopathy score. Further, texture response scores and PCL-R scores together accurately predicted 100% of the sex offender sub-group membership.

In summary, the data confirmed the hypothesis that capacity for attachment was correlated with psychopathy among juvenile sex offenders and that together these two variables predicted sub-group membership of the offender group, non-offender group, and sub-group membership. The study also showed that impaired capacity for attachment is strongly correlated with juvenile sex offending and is differentially correlated with sub-groups of offenders. In particular, the adult-victim offender sub-group showed the least capacity for attachment and the highest level of psychopathy.

Capacity for attachment and the extent of psychopathology

The current data also revealed significant interrelationships between an individual's capacity for attachment and the level and extent of his psychopathology. Specifically, the data showed that the adult-victim offender sub-group had the lowest capacity for attachment and the greatest levels and range of psychopathology on the MMPI-A clinical scales and on the PSY 5 scales.

Specifically, the psychopathology described the adult-victim offender sub-group as similar to conduct disordered samples, but with more paranoid and psychotic tendencies. The adult-victim offender sub-group also showed the least capacity for constraint and the poorest ability to experience positive emotion.

Capacity for attachment and human relatedness

Clinically, the capacity for attachment and human relatedness are linked: thus, not surprisingly, when the HEV was plotted against absent texture, the area under the resultant ROC curve was 0.76 and there was a positive bi-variate correlation between HEV and psychopathy ($r = 0.58$, $p < 0.01$), so the association between the two variables was confirmed in this study. Consequently, these variables predicted group membership.

Conclusions

The findings from the current study showed juvenile sex offenders can be distinguished from non-offenders by their results on the MMPI-A, the PCL-R, and the Rorschach. These instruments similarly differentiated a child molester sub-group from offenders with peer-aged and adult victims. The results showed that capacity for attachment and the extent of psychopathy were inversely correlated and were good predictor variables of juvenile sex offender group and sub-group membership. The data confirmed the heterogeneity of juvenile sex offender clinical characteristics and revealed them to have significant psychopathology, which was most pronounced in the adult-victim offender sub-group. Furthermore, the data provided some limited support for the argument that the child molester group could be differentiated by its attachment pathology.

CHAPTER EIGHT

A closer view into the internal world of the juvenile sex offender

"Out of infinite longings, rise finite deeds"

(From "Infinite", Rilke, 2004)

On the basis of their landmark meta-analysis of research involving 3855 adolescent sex offenders, Seto and Lalumière (2010) concluded that "adolescent sex offending cannot be parsimoniously explained as a simple manifestation of anti-social tendencies" (p. 526). Their analysis highlighted that these offenders represent a heterogeneous group with a significant range of psychopathology. Further, many of the factors they isolated as having likely aetiological significance to juvenile sex offending are experiences likely to disrupt their attachment, once again highlighting the probable significance of attachment issues to juvenile sex offending.

The research (reported in Chapter Seven) is the first to demonstrate that sub-types of juvenile sex offenders could be predicted by measures of capacity for attachment, level of relatedness, psychopathy, psychopathology, and empirical correlates of the internal world. This research, which I will hereafter refer to as "my study", showed that attachment capacity and human relatedness were lower in juvenile sex offenders when they were compared to a group of non-offending adolescents. It further showed that these variables, along with psychopathy, differentiated those offenders who molest children from those who have peer-aged or older victims. The results, therefore, suggested the diagnostic relevance of capacity for attachment, level of relatedness (and the associated object relations), and psychopathy with juvenile sex offenders.

The study not only confirmed previous findings concerning the clinical characteristics of juvenile sex offenders, but also indicated that differences in personality and behaviour among these offenders appeared to be linked to their capacity for attachment, level of relatedness, and level of psychopathy. Importantly, these findings help to explain why juvenile sex offenders who offend against children, particularly those characterized by cognitive distortion in relation to their victims (i.e., those who believe that they are "loving" or "helping" their victims) have a different type of attachment pathology than those offenders who have peer-aged or older victims.

Support for an attachment based theory of juvenile sex offending

The results of my study broadly support an attachment-based theory of juvenile sex offending. They link with the finding that, when the developmental experiences and behavioural characteristics of juvenile sex offenders are subjected to path analysis (see Chapter Three), their attachment-related behavioural difficulties can be seen as distal precursors to their sexual recidivism (Kenny, Keogh, & Seidler, 2001). Further, the study supports the view that disrupted attachment experiences are of fundamental aetiological significance in the development of conduct disorder and juvenile offending (Carlson & Sroufe, 1985; Keogh, 2002; Loeber & Hay, 1997). As such, they add weight to the case for a developmental theory of juvenile offending (Atkinson & Zuckermann, 1997; Belsky, Steinberg, & Draper, 1991).

Many of the characteristic problems of juvenile sex offenders, including low self-esteem, reduced capacity for empathy, and a range of social skill difficulties, are known to be linked to insecure attachment (Fonagy, 2001; Lindsey, Carlozzi, & Ellis, 2001; Marshall, 1993; Sperling & Berman, 1994). The findings in my study suggest that the attachment difficulties of *some* juvenile sex offenders might account for characteristics such as their shyness, social isolation, and anxiety, which typify juvenile sex offenders who are less violent, but who are, none the less, impaired in their ability to form satisfying adult relationships. The results also describe another group with less capacity for attachment whose members are typified by their aggression, control. and lack of concern for their victims.

Bowlby (1944) postulated that the individuals who are most detached attempt to control others in relationships, an idea that Crittenden (1997b) developed by demonstrating that such individuals are compromised by their inability to use affect to make judgements. The inability to consider (the states of mind of) others makes it difficult to develop appropriate social skills, contributing to a diminished capacity for intimacy (Marshall, 1993). In terms of implications for treatment, reduced capacity for attachment has been shown to be linked with a reduced ability for "reflective thinking", that is, with difficulties inferring the "states of mind" of others (Fonagy, 1996). Recent evidence suggests that the deficits may vary depending on the nature of the attachment difficulties (Crittenden, 1997b; Fonagy & Luyten, 2009). Ward, Keenan, and Hudson (2000) have noted that such findings have significant implications for understanding how sex offenders might more easily "objectify" and control their victims.

As previously noted, research has shown that adult sex offenders have attachment difficulties which appear to be linked to their offence type (Kear-Colwell, 2001; Ward, Hudson, & Marshall, 1996; Ward, Keenan, & Hudson, 2000). The attachment problems of adult sex offenders who offend against children have been shown to relate to their poor coping skills (Cortoni & Marshall, 1998), the nature of their coping difficulties (Marshall, 1993), and their difficulties in developing sexual intimacy with adults (Marshall, Cripps, Anderson, & Cortoni, 1999; Ward, Keenan, & Hudson, 2000). My study not only supports such findings, but underlines the probable aetiological importance of capacity for attachment and relatedness to others, to juvenile sex offending.

More light on the internal world of
psychopathic juvenile sex offenders

Psychopathy, which has emerged during recent decades as an important predictor of repeat violent and sexual crime (especially rape) in adult samples, appears from the results of my study, as being likely *to have similar predictive ability with juvenile sex offenders.*

My study showed that in a sub-group of juvenile sex offenders characterized as more psychopathic, there is a poor level of internalized (psychic) representation of "others", the representation of which is known to be a necessary precursor for achieving closeness and intimacy with others. It revealed that the adult-victim offender sub-group, in particular, had the least co-operative human representation and a significantly reduced human (H) response rate as measured by Rorschach variables, suggestive of a poor level of individuation and separate identity formation. These offenders were, thus, shown to be individuals whose internal world makes them prone to behaving in violently sexualized ways (Blos, 1967; Chorn & Parekh, 1997).

Many juvenile sex offenders have histories of conduct problems (Kavoussi, Kaplan, & Becker, 1988; Kenny, Keogh, & Seidler, 2001). Clinical descriptions of them in the literature (e.g., Dolan, Holloway, Bailey, & Kroll, 1996; Lakey, 1994) have suggested that a significant incidence of incipient psychopathy is to be found in this group, as indicated by their high levels of conduct disorder. Not surprisingly, therefore, behaviours related to psychopathy, such as lack of remorse for offending and lack of empathy for victims, are commonly found in juvenile sex offenders.

Although no comparative data exist regarding juvenile sex offenders, research with adult sex offenders emphasizes the importance of psychopathy to sex offending and shows that sexual deviance and psychopathy largely account for the variance in sexual recidivism (Harris & Rice, 1996). In regard to adult sex offenders, sub-group differences exist with rapists or mixed child molester/rapists, showing higher levels of psychopathy than among the child molester only offenders (Porter et al., 2000). This suggests there might be further within-group differences to be found in the child molester sub-group.

The findings of the study corroborate other studies that show that among juvenile sex offenders, rapists with peer-aged or older victims are the most psychopathic group of offenders. Individuals with high levels of psychopathy are, as Bowlby (1944) suggested, dismissing of relationship and are "non-relationship" seeking. This is also consistent with De Masi's (2003) view of the sadomasochistic perversion, wherein he sees that there is a "no-object relating" context to sadism.

Offenders who deny, and are hostile about, their need for attachment, trust no one and are "unable to appreciate the way in which they are traumatising their victims" because of their lack of emotional contact with others (Hodges, Lanyado, & Andreou, 1994, p. 304). The poor quality or incapacity for empathy, so frequently noted, can be explained by their related mental representations of self, other, and relationship (their internal world).

Such ideas link with the notion of the relevance of the "storyline" in sexual fantasies (Stoller, 1975), with rapists showing themes of domination, control, and violence, and child molesters showing cognitive distortion related to ambivalence about reciprocal human relationship. Stoller argues that in the sexual fantasies associated with perversion, there is, to a greater or lesser degree, an attempt to achieve a victory over an original trauma. De Masi (2003), as discussed in Chapter Five, has challenged the importance of trauma in perversions, suggesting instead the importance of a primary destructiveness. As previously noted, while this idea fits with the findings concerning the psychopathic sex offender for whom sexualized needs for attachment might not be the primary motivator, it does not so easily account for the motivations of the child molester who appears to have pathological attachment needs, wherein the desire for the other is a central feature of his behaviour.

In summary, the findings vindicate the importance of understanding and differentiating juvenile sex offenders and their sub-groups. As such, they have important implications for the aetiology of juvenile sex offending, as well as for assessment and intervention.

The "attachment hungry" juvenile sex offender and his object relations

The findings of my study were consistent with classificatory schema that have categorized such offenders as, variously, sexually and socially inexperienced, socially timid and neurotic, or severely anti-social, aggressive, and peer group-influenced (O'Brien & Bera, 1986). In terms of Bartholomew's (1990) schema of adult attachment, psychopathic offenders represent a group of individuals who have an extremely low (or no) level of dependence on others and an extremely high level of avoidance of relationship. Their behaviour (sexually violent and destructive), however, is in direct contrast to the intra-familial child molester who cites, as one of the (cognitively distorted) reasons for his offending, his "need for affection".

The mixed findings concerning psychopathy among juvenile sex offenders were consistent with reports that over 60% of these offenders reveal little or no empathy for their victims, while more than 30% of them think of sex as a way of showing love or caring for others (Ryan, Miyioshi, Metzner, Krugman, & Fryer, 1996). Those paedophilic offenders who *forcibly rape* appear to be the offenders who have the highest levels of psychopathy; those who molest, who have distorted cognitions concerning their "love" for their victims and who have "attachment hunger", appear to have the lowest levels. In light of my findings, it appears that there might be within-paedophilic group differences in attachment issues associated with different offending motives. Adult sex offender attachment research shows that there are intragroup differences in attachment patterns among paedophiles, which also suggests that some of them are much less psychopathic, but, none the less, seriously disturbed (Bridges, Wilson, & Gacono, 1998).

My study suggests that a significant group of juvenile sex offenders who molest children appear to be ambivalent (preoccupied) about relationships, hungry for attachment, and less confident about negotiating satisfying reciprocal adult relationships. That is, they have a relationship with the "object", but this is highly enmeshed. Such offenders are, thus, very dependent on the object for maintaining their sense of self. The self in this case is a psychosomatic, sensation-dominated self, which has not developed any capacity as a representational (lexical) self. This creates major dilemmas for such offenders in achieving meaningful, reciprocal, and emotionally satisfying relationships. Their object relations are expressed in their unique, clinical characteristics. The current findings regarding this sub-group support the view that they are socially isolated, have difficulties communicating with adults, and often experience aberrant modelling as a result of sexual abuse and related experiences (including possible exposure to pornography). These difficulties link to their turning to children as objects of sexual satisfaction. Crittenden (1997a) has articulated how disturbances to affect (hyper-activation of the attachment system) and cognition (distorted and not based in reality), associated with an insecure attachment style, along with other social maturity deficits, can lead to offenders *choosing* child victims.

In terms of the sub-groupings identified in my study, the path analysis of factors contributing to recidivism (Kenny, Keogh, & Seidler, 2001), which highlights the salience of social skill deficits and cognitive distortions linked with deviant sexual fantasies, might have special relevance to this attachment hungry sub-group. All of this has major implications for intervention and again suggests the need for different foci in the treatment of these sub-groups of juvenile sex offenders.

Psychopathology, juvenile sex offending, and recidivism

Juvenile sex offenders have previously been found to have significantly more psychopathology than non-offending adolescents (van Wijk, van Horn, Bullens, Bijleveld, & Doreleijers, 2005). My study corroborated this finding and showed that, as a group, they had a clinically significant profile of conduct disorder and depressive traits. They were also found to be significantly more defensive, with a non-acquiescent (non-compliant) style associated with impression management. Further, they showed a greater propensity to lie and fake responses and to have lowered capacity for constraint and to be less likely to experience positive emotion.

The findings are consistent with other data that suggest that such offenders have poor psychological adjustment and personality related problems. They also confirm the view of a number of authors whose research demonstrates significant mental health problems in this group (Kavoussi, Kaplan, & Becker, 1988; Kenny, Keogh, Seidler, & Blaszczynski, 2000; Seto & Lalumière, 2010). The fact that juvenile sex offenders have been shown to have depressive features (Becker, Kaplan, Cunningham-Rathner, & Kavoussi, 1991; Herkov, Gynther, Thomas, & Myers, 1996; Kenny, Keogh, & Seidler, 2001) was also confirmed in the study and was an important finding, as depression can often be overlooked in adolescents who are acting out, because of the links involving self-esteem, educational difficulties, and depression.

The significant levels of conduct problems among this offender group, and their low levels of constraint found in my study, also fit with the fact that some juvenile sex offenders have been found to engage in other forms of offending and to have other conspicuous conduct disorder features (Carpenter, Peed, & Eastman, 1995;

Kempton & Forehand, 1992). The research is, thus, in line with descriptions of such offenders as impulsive and as having difficulties regulating their affect (Kavoussi, Kaplan, & Becker, 1988), as well as having histories of disruptive behaviour at school where they display poor levels of motivation (Lakey, 1994).

Overall, juvenile sex offenders in the study were shown to be a poorly adjusted group in terms of their personalities; my study corroborates the clinical picture of them as having difficulties achieving satisfying reciprocal relationships with others (consistent with a poor history of attachment and bonding). Increased psychopathology is also correlated with increased sexual deviancy (Harris & Rice, 1996). As sexual deviancy is implicated with attachment disruption in the prediction of juvenile sexual recidivism (Kenny, Keogh, & Seidler, 2001), impaired capacity for attachment appears once again to be the common link. Moreover, the data are consistent with accounts of adult sexual recidivism that stress the aetiological role of sexual deviance (Hanson & Bussière, 1998).

The significance of differences in offender sub-group psychopathology

My study revealed distinctive personality issues and motivations in the adult-victim offender (largely rapist) sub-group. This sub-group was found to be the most aggressive, antisocial, paranoid, to have the least reality sense, and to be the least constrained in their behaviour among the groups examined. These data suggest that those in this sub-group are likely to be prone to primitive defence mechanisms such as splitting, primitive idealization (and related devaluation) and projection, as well as omnipotent behaviour (Gacono & Meloy, 1994), all of which are features of malignant narcissism.

The child molester sub-group comprised a largely non-sodomist and non-rapist group. Sodomists and rapists are reported in other studies to have the highest Scale 4 (psychopathic–deviate) elevations. Porter and colleagues' (2000) findings, which show that child molesters who do not rape have lower psychopathy scores than those who rape, also support the notion of a difference in the psychopathology of the two sub-groups and within-group differences among child sex offenders.

Adult sex offenders who are sodomists (who, in turn, have a much higher likelihood of having been sodomized themselves) display the highest levels of psychopathology (Herkov, Gynther, Thomas, & Myers, 1996). Further, a relatively rare sub-group of juvenile sexual homicide perpetrators are also characterized by extensive psychopathology (Gacono & Meloy, 1994). Although studies show some variation in the extent and level of psychopathology among adult and juvenile sex offenders, rapists always show the greatest extent and level of disturbance (Kavoussi, Kaplan & Becker, 1988; O'Brien & Bera, 1996).

In my study, juvenile sex offenders with peer-aged or adult victims (predominantly involving rape) had the greatest levels of psychopathology. This is obviously an important consideration when profiling offenders, especially those who might offend non-sexually and who are being assessed for such non-sexual offences. Further research might show that such data also support the finding that sexual deviance, psychopathy (and malignant narcissism), and attachment difficulties together best predict sexual recidivism among juvenile sex offenders.

In summary, the study found that the range and level of psychopathology among juvenile sex offenders are broadly consistent with findings in the literature which reveal overall significant deficits in interpersonal functioning. It also confirms that rapists (and probably sodomists in particular) have the highest levels of psychopathology.

Implications for assessment and treatment

The findings of the study provide evidence that the capacity for attachment and psychopathy, *together* with empirically based indices of object relations, appear to be particularly useful in understanding the motivations of juvenile sex offenders. This evidence connects with findings concerning adult sex offenders which have shown that those who are preoccupied (or, in some cases, fearful) in their attachment are usually child sex offenders, while those who are more dismissive and coercive are usually those with adult victims (Kear-Colwell & Sawle, 2001; Ward, Hudson, & Marshall, 1996). A dismissive attachment style in adulthood is associated with higher levels of psychopathology (including psychopathy), especially violence and criminality (Fonagy et al., 1996).

What is clear from my study, thus, is that juvenile sex offenders cannot be adequately or effectively assessed without reference to their capacity for attachment and their level of psychopathy (and associated object relations). The finding that these measures are correlated and predict offender sub-group membership in this offender group appears to be a new finding in the juvenile sex offender research field. The study indicates the importance of assessing the level and range of psychopathology in juvenile sex offenders and identifies different targets when intervening therapeutically with them. *This should be done with a consideration of the nature of the offender's victim and offence type.*

The interrelationships among the level of psychopathy, capacity for attachment, level of relatedness, and other psychopathology, therefore, appear pivotal in predicting recidivism by juvenile sex offenders. There is much attention given in the literature to the role of psychopathy (generally, as well as specifically with sex offenders) in determining the level of dangerousness and amenability to treatment. Attachment capacity, when used in conjunction with a measure of psychopathy and empirical correlates of the internal world, can assist differential diagnosis, provide rich insights into offender motivation, direction for treatment, and early intervention for juvenile sex offenders.

The data also suggest that interventions for attachment-hungry child molesters, in contrast to those offenders with adult (and peer-aged) victims, need to address attachment system hyper-activation issues (and, in some cases, fear of closeness), their sense of inadequacy, victim experiences, and capacity for emotional regulation. Fonagy (1996) presents a useful schema to address such issues in his model of mentalization based therapy (MBT) (see Chapter Eleven).

Adult child sex molesters are known to be hard to engage in therapy and their ambivalence and/or avoidance creates considerable therapeutic challenges for the therapist (Kear-Colwell & Sawle, 2001). These difficulties are, none the less, fewer than those encountered with the psychopath, who, because of his grandiosity and unwillingness to form relationships, presents the greatest challenge to those attempting to provide treatment. There have been some attempts to develop treatment for psychopaths, but this area is in its infancy. There have also been concerns that psychopathy might be treatment-resistant (Wong & Hare, 2002). Researchers who seek a biological explanation argue that a positive treatment outcome is unlikely for this group and that protection of the community from such individuals is the only helpful strategy. There is, however, some evidence (including my research) that psychopathy is developmentally determined, dimensional, and amenable to treatment, especially in young offenders (Salekin, Worley, & Grimes, 2010) (see also Chapter Nine). McWilliams (1994) has argued the importance of seeing psychopathy as a continuum, so that some psychopathic offenders have more potential for treatment than others. Using this argument, differential treatment outcomes, depending on the extent of psychopathy, are a more realistic prediction.

Moreover, the study's findings are consistent with others which show that rapists are likely to have encountered particularly harsh, violent, inconsistent, and frightening discipline (Polaschek, Hudson, Ward, & Seigert, 2001; Worling, 1995) and, as such, once again suggests that rapists have a different type of attachment problem. Early abuse experience is known to damage the (social) brain, which can inhibit the brain's capacity to benefit from subsequent developmental experiences. Ongoing compounding developmental experiences could combine to produce further deficits, which predispose individuals to juvenile sex offending. Evidence of such difficulties does not, however, necessarily preclude psychotherapeutic intervention with such offenders (see Chapter Six).

Some conclusions

Overall, the current findings support a bio-psycho-social model of causation of juvenile sex offending, but suggest that developmental experiences play a key role in the formation of paraphilias and asociated perversions found in rape and paedophilia. This is not only consistent with the increasing body of evidence concerning epigenetics, but with the vast body of literature on attachment and empirically supported, causal connections between the experiences in the primary care-giving relationships and the development of psychopathology.

Importantly, my study adds to an emerging empirical database that suggests that internalized schema (or psychic representations), based on such experiences, become powerful epigenetic factors which strongly shape views about oneself, others, and relationships. Such templates help to explain the motivations of juvenile sex offenders, which are reflected in their sexual fantasies and can become powerfully reinforced neurochemically (see also Chapter Six) to become key mediators of sex offending (Marshall, 1993).

The data clearly implicate differential developmental trajectories to sexual offending, while providing evidence in favour of a general developmental model of offending behaviour. The data specifically support the notion that particular cohorts of offenders develop early behavioural problems, such as attention deficit disorder, oppositional defiant disorder, conduct disorder, substance abuse disorder, antisocial personality disorder, and psychopathy (Keogh, 2002). In this regard, there is extensive research demonstrating the trajectory of violent behaviour in children and adolescents (Loeber & Hay, 1997), yet little has been articulated in terms of a developmental pathway for juvenile sex offending. Lyons-Ruth (1996) has shown that attachment style can predict aggression in adolescence, but patterns of attachment have not, until recently, been implicated empirically in adult sex offending (Becker, 1998; Marshall, 1993; Marshall, Geris, & Cortoni, 2000) and even more recently with juvenile sex offending (Kenny, Keogh, & Seidler, 2001; Keogh, 2004; Leguizamo, 2000).

Moreover, the current findings also support the general profile in the literature of the disparate and somewhat contradictory nature of personality features, behavioural characteristics, and the clinical presentation of juvenile sex offenders (Lakey, 1994), which suggests multiple causation of juvenile sex offending (and links to the associated typologies of their offending) (O'Brien & Bera, 1986). Related to these considerations, the data have potentially important implications for future research which might identify developmental *psychodynamic* risk factors which could inform early intervention programmes that might help to prevent otherwise inevitable trajectories to juvenile sex offending.

Overall the current research suggests that attachment theory, combined with object relations theory, provides a potentially useful empirically based, aetiological, and diagnostic framework for explaining the development of sub-types of juvenile sex offending.

The potential applications of these findings to the assessment and treatment of the juvenile sex offender will be discussed in Part IV of this book.

PART IV
PRACTICE AND APPLICATION

CHAPTER NINE

Implications for the assessment of the juvenile sex offender

The results of my study (discussed in Chapters Seven and Eight), along with the broad research literature base concerning juvenile sex offenders, make a case for the importance of assessing their capacity for attachment, level of detachment (psychopathy), psychopathology and empirical correlates of their internal world. In this chapter, I highlight some important issues in the assessment of juvenile sex offenders and recommend a battery of tests that facilitates the assessment of these constructs. I describe in some detail aspects of these instruments which I feel are particularly useful in articulating relevant motivational factors behind their offending. As the Rorschach (a part of the battery of tests I recommend) has been a somewhat controversial psycho-diagnostic test (despite the richness of assessment data it can yield), I also take up something of the controversy around the use of this instrument.

Starting with the proposition that juvenile sex offenders are not a homogeneous group in terms of their psychopathology, a careful assessment of differential offending-related variables is necessary to ensure the appropriateness of the approach to, and content of, their treatment. It is also important to determine who is most suitable for treatment and, in some rare instances, whether treatment is not indicated or is not feasible. These considerations relate in part to the issue of what has become known as treatment "responsivity".

The assessment process I advocate is based on a bio-psycho-social model of juvenile sex offending. It also stresses the need for a psychodynamic formulation to facilitate a better understanding of the motivations of the juvenile sex offender and the meaning of his victim choices. I believe that such an assessment provides a valuable addition to the conventional assessment of "dynamic risk factors".

Risk assessment with juvenile sex offenders

Pertinent to the assessment of juvenile sex and other offenders is the important issue of the risk of reoffending. Risk assessment has become an industry in the field of criminology and such assessments are now common inclusions in forensic reports prepared by experts in the criminal justice field. While robust, scholarly reviews of this subject have been provided (e.g., Rich, 2009) and a comprehensive review of risk assessment of juvenile sex offenders is beyond the scope of this book, a consideration of some of the fundamental issues is risk assessment requires attention.

Risk assessments are used to determine the priority and need for treatment in the adjudication process, as well as for release, and parole determinations, where public safety must be kept in mind. There are a limited number of validated risk instruments that are currently used with sex offenders. These instruments are either used alone or in combination with clinician interpretation.

The *Static-99* used with adult sex offenders, for example, is a second-generation risk assessment instrument and only uses a strictly evidence-based, ten-item scale to assess risk behaviour. Other, more recent, approaches involve what is called a "third-generation approach", that is, one that involves what is called "structured professional judgement" (SPJ). This involves a professional interpretation of factors such as the severity, frequency, or duration of those predetermined risk factors and allows the clinician to take into account individual-specific details of an offender. In the risk assessment of juvenile sex offenders, commonly used instruments are: The Juvenile Sex Offender Risk Protocol (J-SOAP-II) (Prentky & Righthand, 2003), the Juvenile Sexual Offense Recidivism Tool (JSORRAT-II) (Epperson,

Ralston, Fowers, DeWitt, & Gore, 2005) and the Estimate of Risk of Adolescent Sex Offense Recidivism (ERASOR) (Worling & Curwen, 2001). The J-SOAP is used with adolescents between the ages of twelve and eighteen years and can be used to assess reoffence risks for adjudicated or non-adjudicated youth. It now has twenty-eight items, the majority of which tap into static risk factors. It is recommended that the J-SOAP Scales 3 and 4, which contain twelve dynamic risk factor items, should be reassessed after six months, and earlier if risk-relevant changes are seen to have occurred. The JSORRAT-II is a twelve-item actuarial risk tool which has impressive interrater reliability and validation studies to support it. The ERASOR 2.0 also aims at predicting risk in juvenile sex offenders aged 12–18 years who have previously committed sexual assaults. It was developed using an empirically guided, clinical judgement approach. The majority of its questions (sixteen of the twenty-five) explore dynamic risk factors.

The Youth Level of Service Inventory/Case Management Inventory (Hoge & Andrews, 1994, 1996), also a frequently used instrument with juvenile sex offenders, is a general measure of risk and focuses more on antisocial factors. It is not sex offender-specific, but includes an assessment of what are regarded as the big eight factors: antisocial attitudes, antisocial thoughts, cognitions, and ways of thinking, antisocial personality, antisocial history, employment, family, leisure, and recreational activities, substance abuse problems, and antisocial peers or criminal associates. It is a *third generation* approach, which involves structured clinician judgement. The use of such an instrument makes more sense where a sex offender is likely to have more psychopathic features.

It is increasingly recognized that the assessment of dynamic risk factors, *with* clinician rating of their importance, is crucial in determining current, or what I would call "real time", risk factors. Gottfredson and Moriarty (2006), having reviewed the evidence for actuarial prediction, note,

> Specialists must have a role in decision making that goes beyond the mere administering of the risk-assessment devices. There is a place for human judgment and experience in the decision-making process, and we must value their continued consideration. [p. 17]

They note that statistically rare events can have an impact on the risk equation.

"Real time" psychodynamic risk factors

From what is known about the characteristics and profile of the juvenile sex offender, there is a clear indication of the need to assess the level of their psychopathy, the nature of their psychopathology, and to understand something of their need and capacity for attachment, in particular whether this is absent or exaggerated. In turn, from a psychoanalytic point of view, it is also important to *understand the nature of the psychic phantasies that are currently driving their variously impulsive, violently sexualized or compulsively sexualized behaviours.* My study (see Chapters Seven and Eight) revealed that that not only will this help to more clearly identify the offender type, but information concerning the idiosyncrasies of the internal world of the offender can form part of a decision-making tree concerning disposition and treatment.

Including a psychoanalytically based assessment also adds significant and meaningful information about risk of reoffending.

On the basis of such considerations, and in line with the central proposition of this book, I recommend a combination of actuarial measures such as the PCL-R, combined with a *real time* assessment of the psychic structure and related (conscious and unconscious) fantasies of the juvenile sex offender, in order to facilitate a more refined picture of *psycho*-dynamic risk factors.

When it comes to reoffending, it is acknowledged that antisocial (psychopathic) traits are highly predictive of future offending. The immediate relevance of assessments, which tap into such traits, whether via static or dynamic factors, is, thus, also clear. With juvenile sex offending, I have argued the need for a sub-group of juvenile sex offenders to be distinguished from other offenders on the basis of their level of antisocial traits. The other group of offenders can be distinguished by their pathological need for attachment, which causes them to distort reality. The assessment of the risk of reoffending of such a sub-group of offenders can be enhanced by a psychodynamic formulation, including psychodynamic risk factors.

Psycho-dynamic risk factors, or what I am calling "real time" risk factors (derived from indices of the level and type of mental representation of human content and relatedness), represent appropriate and useful components of risk assessment. When used in conjunction with other actuarial-based measures that tap into static and dynamic behavioural factors and other standardized psychometric measures of personality functioning, especially *gold standard* ones such as the MMPI-A, they substantially increase the quality of risk prediction. The effort involved in conducting such assessments pays many dividends and can lead to more cost-effective interventions.

A suggested psycho-diagnostic test battery

With these issues in mind, I recommend an assessment battery for the psychodynamically orientated clinician who wants to be able to describe and predict risk, describe the motivations of the offender, and propose the most useful interventions. Such a battery would include:

1. The Minnesota Multi-Phasic Personality Inventory for Adolescents (MMPI-A), including the PSY-5 scales;
2. The Hare Psychopathy Checklist-Revised (PCL-R)[1];
3. The Rorschach (with a particular focus on the HEV variable and texture response);
4. A risk assessment instrument such as the JSORRAT-II, J-SOAP, or the ERASOR;
5. An assessment of countertransference reactions, which might help to assess suitability of treatment (discussed at the end of this chapter).

It is relevant to describe the MMPI-A, PCL-R, and the Rorschach in some greater detail, highlighting the particular aspects of these instruments that can be useful in assessing the nuances in motivations among juvenile sex offenders.

The Minnesota Multiphasic Personality Inventory for use with Adolescents (MMPI-A)

The MMPI is one of the most widely used tests for the assessment of adolescents and, in particular, one of the most used tests in forensic settings (Archer, Maurish, Imhof, & Piotrowski, 1991). The test was originally developed during the 1930s as a screening instrument for the differential diagnosis of psychopathology. The MMPI has a long history of use as a predictor or correlate of criminal behaviour. Scale 4 (psychopathic–deviate), in particular, predicts a category of individuals who demonstrate criminal behaviours (McKinley & Hathaway, 1944). This scale has an ability to predict characteristics of individuals now referred to as having conduct disorder, which is often a precursor to psychopathy (Loeber & Hay, 1997). Subsequently, Hathaway and Monachesi (1957) demonstrate that other clinical scales, notably Scale 8 (schizophrenia), Scale 9 (hypomania), and Scale 0 (social introversion), are able to assist in correctly identifying juvenile delinquents. Scale 2 (depression) and Scale 5 (masculinity–femininity) are also found to identify such participants, but less effectively.

The validity scales of the MMPI also influence the forensic utility of the instrument (Lang & Langevin, 1996a,b). The lie (L) scale, for example, measures overly positive presentation or so-called "faking good", while the F scale identifies deviant test protocols. The K scale, completing the original trio of validity scales, measures defensiveness. Two other validity scales were added in the subsequently revised MMPI (MMPI-2) and MMPI-A: the true response inconsistency scale (TRIN) and the variable response inconsistency scale (VRIN). The VRIN scale adds to the validity profile by giving a measure of tendencies to respond inconsistently, while the TRIN scale measures inconsistent false responding (non-acquiescence) or inconsistent true responding (acquiescence).

The MMPI-A was originally developed as a screening instrument for differential diagnostics, but more recently a version for adolescents has been developed. In developing the MMPI-A, 704 items were piloted. The F scale, in particular, is considerably modified because it was seen to be relatively ineffective with adolescents. With other various modifications, the resulting inventory contains 478 items. The normative sample is based on 805 boys and 815 girls, ranging in age from fourteen to eighteen years, selected randomly from seven states throughout the USA.

Reliability and validity of the MMPI-A scales

Butcher and colleagues (1992) provide reliability coefficients and temporal stability coefficients for the MMPI-A clinical and validity scales in the normative sample. For boys, the internal consistency Cronbach alphas range from 0.43 to 0.88. For the validity scales, the temporal stability coefficients for test–retest reliability are in the 0.70 to 0.84 range. The scores are in line with the general finding of lower temporal stability of personality test scores for adolescents. The MMPI-A is as accurate as the MMPI in terms of its test–retest reliability (Graham, 1993). Each of the scales in the MMPI-A has undergone extensive construct validity research (Butcher et al., 1992).

Interpretations of MMPI-A scale results

The normative data derive T-scores from raw scores. A T-score of 50 is considered a normative score. Scores above and below this score can be of clinical significance. High scores are usually defined as greater than or equal to a T-score of 65 for the clinical scales. For the validity scales, a T-score equal to or greater than 55 can indicate the likely presence of behaviours and traits associated with the scale.

High scale scores on the clinical scales usually indicate the probable presence of clinical symptoms associated with the scales. Moderate clinical scale scores (usually T-scores 60–64) predict the presence of the symptoms and behaviours associated with the particular scale, but with less confidence. T-scores of below 55 on the clinical scale are not considered to be of clinical significance.

Psychopathology five (PSY-5) scales

The PSY-5 scales consist of five scales derived from MMPI-A items (McEntee, 1999; Williams & Carolyn, 1997), whose construct validity has been established by external correlation with the record review form (RRF), the child behaviour checklist (CBCL) and the Devereux adolescent behaviour rating scale (DAB). The pattern of correlations with MMPI-A scales showed appropriate convergence with the PSY-5 constructs (McNulty, Harkness, Ben-Porath, & Williams, 1997).

The PSY-5 scales consist of five scales: the aggressiveness scale, the psychoticism scale, the constraint scale, the negative emotionality/ neuroticism scale, and the positive emotionality/extraversion scale. The PSY-5 scales are designed to capture broader personality dispositions rather than specific psychopathological characteristics. The scales demonstrate good internal consistency coefficients and good criterion group validity (McNulty, Harkness, Ben-Porath, & Williams, 1997).

The Rorschach inkblot method

The Rorschach can be easily administered and, once coded, a computer generated report produces many qualitative findings that are extremely useful in uncovering the internal world of juvenile sex offenders. The beauty of the Rorschach lies in the fact that it is a projective test, which is hard to feign and which gives extensive data concerning motivation (Hent, Harte, & Weenink, 1999).

The Rorschach inkblot test, originally developed by Hermann Rorschach (1921), has undergone many changes in its use and interpretation. The first scoring systems were developed in the USA (Beck, 1943; Hertz, 1941; Piotrowski, 1957; Rapaport, Gill, & Schafer, 1945). The comprehensive system (CS) is, however, a standardized scoring and interpretive system with associated normative data. Following Exner's (2003) development of the CS for scoring the Rorschach, the instrument has become a reliable and valid instrument that has taken its place alongside traditionally more respected and empirically based instruments such as the MMPI (Gacono & Meloy, 1994). The CS derives from the integration and standardization of the previous five most common scoring systems.

Standardization, reliability, and validity

The standardization of the test is based on a stratified sample of 1,390 children and adolescents aged between five and sixteen years. In addition, extensive samples for adults, with clinical samples including 180 outpatients with character disorders, add to the standardization of the test (Exner, 2003). This represents considerably more standardization data than are available for other more commonly used psychological tests.

The reliability and validity of the instrument as a whole, when administered and scored in accordance with the CS, is demonstrated by a number of studies. McDowell and Acklin (1996) demonstrate an overall mean percentage agreement of 87% for interrater reliability. With respect to the overall test–retest reliability, Exner and Weiner

(1995) demonstrate stability coefficients of 0.80 or greater on thirteen core variables at a three-year retest. More recent reviews of validity and reliability confirm these findings.

Administration, properties, and the scoring of the Rorschach inkblot test

The Rorschach consists of ten cards on which there are inkblots and to which the test participants are required to respond. The aim of the test administrator is to record the participant's initial responses and then the responses to an "enquiry" about each card. All of these response data are then encoded according to the specific directions laid out in the scoring manual.

The Human Experience Variable (HEV)

The HEV (derived from Rorschach scores) measures interest in human relationships or the extent of "relatedness" to others that an individual experiences. The variable (essentially a regression equation) is a composite variable that looks at the level of internalized representation of human relationship (the human content responses) and the quality of these responses in terms of the extent to which they represent reciprocal human relationship.

There is a substantial body of research concerning the Rorschach, revealing that the lack or poor quality of human content responses is associated with psychopathology (Exner, 2003). This research contains, in common with a vast body of attachment research, the notion that experience of human relationship with primary caregivers during early development becomes an important factor in perception and expectation about experience with other human relationships.

Exner concludes that a number of factors determine the likelihood of psychopathology in terms of the human content representation. These include whether the human content is represented in a whole way, whether it is a realistic representation or an imaginary one, and whether it is a confused representation (which might possibly result in special scores). Such findings have stimulated the research of Perry and Viglione (1991), who derive a variable originally known as the "ego impairment index" and later refine their finding and describe the human experience variable (HEV) (Perry, Viglione, & Braff, 1992).

The HEV might be used as an index of the quality of an individual's interpersonal relationships and relatedness (Burns & Viglione, 1996). Prior research into human representation has lacked appropriate controls. Burns and Viglione (1996) have remedied this problem and have provided not only a validation study, but also a construct validity study of the human (object) representation. In this study, the HEV is validated against the Bell Object Relations Inventory (BORI). An empirical validation study shows that the HEV is significantly related to the quality of interpersonal relatedness (attachment). To validate the HEV, Burns and Viglione (1996) had participants who were scored on the variable rated by their partners on a modified BORI and the emotional maturity rating form. The HEV is significantly correlated to the quality of interpersonal relatedness as measured by these instruments. The study validates the Rorschach's capacity to account for variance in the prediction of the quality of interpersonal relationships.

The variable has good face validity and is well founded in terms of theory and related empirical findings. The authors of the HEV have also provided a normative sample for the variable (Burns & Viglione, 1996).

HEV reliability and validity

The HEV variable, which measures the quality of internalized human representation, has good temporal stability and correlates with a range of psychopathology, notably depression and schizophrenia (Perry, McDougall, & Viglione 1995; Perry, Viglione, & Braff, 1992). In the original study on the variable (Burns & Viglione, 1991), the test–retest reliability of the HEV is 0.78 and at a five-year follow-up was 0.68 (Perry, McDougall, & Viglione, 1995). The results of a further study by these authors (Burns & Viglione, 1996) show that the HEV is able to distinguish between high and low interpersonal relatedness.

More broadly, the Burns and Viglione (1996) study is significant because it provides a source of empirical validation for attachment theory and object relations theory. Specifically, the findings "support the notion that intra-psychic representations of self and other, accessed through visual perceptions on the Rorschach, are related to the quality of external relationships" (p. 97).

For these reasons, the HEV is included as a measure in the research and its scores are expected to be inversely related to psychopathy.

The texture (determinant) response

Of all the determinants discussed, the texture determinant has been found to reliably distinguish psychopathic offenders from non-psychopathic offenders and it is, therefore, a particularly useful measure in identifying groups of juvenile sex offenders, especially where combined with other measures. Texture responses refer to tactile responses such as soft, hard, furry, fuzzy, silky, smooth, sticky, and greasy, and which use shading responses in the service of synthesizing tactile impressions. It is particularly common for younger-aged participants to touch the blot to indicate the presence of the texture variable.

The texture response relates to a reliance on tactile cues and to categorizing cognitively in terms of texture and behaviourally by stroking and touching (Marsh & Viglione, 1992). The authors have been able to demonstrate a link between these modes of information processing and a need for touching and stroking in establishing the validity of texture as a measure of attachment. (It was on the basis of such findings that participants in the current research who score higher on the PCL-R and who might have elevations on Scale 4 (psychopathic–deviate) of the MMPI-A would be found to be most likely to have no texture response on the Rorschach.)

Texture identifies the need for (attachment) closeness to or distance from others (Meloy, 1997). Most recently, *texture has been shown to predict attachment style*, with over-production of texture predicting preoccupied attachment style and lack of texture predictive of dismissing attachment style (Iwasa & Ogawa, 2010). Participants who produce no texture response have been found to be selfish and uncaring, more guarded and distant in their interpersonal relationships. In a sample of 100 conduct-disordered adolescents, texture responses were absent in 87% of cases (Loving & Russell, 2000). Similar findings were reported with a range of antisocial samples (Bridges, Wilson, & Gacono, 1998), with capacity for attachment strikingly absent in conduct-disordered adolescents. In adult samples of psychopaths, texture is absent in all the responses to the blots (Gacono & Meloy, 1994). These findings are significant sources of construct validity for this variable.

The texture response has been found to have an internal reliability coefficient of >0.80 (Exner & Weiner, 1995) and has shown test–retest reliability coefficients of 0.87 (at three years), 0.91 (at one year), 0.96 (at three weeks), and 0.86 (at seven days). As such, the texture response meets the criteria set for clinical and research use by the American Psychological Association.

Controversy concerning the reliability and validity of the Rorschach

Vigorous debate in the scientific assessment literature has continued in regard to the validity and reliability of the Rorschach, with claims that the Rorschach can be found lacking (Wood, Lilienfeld, Nezworski, & Garb, 2001). Despite these claims, other authors have continued to garner considerable evidence in support of the Rorschach's reliability and validity (Exner, 2003; Mattlar, 2004). The Rorschach has a long history of controversy, yet it remains one of the most widely used psychometric instruments for forensic assessment in the USA. Claims concerning the subjective nature of scoring the Rorschach have been addressed by the introduction of the "comprehensive system" (Exner, 2003). Despite the fact that the introduction of the comprehensive system has addressed concerns about the Rorschach's overall validity and reliability, there has been ongoing debate about these issues. Consequently, the verdict regarding the clinical utility of the Rorschach is equivocal and the debate continues to be spirited.

A number of journals have presented special sections dedicated to the debate concerning the psychometric properties of the Rorschach. A special section appeared in the *Journal of Personality Assessment* (2001), preceded by special sections in issues of *Psychological Assessment*, *Journal of Clinical Psychology* and *Assessment* in 1999 and 2000. The main areas of criticism focus on the adequacy of the comprehensive system norms, issues of cultural generalizability, scoring reliability, test–retest reliability, the problem of response rate bias, the factor structure of Rorschach scores, and validity issues (including the incremental validity of the comprehensive system).

There have been concerns that the comprehensive system norms are not so extensive and broad in scope as those for other widely used psychometric instruments such as the Wechsler adult intelligence scale. Critics also claim that many of the norms for the Rorschach are out of date and tend to over-pathologize normal adults (Lilienfeld, Wood, & Howard, 2000; Wood, Nezworski, & Garb, 2003). In response, Rorschach researchers have claimed that the norms are as comprehensive as many of those used to support other instruments and that individual variables, such as reflection responses, have to be interpreted by the context in which they appear, not just whether or not they are scored. As such, the criticisms of the norms potentially over-pathologizing individuals were considered by Weiner (1997) to be a statement of ignorance about the nature of Rorschach variables and their meaning. He particularly emphasizes the need to examine the properties of individual variables, such as texture, in order to examine reliability and validity issues.

Lilienfeld, Wood, and Howard (2000) marshalled evidence that half of the Rorschach variables achieve less than the 0.85 interrater reliability criterion, which is considered the minimum threshold for reliability. None the less, they note that "practitioners who use the Rorschach can be confident that about half of Comprehensive System variables can be potentially scored at a level of reliability for clinical work" (p. 33).

In relation to test–retest reliability, Wood, Nezworski, and Stejskal (1996) claimed that the reliability of the Rorschach as a whole does not meet test standards of the American Psychological Association, and that its reliability has not been adequately established. Meyer (1997) provides a meta-analysis of published studies concerning interrater reliability and demonstrates that the comprehensive system has excellent interrater reliability. Lilienfeld, Wood, and Howard (2000) subsequently claimed that these research findings do not address the interrater reliability of the non-research use of the instrument. Ganellen (2001) suggested that such criticism is harsh, given that such criteria have not been applied to other instruments where complex decision-making about scoring is required. The interrater reliabilities for variables used in my study are, none the less, sufficient to justify their use for research.

Wood, Nezworski, Stejskal, Garven, and West (1999) have also taken issue with the Rorschach's validity and claim that the validity of the instrument has not been adequately established. Much of their critique cited studies that have looked at the relative merits of the Rorschach and the MMPI. They took findings, which showed a lack of correlation of Rorschach variables with MMPI variables, to suggest the poor validity of the Rorschach. That method, as Ganellen (2001) pointed out, is an inappropriate basis from which to establish such an argument. In relation to this point, Hiller, Rosenthal, Bornstein, Berry, and Brunell-Neuleib (1999) showed that the global validity coefficients for the two measures are comparable, and also that the Rorschach had larger validity coefficients than the MMPI for studies using objective criterion variables.

Taken together, these findings suggest that the Rorschach, specifically the measures targeted in the current research, has sufficient reliability and validity to be used for research purposes.

The Hare Psychopathy Checklist-Revised (PCL-R)

The Hare Psychopathy Checklist—Revised (PCL-R) is a behavioural rating scale designed by Robert Hare (1991) for use with male forensic populations. Its aim is to assess behaviours and personality traits that are related to the clinical concept of psychopathy. Previous approaches to the task of assessing psychopathy are criticized as lacking reliability and validity. The PCL-R is now seen as the method *par excellence* to measure psychopathy.

The PCL-R provides two factor scores:

Factor 1 scores: According to the administration manual, factor 1 measures "selfish, callous, and remorseless use of others". This is a cluster of personality factors considered by Hare (1991) to be fundamental to the concept of psychopathy. The scale taps a participant's level of affect and interpersonal and verbal style and includes items that assess lack of remorse and pathological lying.

Factor 2 scores: Factor 2, which includes items such as juvenile delinquency, irresponsibility, and early behavioural problems, assesses behaviours that are indicative of unstable and antisocial lifestyle and behaviours that are socially deviant. The checklist comprises twenty items that are scored 0, 1, or 2, with the highest score representing the greatest evidence of psychopathy.

The items are derived from features of psychopathic behaviour and personality that are described by Cleckly (1941) in his classic work, *The Mask of Sanity*. The current PCL-R is based on a revision of the original PCL (Hare, 1991). As a result of extensive analysis of normative data, a cut-off score is established for the PCL-R so that a score of 30 or more is used to classify individuals as psychopathic. Using this cut-off, Hare (1991) finds in a sample of 229 inmates that the accuracy rate of the PCL was 0.85 (kappa=0. 67). This cut-off is used in most research studies and produces consistently high, significant differences between psychopaths and others in relation to a variety of behavioural, self-reported, and experimental variables.

Overall, interrater reliability demonstrates a coefficient of 0.93 for pooled forensic patient samples (Hare, 1991). In terms of internal consistency, the values are shown to be 0.85 for the alpha co-efficient and 0.22 for the mean inter-item correlation for the pooled forensic patient sample. The test–retest reliability is 0.94 for the PCL-R total scores.

A number of studies summarized by Hare (1991, 1998b) (mainly correlation studies of the PCL-R with *DSM-III* diagnoses) attest to the construct validity of the PCL-R. Also, especially relevant to the current study, are the reported correlations of the PCL-R with the MMPI, which reveal that the PCL-R is positively correlated with MMPI Scales 4 (psychopathic–deviate) and Scale 9 (hypomania), but negatively correlated with other scales, especially Scale 5 (masculinity–femininity) (Hare, 1998c).

Administration, properties, and scoring of the PCL-R

The PCL-R materials consist of a twenty-item rating scale with a manual, which provides a guide to scoring. Items are scored 0 = No, 1 = maybe/in some instances, or 2 = yes, depending on the extent of the evidence for the particular behaviour. For example, on Item 1, if a subject is sincere and straightforward, he would be scored 0.

The information gathered to complete the rating scale is commonly derived from an interview and from collateral data (usually file notes, reports, and institutional logs). If the quality of the collateral data is sufficient, collateral alone can be used.

A note about the assessment of suitability for
treatment of psychopathic sex offenders

The issue of assessing psychopathy is closely related to the issue of suitability for treatment. Despite the rather serious psychological difficulties with which many psychopathic sex offenders present, there is some encouraging evidence of positive treatment outcomes (including psychoanalytic interventions) with such offenders (McGauley, Adshead, & Sarkar, 2007). For example, Salekin, Worley, and Grimes (2010) report that, in a review of forty-two treatment studies on psychopathy, there was little scientific basis for the belief that psychopathy is an untreatable disorder and that outcomes of treatment with adolescents show promising results.

Skeem, Monahan, and Mulvey (2002) also reported, based on a review of a sample of 871 psychopathic offenders, that "Psychopathic patients appear as likely as non-psychopathic patients to benefit from adequate doses of treatment, in terms of violence reduction" (p. 577). They noted that such patients need longer-term treatment.

In terms of psychoanalytic interventions, in addition to individual case reports (e.g., Hyatt-Williams, 1998), Fonagy, Roth, and Higgitt (2005) has also shown significant outcomes in terms of impulse control and affect regulation in antisocial adolescents using mentalization-based interventions.

Consideration of suitability for treatment is, however, a vexed issue and is related to what might be regarded as the politics of psychopathy. As the nature of psychopathic crimes is often repulsive and frightening, there is an understandable tendency for people to want to distance themselves from these crimes. The concept of psychopathy has allowed for categorization and labelling of such offenders, which has often been used in a negative way.

The best that can be said within the current state of knowledge is that there is a need to think in terms of levels of psychopathy, as well as the capacity for attachment and interest in human relatedness. In terms of assessment of suitability for treatment, therefore, with psychopathic offenders who score at the higher level on measures of psychopathy, at a minimum there needs to be a careful consideration of criteria for suitability for interventions.

I believe the best criteria available are those developed by Meloy (1997), which encompass:

- a rejection criterion of anyone with a score greater than or equal to 30 on the PCL-R;
- the consideration of countertransference reactions that encompass an atavistic fear of predation;
- evidence in the patient of a complete absence of remorse;
- a history of sadistic offending, which has resulted in maiming or in death.

As it has been shown that there are cruel, violent, and murderous individuals who have psychic constellations associated with violent conflicts relating to separateness and symbiosis, there is a need to carefully and comprehensively assess juvenile sex offenders whose presentation suggests the existence of such problems. This is not only because they are likely to be at extreme risk for reoffending, but also because treatment recommendations for them need to be informed and realistic.

Related to this one needs, however, to avoid overly judgemental approaches to offenders who are psychopathic, but instead to carefully assess them and intervene where it is appropriate and safe to do so.

Note

1. I recommend the PCL-R on the basis of the extensive research underpinning it and because of my experience of its clinical and research utility. I nonetheless draw the reader's attention to the Psychopathy Checklist:Youth Version (PCL:YV) (Forth, Kosson, & Hare, 2003) which was derived from the PCL-R and taps into similar factors predictive of psychopathy.

CHAPTER TEN

The tale of two psyches: case histories of juvenile sex offenders

"That self, that life of one's own . . . is a composite structure which has been and is being formed and built up since the day of our birth, out of countless never-ending influences and exchanges between ourselves and others"

(Riviere, 1985, p. 358)

I n this chapter, I present two case histories representing one from each of the two broad categories of young sexual offenders that have been discussed in previous chapters. In the case of the psychopathic offender, relating to others is achieved primarily through violence and sexualized violence. Psychopathic offenders divest themselves of any emotional investment in the other. Affect, the mediator between the somatic and psychological self, has been removed as a means of maintaining psychological equilibrium (McDougall, 1995). This is one solution which also has a unique psycho-biology. It is the endpoint of a developmental trajectory which has undoubtedly involved a threatening emotional environment lacking in safety and security and one in which the individual has had to defend himself against an object on which he ought to have been able to rely. Such a background often involves severe neglect and abuse, usually early in development and often continuing for lengthy periods of the child's life. This developmental context results in the development of what Meloy (1997) refers to as the *stranger self-object*.

With the attachment-hungry (preoccupied attachment) juvenile sex offender, sexuality is used as the means of achieving (a pathological form of) attachment. As a result of the offender's trauma-linked identifications with children and his difficulties managing affect, a child can become the object of a sexualized form of attachment (Crtittenden, 1997b). This pathology suggests a developmental arrest involving a failure to psychically represent somatic states (mentalize) and to subsequently develop a sense of self-identity. This compulsive type of individual has not been able to internalize a capacity to soothe and regulate himself emotionally *by internalizing* a containing maternal object, but instead has remained reliant on external sources of somatic (sexual) satisfaction which provide only a temporary stabilization of the sense of self (McDougall, 1995). As McDougall suggests, there has been little development in such individuals from a sensation-dominated self to a psychological (lexical/agentive) self.

From a psychoanalytical standpoint, both of these pathologies involve the universal dilemma of dealing with love and hate towards the object of attachment (with one solution involving a detachment from the object). In normal development, when there has been a sufficiently loving environment, hate is contained by love. The infant gradually realizes that he loves and hates the same object (whom he has inevitably experienced as both providing for, and at other times frustrating, his needs). When abuse, neglect, or intrusiveness by the object has derailed psychological development, an integration of these feelings is disrupted. Psychic survival and a (precarious) sense of self can only be achieved by a limited range of (psychologically costly) outcomes. One of these involves detachment, identifying with the frightening object and becoming grandiose and, in the case of the psychopathic offender, predatory. Another outcome involves an enmeshed attachment with an object in order to satisfy somatically felt anxieties. That is, they become attached but cannot separate. Such individuals have little ability to be soothed by a lexical (separate) self. This is the situation with the "attachment hungry" juvenile sex offender and what gives his relationship with his victim a compulsive/addictive quality.

These descriptions do not preclude a psychopathically disposed paedophilic offender whose child victims become for him objects of sexualized aggression, often sadistic and murderous in nature. Some paedophilic offenders might also represent a fearful attachment style, which represents both a negative view of the self and the other. In this chapter, I do not explore the dynamics of this group in any detail other but note that these offenders are likely to appear to have some capacity for attachment and interest in relatedness. Instead, I focus on the two categories of offenders who represent almost opposite (and pathological) poles of the attachment spectrum.

Object manipulation and force: the case of Aaron

Aaron was seventeen years old at the time of his assessment for being charged with sexual offences. As full details of his background were unavailable, facts about his very early development were not known. It was disclosed, however, that he had been taken into care as a young child of four years of age and not returned to his single (biological) mother who, along with her *de facto* husband, had physically abused him as an infant. The abuse was extreme and he had marks from cigarette burns he had suffered as a child. He was finally placed with a foster family, after a number of foster arrangements, when he was nearly five and a half years old. His adoptive parents relinquished their care of him at age ten years, after he had tried to set fire to their house. He had been brought to the attention of the school for bullying other children and was finally expelled for stealing. He was placed in residential care. There was some thought that, later in childhood, he might have been a victim of sexual abuse, which was known to have been prevalent at the time he resided in one particular institution.

When he was eleven years old, he came into contact with the juvenile justice system as a result of a stealing offence. He later became involved with a deviant peer group and this involvement also saw him become a regular user of THC, alcohol, and amphetamines. During his mid-teens, he was subsequently charged with a number of breaking and entering offences and was sexually promiscuous. When he was seventeen years old, he and a group of other young men engaged in the rape of two peer-aged girls after encouraging them to take psychotropic drugs. He was charged with two counts of rape. He seemed unmoved by the accounts of distress of the girls and their families subsequent to the rape, claiming they had asked for sex.

His background revealed a trajectory that is fairly typical of a boy who develops conduct disorder and psychopathic behaviour. There was a background of disrupted attachment, with the development of early behavioural problems and hyperactivity which progressed to what can be diagnosed as oppositional defiant disorder (ODD) through to conduct disorder (CD), the development of drug and alcohol problems in adolescence, and then an increasingly serious pattern of offending (Keogh, 2002). (See Chapter Eleven, Figure 4.) In his case, his offending also encompassed sexual offending, namely, forcible rape.

Aaron's psychometric assessment

Aaron was assessed using the MMPI-A, the PCL-R, and the Rorschach. His MMPI-A scale results showed a valid profile, although there was an elevated Lie scale. His clinical scale profile revealed him as having an extremely elevated Pd (psychopathic–deviate) scale as well as a significantly elevated Ma (hypomania) scale. This two code point (4–9) profile describes someone who shows a significant disregard for social convention, rules, and standards and is frequently in trouble with legal and other authorities for his antisocial behaviour. Such an individual is seen to have a poorly developed conscience and is often characterized by abuse of non-prescription drugs and alcohol and by violent behaviour, as was the case with Aaron. Not surprisingly, such individuals are seen to be narcissistic and self-indulgent and to have difficulty with controlling their impulses.

Such subjects are seen to have a low tolerance for frustration and often erupt into outbursts of anger and hostility. Like Aaron, they blame others for everything that is wrong and tend to be exploitative in their relationships. Importantly, they are seen to be poor at, if not incapable of, forming relationships or closeness with others and appear not to be interested in relationship. A diagnosis of antisocial personality is common in people with higher elevations on this scale (elevations which characterized Aaron). This code point also typifies someone who is not willing to take responsibility for his actions and who has a poor level of empathy for others. Difficulty in learning from experience is another characteristic tendency.

The Psychopathology Five scales showed that Aaron had clinically significant elevations of the aggression scale and the constraint scale. Scores such as his describe someone who has a tendency to behave combatively with a disposition towards anger, as well as someone who displays grandiosity and has a desire for power and social domination. It further suggests a tendency to be rule breaking and to be impulsive, rather than following plans and being ordered in his behaviour. It also suggests a leaning towards criminality and risk-taking behaviour and a rejection of traditional morality.

Aaron's PCL-R score was 27: close to the cut-off score of 30 recognized as a definitive score for psychopathy. Of interest is that he achieved a maximum score on all items of Factor 1, which taps psychopathic (aggressive narcissistic) personality traits.

On the Rorschach, he had sufficient responses for a valid interpretation. His Rorschach summary revealed that his responses to the plates were completely devoid of texture (T). There was no human representation (H) in his responses, which otherwise contained themes of aggression and mutilation (e.g., animals "ripped apart" or parts "torn off"). There was also no co-operative response (COP). There were, however, a number of reflection responses (Fr, rF) (e.g., "this looks like a mirror"), which load into an egocentricity index, in his case indicating the presence of pathological narcissism.

Taken together, his results suggest the absence of affectional bonds, the presence of aggression, and merging and violent symbiosis in his object relations. The low HEV score also substantiated the picture of someone with little interest in (or capacity for) relationship. The results overall suggest a poor level of individuation (Exner & Erdberg, 2003).

Aaron's profile is similar to the Rorschach profile of conduct-disordered adolescents as described by Gacono and Meloy (1994). They note,

> Consistent with previous research on delinquency and human content (H) . . . the low frequency of H (*Human responses*) in our *Conduct Disorder* (CD) sample may indicate an indifference to others as whole, real and meaningful objects, and *an absent capacity to internally represent others as such* . . . For some of these CDs the beginning stabilization of certain regulatory defensive operations, such as acting out and grandiosity in warding off threats to internalized object relations may be indicated, rather than the neurotic use of signal anxiety to manage internal conflict. [pp. 56–57, my italics]

And they continue,

> Despite the likelihood of greater heterogeneity among the CD adoles-
> cent subjects than among the incarcerated Anti-Social Personality
> Disorder subjects we have utilized in the samples, similarities in the
> quantitative analysis of selected variables among the child, adolescent
> and adult samples supported *a developmental continuum for the anti-
> social pattern*. The similarities include, but are not limited to, *attachment
> deficits*, lessened anxiety and deficits in whole object internalization.
> [p. 57, my italics]

The overall picture emerging from Aaron's assessment is that of an
individual with high levels of psychopathic traits, little interest in relationship and attachment, and an approach to people based on a view
of them as objects for manipulation (and force). It is an internal world
where the need for others is denied. Sexual satisfaction in such an
individual is usually devoid of any regard for the other. My experience (countertransference) in being with him was that I felt no warmth
towards him and that there was something disturbing about the
emotionless manner in which he talked about others. I found myself
being aware of something frighteningly violent in him.

In terms of attachment, in many ways he expressed a positive
view about himself, but a consistent disinterest or disdain for others,
placing him in the most extreme position of the dismissing attachment
quadrant. Supporting this, he was aggressive in his interpersonal style
and he expressed scepticism about the value of human relationships.
His developmental experiences of abuse and neglect can be seen to
have been devastating to the development of his sense of self, and
instead to have fostered his very negative view of others and turning
to the self as the object. His behaviour and attitudes reveal little
psychic representation of human interaction and no developed social
representation such as reciprocal or co-operative behaviour. It can be
seen that he had little psychological containment as an infant and that
his early development would have been totally disruptive of the
normal development of the social brain. Albeit in a different way to the
enmeshed and poorly individuated offender with a preoccupied
attachment style, his capacity to move to the development of an agentive self would have been severely compromised by this turning to
himself as the object. This would have left him devoid of opportunities

to learn about himself and about relationships and sexuality in the maternal crucible of attachment.

Object distortion and perversion: the case of Paulie

In contrast to the physically slim and wiry presentation of Aaron, Paulie was a tall, rather overweight, socially introverted, and awkward-looking fifteen-year-old when he was assessed as a result of charges of paedophilic sexual offences against a seven-year-old boy. He seemed to spend his time in a rather withdrawn state, focused on his fantasy life, much of which, the assessment revealed, centred on sexual fantasy about children, mostly boys aged around seven years. These fantasies were, for his average level of intelligence, quite elaborate.

Paulie was the eldest child in his family and had a sister two years younger than himself. His mother had seemed inconsistent in her affections for him and treated him as her confidant, especially in terms of her negative feelings towards her cold and critical husband. Paulie felt that his mother's affection for him was always bound up in her own need to be comforted. He felt responsible for her. His father was an abrupt man who was emotionally distant. Paulie's mother revealed that the father was disappointed that his son was not more sports minded. Paulie had always been shy, according to his mother, and was not very sociable. His mother painted a picture of his being a rather intense and withdrawn boy who always seemed to play with younger boys. He underachieved at school. Relatedly, he missed many days of school. His mother seems to have colluded with his school absences, preferring to have him at home with her. At school he was not otherwise a problem. His school reports, however, suggested he was quiet and socially isolated and engaged poorly in class.

Somewhere between the ages of five and nine years, he was sexually abused by an uncle who lived nearby. He was never able to tell anyone about this, not because he was threatened, but because the perpetrator told him he would not be believed and would be seen as causing trouble, which would anger his father. He was also aware that his father had quite a collection of pornography, which he was easily able to access. He felt that he was accessing something of his father when he looked at this pornography, which was "hard core".

Paulie said that he started to have romantic fantasies about younger children, whom he felt wanted to be with him. He felt they shared a common secret bond. He masturbated endlessly with the masturbation fantasies centring on encouraging young boys into this "special" behaviour with him.

After being charged with sexually molesting a seven-year-old boy whom he fondled and encouraged into fellatio, he confessed that this was not the first time that he had done this. Investigations revealed that there were at least four other young boys who were his victims. He was ordered to serve a brief custodial sentence and then a community based order with a requirement for him to enter into a treatment programme for sex offenders. He had no other non-sexual offending history. He was at risk of assault in the custodial system because he was identified as a sex offender and because of his timid disposition.

Paulie's psychometric assessment

Paulie had a marked fake good profile on the MMPI-A, but it was, none the less, valid. He seemed to want to make a favourable impression. He revealed clinically significant elevations on Scales 2 (depression), 8, and 0 (social introversion). His clinically significant Scale 2 score describes someone who often feels pessimistic about the future, who lacks confidence, feels useless, and is unable to function in social situations, from which such a person tends to retreat. The lives of those with this type of profile are usually typified by social withdrawal and by a lack of intimate relationships.

High scorers such as Paulie tend also to be shy and retiring. Generally, they are seen to have high levels of distress, but in their favour they are often amenable to psychotherapy or counselling. The clinically significant Scale 8 elevation suggested schizoid features. Individuals like Paulie, with such scores, often have sexual preoccupations and are confused about their sexuality. They typically respond to stress by daydreaming. They can also be impulsive, non-conforming, and unusual. They often feel alienated and unaccepted by their peers.

The high score on Scale 0 speaks to the presence of a significant level of social introversion. Such individuals tend to be very uncomfortable in negotiating sexual intimacy and, if heterosexual, very

THE TALE OF TWO PSYCHES 149

uncomfortable around peer-aged members of the opposite sex. Apart from being shy and socially withdrawn, they tend to be sensitive about what people think of them and tend to feel most comfortable when they are alone.

Consistent with these scores was the fact that Paulie achieved clinically significant elevations on the psychoticism and the introversion (PSY-5) scales, but showed no significant elevations on the aggression and constraint (PSY-5) scales. In terms of his introversion score, there were a number of bizarre items endorsed, suggesting some psychotic-like functioning. Overall, his MMPI profile revealed considerable psychopathology, but yet it was not a profile that would be typically found in a juvenile offender.

His PCL-R score of 12 was consistent with his lack of significant elevation on the Pd scale of the MMPI-A. There were only very few of the items of Factor I (psychopathic personality) traits endorsed. This is consistent with MPPI-A studies of juvenile sex offenders that reveal no such Scale 4 elevations (Freeman, Dexter-Mazza, & Hoffman, 2005).

Paulie's Rorschach results were also very revealing, showing an over production of texture (T) responses found in cases of so-called "attachment hunger" (Gacono, Meloy, & Bridges, 2000; Meloy, 1997). He also revealed a number of shading responses (Y), consistent with his Scale 2 (depression) scores on the MMPI-A. There were also numerous morbid responses (MOR) that have been linked to self-hate (Exner & Erdberg, 2003).

In terms of his attachment status, he endorsed many statements that suggested he had preoccupied attachment status. In terms of the broad dimensions of view of self and others, he had a less favourable view of himself than others, with an overly dependent style and with palpable feelings of low self-esteem and unworthiness. In sessions with him, I felt a sense of connection and some warmth towards him.

Differences in psychic structure and object relations

There are notable differences in the psychic structures (object relations) of these two offenders that serve to illustrate the differences between juvenile sex offenders who offend against the background of an antisocial personality style and those with significant psychopathology, which leads them into escalating compulsive sexual behaviour. In a psychoanalytic sense, both types of offenders are impelled to act in the manner they do as a means of maintaining psychic survival and dealing with their internal object relations. There is, in both cases, a complex enactment of internal object relations via an identification with a variously intrusive or threatening object (associated with varying levels of abuse and violence), where the victim represents the split-off (psychically traumatized) aspect of the self. These represent important aspects of a psychic "real time" assessment of risk.

In the case of the psychopath, the means of psychic survival has been to identify with a destructive, omnipotent, and grandiose self. In terms of the Rorschach responses in Aaron's case, these were revealed most clearly through the lack of texture response (T), his high egocentricity index, the level of PER (personal responses) which reflect grandiosity, and the absence of affect, notably through the absence of reflection responses (Fr, rF). These results were corroborated by his profile and were revealed by the other diagnostic tests (MMPI-A and Hare PCL-R) used in Aaron's assessment case and in the study.

In Aaron's case we can see that his early development involved a significant lack of trust and basic safety. His objects were frightening and unpredictable. Objects of attachment that should have been the sources of safety and security were instead sources of fear and insecurity. The child, in order to survive, has to identify with this frightening or aggressive object. The child has to turn to the self as an object. Meloy's (1997) *stranger self object* captures this concept of the frightening, malevolent object that is identified with in order to survive relentless abuse and cruelty. The psychopathic individual develops a grandiose omnipotent self, which feels, in fantasy, invulnerable. Relatedness is achieved through aggression and violence.

In Paulie's case, attachment is achieved primarily through sexuality, which is experienced in a compulsive way. There is an intense identification with the object of sexual arousal. The victim is experienced as vital for psychic survival and balance. In addition, and because of a limited capacity (due to failures of separation and individuation) to relate to adults, attachment is achieved by sexualizing the relationship with the child victim (who is identified with in complex ways that are often relevant to the child victim's age, which might, for example, be the age of the perpetrator at the time of his own sexual abuse). In Paulie's case, his overall background was more conducive to attachment than was Aaron's. None the less, the sensation-dominated self, not allowed to develop into a psychological self as the pathway to separation and individuation, was corroded by intrusive mothering, which caused him to develop what Fonagy, Gergely, Jurist, and Target (2004) have referred to as an *alien self*. This self develops in response to failed maternal containment or misattunement. This alien self is seen to create a particular vulnerability to trauma in middle childhood, which it did in the case of Paulie. His experience of sexual abuse, in the context of intrusive mothering and an unavailable father, caused him also to associate relatedness with intrusive sexuality.

As he developed into adolescence, he started to have sexual fantasies about young children. He thought a lot about relationships with children. This desire to be close to children in a sexually perverse way dominated his thinking and masturbatory fantasies. In the case of the compulsive adolescent (dominated by high levels of dopamine, which, in turn, reward the brain for the compulsive sexual behaviour), he was totally reliant on the external environment for the regulation of his emotional world and psychic equilibrium. As McDougall (1995) has so clearly pointed out, the sensation-dominated individual has never developed an agentive self. This was linked to his difficulty in separating (psychologically) from a mother who, for a variety of reasons, might herself need to remain fused with her child.

The consequences of this were great, as it impacted adversely on Paulie's development of his identity and his ability to see and relate to others as individuals separate to himself. As McDougall (1995) points out,

> The two challenges that confront every human being – the compli-
> cated process of acquiring and assuming a sense of individual iden-
> tity, followed by coming to terms with one's gender identity and
> assuming a future sexual role – both involve a mourning process ...
> individuality and mono-sexuality are major narcissistic wounds to the
> megalomaniac psyche of the child, but there are rich compensations.
> Overcoming the claim of fusional rights involves renouncing the
> omnipotent expectation of a magical fulfilment of one's wishes, as
> occurred in infancy, when wishes were met without having to pass
> through the code of language. However, this renouncement is

rewarded with a sense of self identity and freedom from the counter-fantasy of being omnipotently controlled by the mother . . . this loss is compensated by the gift of sexual desire and satisfying adult love relations. [p. 155]

For Paulie, he could not be free from being ("preoccupied" with and) omnipotently controlled by his mother (and, in a sense, now his victims). His attachment insecurity leaves him in a state of dependent symbiosis with his objects. In contrast, Aaron has triumphed over and has taken himself as the object: a grandiose object that contains all that is desired. His megalomaniacal psyche is maintained, as he has perfect merging with the object in a manner that allows him freedom from his envy and can obfuscate the need for all others, who, instead, are controlled and coerced in the service of his needs.

In summary, the differences in interest in attachment and relationship in the two cases are clear. In Aaron's case, he felt he needed no one and was self sufficient; in Paulie's case, he spent hours in perverse sexual fantasies about children he convinced himself would want to be with him and on whom he depended for his sense of self. At the same time, he expressed no interest in peer-aged friendships and seemed more and more incapable of the demands of adulthood as he became older. In contrast, as Aaron arrived at adolescence, he became more interested in seeking stimulation and self-gratification and took an increasing disinterest in attachment and relatedness.

Adolescence as second chance at separation and individuation

In the two above-mentioned subjects, as is typical with such offenders, their offending commenced and escalated in adolescence. Often this phenomenon is attributed simply to puberty and the effect of sexual maturation along with other biological changes. It also often linked to the increase in risk-taking behaviour common at this stage of development. This is associated with the fact (as discussed in Chapter Six) that the amygdala, a sub-cortical structure in the brain, develops in advance of the frontal cortex, so that strong feeling states in the adolescent are often not well tempered by appropriate levels of considered behaviour.

Notwithstanding these considerations, there are important psychological issues which come into play. With psychopathology, including that which encompasses sexual offending, there is a complex set of reasons why problems that may have been incubating throughout middle childhood suddenly erupt in the way they do in adolescence. Psychoanalysts have long known that the turmoil of adolescence is due in large part to the psychological developmental challenges that adolescence presents, as much as the physical hormonal maturation. Blos (1967), for example, has argued that adolescence in particular represents a further challenge concerning separation and individuation, which Fonagy, Gergely, Jurist, and Target (2004) regard as the primary task in adolescence. In middle childhood, failure at individuation and separation can be disguised, but when the adolescents have to finally separate from their attachment figures, those who have failed to achieve the requisite levels of separation and individuation can experience a serious breakdown in their psychological functioning. In juvenile sex offenders, this might be acted out in their sex offending.

Erikson (1968) suggests that the challenge of adolescent development is the resolution of the question, "Who am I?" He argues that it is a stage of development where the adolescent has to become clear about his personal identity. This crossroad of development and the possibility of entry into adulthood are dependent upon how this stage of development is navigated. Gross (1987) has noted that what is particular about this phase of identity development is that

> It is a special sort of synthesis of earlier stages and a special sort of anticipation of later ones. Youth has a certain unique quality in a person's life; it is a bridge between childhood and adulthood. Youth is a time of radical change—the great body changes accompanying puberty, the ability of the mind to search one's own intentions and the intentions of others, the suddenly sharpened awareness of the roles society has offered for later life. [p. 47]

The "special sort of synthesis of earlier stages" can be seen as the re-emergence, not only of difficulties with separation and individuation, but linked to it, the dilemma, as Fonagy, Gergely, Jurist, and Target (2004) see it, as to what to do with the alien self that has resulted from difficulties with misattunement:

> The infant has been forced to internalize the representation of the object's state of mind as a core part of himself. When he has to finally

separate from his parents, he is no longer able to resort to projecting this aspect of himself into them. [p. 320]

In addition to this challenge, they note that the adolescent finds increasing complexity developing in his emotional world. This results from a developing cognitive capacity for abstract thinking, which can create overwhelming anxiety. The adolescent who has not achieved a secure attachment status and who has not achieved psychological separation and individuation is thrown back into regressive forms of psychic functioning. He is thrown into the two unintegrated forms of psychological functioning: the equivalence and pretend modes.

In the psychic equivalence mode, what is psychically represented internally is equivalent to that which is externally experienced. In a young child, mental events are equivalent to events in their physical world, especially in terms of causality and meaning. In the pretend mode, internal experience is disconnected from the external reality. The child can experience feelings and ideas as completely representational, with no implication for the external world. That is, their thinking is bound up with an inner world of fantasy.

Paedophilic juvenile sex offenders who are attachment hungry rely heavily on the pretend mode of functioning, while the psychopathic offenders rely more heavily on an equivalence mode. In the pretend mode, there is a heavy reliance on fantasy (including sexual fantasy); with the psychopathic offender, there is a reliance on the psychic equivalence mode, whereby one's ideas are not seen as representation of reality, but as realities themselves. There is no ability to appreciate the difference between internal and external reality, between the internal and external predator. The internal threat is perceived as an external one which has to be destroyed. Many of these more contemporary theoretical ideas fit well with earlier object relations oirented accounts of sex offending (Fairbairn, 1952; Fairbairn, Scharff, & Birtles, 1994).

Conclusions

The two cases studies I have discussed represent examples of what appear to be two distinct categories of juvenile sex offenders. The first is characterized by a background of conduct disorder and antisocial (psychopathic) personality development. The other is characterized by psychopathology, which gives rise to compulsive sexual behaviour in an individual dominated by fantasy and incapable of age-appropriate social behaviour. These cases do not preclude a juvenile sex offender who might have a fearful (disorganized) attachment style, who may have less interest in relationship and less capacity for attachment and who, because of social immaturity and inadequacy with adult sexual relationships, might sexually offend against children in a more coercive way.

The different orientations to relationships, combined with the widely differing object relations seen from the vertex of these two individual case studies, illustrate vividly the importance of understanding the very different psychodynamics and motivations of each offender, which has implications for differential treatment approaches. What both cases have in common, as a result of the disruption to the development of their respective socio-emotional selves, is an impaired capacity for mentalization which has led to the very different under- and over-regulated emotional lives of each and their consequent inability to form meaningful, reciprocal, human relationships. As such, treatments that focus purely on cognitive strategies are unlikely to have sustained treatment effect. This relates to the fact that these treatments do not have the capacity to get to the essential (and specific) deficits in such individuals. Such issues are reflected in the findings (see Chapter Eleven) concerning the effectiveness of contemporary treatments for juvenile sex offenders which suggest that the specific and individual needs of offenders are perhaps not addressed by such interventions.

Above all, the close lens on these two cases reveals the need for differential approaches to treatment. Modern psychoanalytic interventions, especially mentalization-based treatments, linked as they are to research findings, appear to hold promise for the treatment of this challenging group of offenders.

Mentalization based therapy (MBT) and other psychoanalytic treatment

"The self and its boundaries are at the heart of philosophical speculation on human nature, and the sense of self and its counterpart, the sense of other, are universal phenomena that profoundly influence all our social experience"

(Stern, 1985, p. 5)

The psychological profiles of psychopathic and affect-hungry juvenile sex offenders discussed in Chapter Eleven can be differentiated on the basis of their level of psychopathology, psychopathy, and their capacity for attachment and relatedness. In turn, these differences are reflected in their psychic structure and object relation configurations and associated psychological defences. These underpin distinct motivations reflected in different offence types. This has important implications for the type of psychological interventions selected for sub-groups of juvenile sex offenders.

Treatment and treatment outcome with juvenile sex offenders

The contemporary psychological interventions invoked with juvenile sex offenders have been predominantly cognitive–behavioural and skill-based approaches. Of these multi-systemic therapy (MST), which has socio-ecological components and works with different systems with which the juvenile sex offender comes into contact, has been the most successful (Henggeler & Borduin, 1995; Henggeler, Schoenwald, Borduin, Rowland, & Cunningham, 1998). All these approaches have tended to regard juvenile sex offenders as a homogenous group with the same treatment needs. The average effect size for treatment approaches with juvenile sex offenders overall has been estimated at 0.43, with a lack of superiority for cognitive–behavioural interventions found. Meta-analytic reviews of treatment outcomes for juvenile sex offenders have noted that a confounding variable concerning effect sizes might be the "one size fits all" approach to treatment (Reitzel & Carbonell, 2006).

More generally, research indicates that the benefits of cognitive–behavioural type interventions are not necessarily any greater than psychodynamic interventions (Arkowitz & Lilienfeld, 2006; Leichsenring & Leibing, 2007; Leichsenring & Rabung, 2008) and that the durability of the treatment outcomes derived from cognitive–behavioural interventions is questionable (Durham et al., 2005). Further, while treatment outcome research with psychodynamic therapy is a more recent development and has not been voluminous (possibly because cognitive–behavioural paradigms have dominated research institutions), the evidence concerning its effectiveness has shown equal, if not better, outcomes for many psychological conditions (Levy & Ablon, 2009; Fonagy & Kachele, 2009), with indications of more durable and sustained treatment effects (Kenny, 2011; Shedler, 2010). Given such findings, we might expect at least similar treatment effect sizes, using psychodynamic interventions with juvenile sex offenders, to those interventions currently used. Further, it could be argued that if greater specificity in sub-typing offenders on the basis of their capacity for attachment, level of human relatedness, and their level of psychopathy could be achieved, the treatment effect might be increased. This argument is supported by the conclusions of meta-analytic reviews concerning treatment outcomes with juvenile sex offenders (Reitzel & Carbonell, 2006).

I believe these findings make a case for psychodynamic interventions (and, I would add, especially attachment theory-informed psychotherapeutic interventions) to be considered as potentially useful interventions with juvenile sex offenders, given that they are found to have core psychological deficits known to be positively affected by such psychodynamic interventions.

Psychodynamic approaches span a continuum, from interventions such as mentalization based treatment (MBT) (an attachment theory-informed intervention) and other brief psychodynamic interventions, to longer-term psychodynamic psychotherapy and psychoanalysis. The specific evidence base for each of these treatments provides a guide for when a particular treatment might be indicated. A decision concerning treatment choice needs to encompass a consideration of the seriousness, risks, and cost implications of reoffending.

In this chapter I make a case for the utility of MBT as a short term intervention with juvenile sex offenders and for psychoanalysis or psychoanalytic psychotherapy, as intensive treatments, particularly where an equation involving suitability for treatment, risk of reoffending, and costs associated with reoffending suggest a cost benefit for intensive treatment.

Mentalization based therapy (MBT)

Intrinsic to understanding MBT is an understanding of the relevance of mentalizing to mature psychological functioning. Fonagy (2001) notes that

> A normal awareness of the relationship between internal and external reality is not universal, but rather a developmental achievement. It is the consequence of the successful integration of two distinct modes of differentiating internal from external in the young child, intricately tied to the earliest relationships. We see development as an early moving from an experience of psychic reality in which mental states are not related to as representations, to an increasingly complex view of the internal world, which has as its hallmark the capacity to mentalize: to assume thoughts and feelings in others and in oneself and to recognize these connected to outer reality. [pp. 169–170]

MBT as an attachment theory-informed psychotherapy involves the activation of the attachment system of a patient in order to engage the patient in a process whereby his ability to think about the state of mind of another and his own is developed (Allen & Fonagy, 2006). It can be viewed as a way of addressing a developmental disruption that began in the individual during his infant development.

The neurobiology underpinning this development is particularly relevant, as it was originally thought that this was fixed in the early stages of infancy (see Chapter Six). We now know that the brain has plasticity, even in adulthood, and that psychotherapy and analysis can have an impact on this neurobiology (Doidge, 2007; Gross, Stasch, Schmal, Hillenbrand, & Cierpka, 2007). In terms of this neurobiology, it is now known that the right hemisphere grows to twice its size within twenty-four months of birth and is disproportionately developed in comparison to the left hemisphere. It is the orbito-frontal cortex (OFC) in the right hemisphere of the brain that seems to contain a significant component of the neurobiological underpinning of the emotional and relational self (Schore, 2005). If there has not been an appropriate level of emotional attunement, or there has been frank abuse from the care-giver during this time, a sense of self and others (separation and individuation) does not take place. If this is the case, subsequent social development, along with what would otherwise be the pathway to a development of a sense of self and self agency, is adversely affected, resulting in a deepening of attachment difficulties.

MBT aims at the remediation of such disrupted development and the associated difficulties with affect regulation, control of impulses, dysfunctional interpersonal communication, and perception. Although MBT has been particularly well developed with patients who have borderline personality disorder (BPD) (Bateman & Fonagy, 2009), there is evidence of its effectiveness with other populations where affect regulation, control of impulses, and the level and quality of relatedness with others are at the core of the pathology. MBT has also been found to be useful with children and adolescents who experience difficulties with these capacities (Fonagy, Roth, & Higgitt, 2005). It is particularly helpful because mentalizing assists with the development of interpersonal functioning. It develops the ability to mentally represent affect (thinking about one's feelings) and to develop an intentional representation of oneself and one's attachment figures, which facilitate thinking about one's own state of mind and that of others.

MBT is based on an attachment theory-informed psychodynamic developmental theory, which links the psychological processes inherent in attachment to the establishment of a mental representation of the relationship between self and other. In particular, it draws on the theory of mind mechanisms (TOMMs), a theory that suggests that humans can develop the ability to infer the mental state of another person. Although the mind is a theoretical construct because it cannot be seen, the ability to mentalize is correlated with the activation of specific parts of the brain, suggesting a neural basis for the TOMMs. Photo-electron tomography (PET) scan-based research has shown that using verbal and pictorial story comprehension tasks, a set of regions including the medial prefrontal cortex (mPFC) and an area around the posterior superior temporal sulcus (pSTS), sometimes the precuneus and the amygdala/temporolar cortex, can be shown to be involved in this functioning (Gallagher & Frith, 2003).

Based on such understandings, I propose that forms of MBT with differential treatment foci, depending on offender type, might be indicated for juvenile sex offenders. MBT would need to have a different focus, depending on the attachment difficulties of the offenders being treated. The two broad attachment difficulties in juvenile sex offenders that emerged from my own research were an avoidant (child)/ dismissing (adult) attachment style in the more psychopathic sex offenders and an ambivalent (child)/ preoccupied (adult) attachment style in those sex offenders with so-called attachment hunger. It is, of course, likely that, as with adult sex offenders, there might be some sex offenders who offend against children who have a disorganized/ disorientated (child)/fearful (adult) attachment style. I will not discuss this group in detail, but note that they could be also seen as amenable to MBT. I would not see this group as attachment hungry, but as being *fearful* of adult relationships (and, thus, prone to child sex offending).

Turning to the sub-group of juvenile sex offenders who offend against children who are characterized by attachment hunger, I see that these offenders have some similarities to patients with BPD who present with a form of attachment hyper-activation. This hyper-activation of the attachment system appears to result in their sexual offending having a compulsive quality. In contrast, the detachment characteristic of psychopathic offenders has made interventions, which require some form of alliance with a therapist, difficult. An MBT approach to psychopathic offenders would, thus, require a unique approach that might focus on increasing their capacity to think about the states of mind of others as a by-product of a transference based relationship with the therapist. Ultimately, MBT might have more benefits for psychopathic offenders who have developed some minimal capacity for attachment (McWilliams, 1994). The fact that adolescence offers a "second chance", developmentally speaking, and given the consequences of unremitting psychopathic behaviour into adulthood (and the costs associated with it), a case can be made for the cost benefit and cost effectiveness of pursuing such interventions.

Fonagy, Gergely, Jurist, and Target (2004) suggest that the capacity to attribute mental states to the self and others develops within an attachment relationship, whereby an attuned care-giver can emotionally receive the infant in a way that allows the mirroring of the sense of self, so that this can become psychically represented or "internalized" during the rapid right hemisphere development in infancy. They suggest that there are two alternating modes of early experiences (subprocesses) serving this development. These are a mode of "psychic equivalence" and a "pretend" mode (discussed in Chapter Ten). Mentalization requires the integration of these two modes of functioning, which is facilitated by playful interaction with an attachment figure that feels safe. Mentalization is seen to go awry when this safe, playful interaction is not available and there is misattunement and the infant instead is made to internalize an alien self as part of himself. This concept is linked to that of a failure of maternal containment, which Hyatt-Williams (1998) has suggested is a common root problem in violent and murderous offenders.

Mentalizing is, consequently, a social process. In order to develop this capacity, one needs to have the experience of another mind. The capacity to mentalize thus requires "social feedback" and care-giving that involves a sensitivity to interpersonal contingencies so that some sense of self and others can develop.

This sense of self develops through a number of sub-processes. First, there is a sense of self as a physical agent (mental representation of one's own body as separate) and a sense of a self as a social agent. Subsequently, there is also the development of a sense of self who is a teleological agent (i.e., has an understanding of goal-directed, rational action) and a self who can become an "intentional mental agent" (i.e., has the capacity to understand things like desires and intentions in self and other). As development proceeds, there also develops a "representational agent" (i.e., able to understand the representational), along with the formation of an auto-biographical self (Fonagy,

Gergely, Jurist, & Target, 2004). All these developments occur along a continuum from a sense of a merged/autistic state to a more differentiated state of self-object representations and an increasingly more complex sense of self (see Chapter Five).

When development goes well (i.e., when care-giving has emanated from a securely attached care-giver), the result is an *internalized working model* (see Chapter Three) that serves as a template for mutual and reciprocal relationship. A sub-component of this internal model has been proposed which has been termed the "interpersonal interpretative mechanism" (IIM) (Fonagy, Gergely, Jurist, & Target, 2004).

This is seen as "An over-arching hypothetical neural structure, a processing system for social information that underlies reflective function or menatlization . . . which may be the final step in the transcription of genetic influence into a pattern of behaviour" (p. 125).

This genetically based mechanism is seen to have both a cognitive (related to the capacity to interpret epistemic/mental states) and an affective structure (related to the capacity for empathy).

Fonagy and Luyten (2009) have described four polarities that are involved in mentalizing. I propose that these dimensions can also be used to describe the mentalizing deficits of juvenile sex offenders and account for the two sub-types of these offenders that I have described (see Figure 4).

The polarities are:

1. *Automatic to controlled (implicit* vs. *explicit)* mentalizing, where controlled mentalization involves conscious, verbal and reflective functioning and where automatic mentalization is seen to be reflexive, rapid and non-verbal.
2. Mentalizing based on *internal* vs. *external* features of self and others, where internal mentalization requires an ability to directly focus on one's own or another's mental state and where external mentalization involves a focus on external features of self and others.
3. A *cognitive* vs. *affective* reliance, where the polarity refers to the extent to which someone is able to integrate a cognitive and affective appraisal of a social situation. Over-reliance on the cognitive aspect can result in a form of hyper-mentalization.
4. The self–other polarity, which refers to the extent to which there is a reliance on an *imitative style* vs. an ability to rely on *one's own belief/desire.*

Each of these polarities has a particular brain circuitry associated with it (Fonagy, 2010).

Juvenile sex offenders and mentalizing deficits

Misattunement can result in the internalization of an *alien self*, as the infant who is not able to find himself represented in the mother's mind instead has to internalize the object's state of mind as a core part of himself (Fonagy, Gergely, Jurist, & Target, 2004). As a certain amount of non-contingent, emotional response is part of the human condition, such an experience is universal. The extent, however, to which it occurs and the amount of other trauma experienced during development can retard both the capacity for mentalizing and the development of a separate, psychological self.

If there is frank trauma and abuse, the alien self is seen to identify with the aggressor, with the result that the child or adolescent can come to see himself as destructive and behave thus. This notion dovetails with Meloy's (1997) idea (described in Chapter Five) concerning the identification with the "stranger self-object" (a term which carries with it the notion of a fundamental disturbance of the process of separation and individuation).

Among juvenile sex offenders there is evidence of differential solutions to various developmental disruptions. These lead to a failure to develop a sense of self (and develop an alien self) or to identifying with the aggressor (and identifying with the stranger self-object), which results in the use of variously sexualized and/or violently sexualized means of attaching. In those adolescents who are attachment hungry, there appears to be a failure with mentalizing to such an extent that there is a desire to think about the state of mind of another, but an incapacity to do so in anything but a distorted way because of their over-reliance on internal mental states (fantasy), reliance on the pretend mode of functioning, and, from an object relations perspective, their fusion with their object. In the attachment dismissing (psychopathic) offender, there is, in contrast, an unwillingness and an incapacity to think about the state of mind (needs), and instead a desire to manipulate and control them and an inability to move from the psychic equivalence mode.

In the attachment hungry group of offenders, it is as if the victim has been placed (unconsciously) in the role that he, the offender, held as a child when he himself was subject to an "intrusive" other. That is, the victim is forced to accept an alien experience, something that denies who he is. This might be linked to the phenomenon of paedophiles who feel misunderstood by law enforcement officers who do not see their view that the child "really wanted sex" with them. Here, one can see the reliance on the pretend mode of functioning with an excessive reliance on fantasy.

In the case of the psychopathic offender, trauma appears to have been so great that the capacity to infer the victim's state of mind has been obliterated. The individuation and separation of the psychopathic offender is totally disrupted by the need to identify with the aggressor in order to survive, thus becoming malignantly narcissistic. As a result, this offender is only capable of seeing others as an object for the offender's own manipulation and control; internal and external reality (and threats to security) are seen as one and the same.

Implications for the use of MBT with juvenile sex offenders

Although MBT has been primarily used with BPD, Masterson (2005) notes there is commonality of pathological mechanisms underlying all disorders of the self. Juvenile sex offenders can be seen to represent heterogeneity of such disorders of the self. It would appear that matching the research findings concerning the attachment and object relations of juvenile sex offenders with the dimensions of attachment deficits that Fonagy and Luyten (2009) have described in borderlines, a number of conclusions and comparisons can be drawn. (These are schematically represented in Figure 4.) This diagram represents four polarities (continua) of capacities required for mentalizing. An individual who is securely attached would have a balance of such capacities and would be positioned midway on each continuum. The heterogeneous range of deficits found in juvenile sex offenders is depicted in Figure 4.

A number of mentalizing deficits of juvenile sex offenders are represented in the figure. First, psychopathic juvenile sex offenders have an almost total lack of reliance on affect, a core deficit of attachment (i.e., detachment), and a lack of empathy. Like borderlines, they

Implicit (automatic) ←(AH)___(P)_____→ Explicit (controlled)
mentalizing   mentalizing

Internal reliance ←____(AH)_____(P)→ External reliance

Cognitive reliance ←(P)_____ (AH)→ Affective reliance

Imitative style ←(P)____(AH)_____→ Own belief/desire

Figure 4. Hypothetical positioning of attachment hungry (AH) and psychopathic (P) juvenile sex offenders on mentalizing deficits continua.

appear to rely more on cognitive cues, and are very reliant on these external cues; unlike borderlines, they are very adept at reading them. That is, they have a disproportionately developed, cognitive interpersonal interpretive mechanism (IIM-c) compared to their affective interpersonal interpretative mechanism (IIM-a). Their reading of external cues, because it is devoid of affect, leads to a false cognition. They are also adept at being imitative.

In comparison, the attachment hungry group of juvenile sex offenders is much more likely to be unable to regulate affect and (compulsive) behaviour which is influenced by their reliance on their phantasy life. Their reliance on internal phantasy leads them to misread the mental states of their victims. They also appear to have a more under-developed IIMc relative to their IIM-a.

The main implications for modifying the focus of treatment with MBT with psychopaths are, thus, the need to activate the attachment system as, unlike patients with BPD, their attachment systems are "hypo-" or deactivated. Stern (1985) has argued that an infant is hard-wired to cognitively appreciate that his mother is separate from him, and yet emotional realization of this requires attunement from the care-giver for it to be internalized in a way that facilitates interpersonal closeness (relatedness).

Within the MBT framework, this would require an approach in which the therapist utilizes the (malignant) narcissistic/grandiose self as a starting point to gradually introduce the notion of the point of view of the other. That is, the activation of the attachment system would have to be achieved via an alignment with the grandiose self. The transference vicissitudes of this (especially a paranoid transference when the attachment system is activated) would need to be carefully managed.

The attachment hunger (paedophilic) group is a more ready group for MBT, due to the fact that those in this group have an accessible attachment system that can be more readily activated. The problems with the activation of the attachment system in this group are, thus, not an issue in the way they are with the psychopathic group, or, for that matter, with the borderline. One of the main issues here would be that the therapist would need to be a receptive landing pad for projections of the alien self, until it can become integrated.

The key problem with the attachment hungry group lies more in the interplay with the hyper activation of their attachment system in conjunction with their problems in being able to read the mental states of (victims) others. The fact that these offenders attach through sexualized behaviour, and have object relations which involve an alien self, appears to contribute to their inappropriate (sexual offending) behaviour with children.

Notwithstanding these specific issues, it seems that the basic phases (e.g., engagement phase) of MBT could be adapted and utilized to intervene with *both* groups of juvenile sex offenders. For example, there needs to be an active engagement phase to ensure against treatment drop-out. The fact that treatment might be mandated in some instances with juvenile sex offenders could also be helpful in this regard. As part of the intervention, a formulation would be required whereby the nature of the attachment difficulties can be identified. In the case of juvenile sex offenders, I would suggest the use of the assessment battery recommended in Chapter Nine. Following this, a risk pathway would need to be identified, along with an understanding of what "triggers" offending. The use of transference and interpretation could then be used to identify the deficits mentioned above and assist in their remediation through the activation and use of the attachment system in relation to the therapist. The use of group work could also be an advantage, as it would allow offenders to hear the experiences of others, which could facilitate their understanding of how others think. Caution would be required with psychopathic offenders who might use such groups pathologically to gain more insight from other group members on how to hurt victims.

With all these considerations in mind, I see MBT as a potentially robust treatment option for use with juvenile sex offenders. As a short-term, cost-effective intervention, it has much to offer.

The case for intensive psychoanalytic interventions, including psychoanalysis

While I have made a case for MBT as a short to medium term intervention for juvenile sex offenders, there are indications that some offenders could consolidate therapeutic gains made with MBT by graduating to more intensive interventions, including long-term psychoanalytic psychotherapy or psychoanalysis. In this regard, progress and responsiveness with MBT could be used as indications of suitability (along with other assessment findings) for more intensive (and costly) interventions. Given the number of victims juvenile sex offenders offend against and the number of victims affected by an offender by the time he becomes an adult sex offender, one needs to consider that even intensive and costly interventions such as these might still be warranted and, indeed, cost effective.

Putting aside the cost and the average length of the treatment, psychoanalysis also requires the analysand to have some ego strength and resilience to cope with the demands of the process. For these reasons, and because psychoanalysis is a treatment that also involves a willingness and capacity to form a (transference) relationship with the analyst, suitability for this form of intensive intervention might be indicated by good progress with shorter term interventions which have assisted the capacity to form and maintain close relationships. In this regard, brief psychoanalytic psychotherapy (whose aims are discussed below) might be an interim step with offenders who show some potential for deeper analytic work. Typically, the analyst might offer shorter-term psychotherapy and, if a capacity for, and greater interest in, understanding the self emerges, the psychotherapy could be extended into an analysis.

In terms of psychodynamic psychotherapy, the types of functioning that can be targeted and improved by such interventions suggest its utility for selected juvenile sex offenders. In this regard, Shedler (2010) has shown that the following functioning can be enhanced as a result of psychodynamic therapy.

1.   An improved ability to identify and be more in touch with feelings and enhanced ability to express and regulate emotion.
2.   An increased ability to not avoid distressing thoughts and feelings.

3. An ability to identify recurrent themes and patterns in thoughts and feelings as a precursor to change.
4. A capacity to relate the influence of the past on the present, to discover, in particular, how old ways of behaving which might have had, in some cases, survival value in childhood are now hampering adjustment in current relationships.

These changes are achieved in intensive interventions through use of the transference (which is the vehicle for activating/regulating the attachment system). Focus is on the therapy relationship and exploration of wishes and fantasies (phantasies) as means of discovering things about oneself and one's ways of behaving in current relationships in order to attempt to bring about a change in these.

Shedler (2010) reviewed eight meta-analyses, comprising 160 studies of psychodynamic therapy, plus nine meta-analyses of other psychological treatments and antidepressant medications. He focused on effect size, which measures the amount of change produced by each treatment. An effect size of 0.80 is considered a large effect in psychological and medical research, with much lower effect sizes used to justify commonly used medications, such as aspirin. One major meta-analysis of psychodynamic therapy included 1,431 patients with a range of mental health problems and found an effect size of 0.97 for overall symptom improvement. (The therapy was typically once per week and lasted less than a year.) The effect size increased by 50% (to 1.51) when patients were re-evaluated nine or more months after therapy ended. The effect size for the most widely used antidepressant medications is a more modest 0.31.

There is also specific evidence suggesting the value of psychoanalysis and longer-term psychoanalytic psychotherapy in terms of the retention of treatment effects (Gerber et al., 2011; Knet, Lindfors, & Laaksonen, 2008; Lamb & Jones, 2009; Leichsenring & Rabung, 2008; Levy & Ablon, 2009). Indeed, there is significant evidence to suggest that long-term psychodynamic psychotherapy (LTPP) is more effective than short-term therapy for patients (such as juvenile sex offenders) who present with complex mental disorders such as personality disorders (Leichsenring & Rabung, 2008).

While specific outcome data regarding juvenile sex offenders are not available, the general outcome findings, when extrapolated to the sort of problems requiring remediation among juvenile sex offenders, make a strong case for the use of such interventions with this group of offenders. Notwithstanding this, more outcome research is required (including single case design studies, such as those emanating from the Portman Clinic (e.g., Campbell (2010)) to explore more fully the utility of such treatments with this group of offenders.

Epilogue

"For now we see through a glass, darkly,
but then face to face: now I know in part;
but then shall I know, even as also I am known"

(Corinthians: 13)

To become an autonomously functioning person, capable of a reciprocal loving and sexual relationship, is a major developmental task. The evidence reviewed in this book suggests that this outcome is unlikely to occur if one has not experienced a development that has been conducive to secure attachment. Secure attachment, while different to the development of mature sexuality, appears to strongly predict the capacity for a stable adult relationship that can be both loving and sexual. It correlates with an internal world that contains mental representations of whole (human) objects and functional dyadic representations. This implies an *internal world* that contains templates that facilitate the integration of loving and hateful feelings. This allows for an intimate relationship that is passionate and lively.

Mental representations are built up as a result of interactions between the infant's experiences with his primary care-givers, his temperament, and the phantasies that arise in this context. These become epigenetic factors capable of powerfully influencing the genetic potential for secure attachment and mature sexual behaviour. When all goes well, the interplay of these factors has the ability to make us more fully human and, in doing so, probably confers an evolutionary advantage. Without the humanizing experience of love and intimacy and the associated attachment security that experience promotes, it becomes difficult to *internalize a capacity to form a mature sexual and loving relationship*. This can, thus, limit the means of relating to others. With juvenile sex offenders, relating becomes limited to sexualized or violently sexualized modes of relating.

The reality of what juvenile sex offending might represent, when seen in this way, is troubling. In fact, it could explain why, as a society, we have been a long time coming to grips with this problem and perhaps even longer coming to the point of being able to bear to look into the internal world of the juvenile sex offender. This is because the view into their internal world takes us into a dark place in terms of love and humanity. From this perspective, early views of juvenile sex offending, which tended to minimize its importance and seriousness, might be seen as a defence against the disturbing reality it represents.

As we have been able to look at the issue of juvenile sex offending more objectively and in a humane way, we have seen how intricately linked such offending is in maintaining (albeit precariously and or desperately), for the sex offender, his sense of self. In this regard, we come to appreciate the particular relevance and nature of the offender's *link* with his victim. We come to see more clearly how this form of offending is associated with struggles about attaching and attempting to relate to others. All these issues are pertinent to our approach to the juvenile sex offender's disposition and treatment and to our understanding about the future risk of reoffending and of harm to others.

In terms of what we have come to understand about an individual's capacity for attachment, his level of relatedness, and psychopathy, it can be seen that they are useful constructs that appear to help differentiate juvenile sex offenders from non-offending adolescents and account for much of their heterogeneity. Thus, these constructs emerge as having a potentially central relevance to the aetiology of juvenile sex offending, as well as its assessment and treatment.

The study I have reported has provided further empirical evidence regarding the role of internalized templates of human relationships in the aetiology of juvenile sex offending. In particular, these data strongly suggest that the extent to which an individual is seeking relationship is crucial in comprehending the dynamics of juvenile sex offending. This adds weight to the view that sexual drive is not the prime motivator of sexual offending behaviour, but that this drive achieves its expression through links with internalized templates of human experience. It also suggests that we can consider some behaviour (or attempts at relating) as "sexualized", rather than behaviour which represents an ability to relate to another as separate from oneself. In the psychoanalytic sense, this links to the concept of sexualized states of mind (Meltzer, 1979). This distinction also connects with Bowlby's ideas about the distinction between the attachment and sexual behavioural systems and how they might influence each other (Diamond, Blatt, & Lichtenberg, 2007).

Notwithstanding this, the findings do not preclude the influence of neurobiology in the aetiology of juvenile sex offending, but, rather, suggest the salience of developmental experiences. A psychobiological model, which stresses attachment and the relevance of internalized templates of relationship, might best explain the heterogeneity of juvenile sex offenders and account for the different developmental trajectories behind offending involving child molestation or the rape of adults.

In terms of a developmental account of juvenile sex offending, research data suggest that the achievement of psychological individuation and separation is a pivotal junction in adaptive developmental pathways. This links with Fonagy's (1996) view that it is only when such a stage of self-development is reached that self-reflective thought is established, which allows for the state of mind of "the other" to be acknowledged. The current data concerning the level of psychological representation of human interaction, and its links to psychopathy and capacity for attachment, support this view. These data suggest the need for further research into the link between the level of self–other differentiation and the prediction of sub-types of juvenile sex offending.

In terms of assessment, the data would suggest that determining the level of psychopathy and the extent of malignant narcissism (from empirical correlates of the associated object relations) can serve as an important predictor of a juvenile sex offender's likelihood of reoffending. This prediction can also be strengthened when findings concerning the nature of capacity for attachment (and attachment style) are integrated into an assessment formulation. When seen in the context of data from adult sex offender research, the study revealed that not only could this more clearly identify the offender type, but it could form part of a decision-making tree about risk, which, among other things, could inform child protection strategies. As asssessment of juvenile sex offenders serves a number of purposes, including supporting guilt or innocence, guiding adjudication, and informing disposition, including an assessment of psychopathy and capacity for attachment can assist all of these aims and add rich information about risk, the offender's profile, and the type of intervention likely to be helpful.

Currently, there are many interventions with juvenile sex offenders which focus on their social skills and social competence (which relate to their capacity for attachment and related capacity to mentalize), yet it would seem that such competencies and skills are more likely to change as a result of therapy where attachment and mentalization issues are the *focus* of treatment. The emergence of a database concerning the outcomes from psychoanalytically orientated and attachment theory-informed interventions, especially MBT, suggests their likely efficacy as treatments for juvenile sex offenders as a whole and for the "attachment hungry" sub-group of paedophilic offenders in particular, the latter group appearing to have particular difficulties with the hyperactivation of their attachment system.

Further, those offenders who have higher levels of psychopathy (and, from the findings of the current research, are likely to be rapists) appear to need a treatment programme that does not focus on treatment targets that are common in contemporary programmes. Instead of focusing on affect regulation and impulse control, treatments that focus on activating the attachment system and on other issues, such as moral reasoning, might be more helpful. Treatment for psychopathic offenders (whose efficacy is doubted by advocates of a biological theory of psychopathy) is still, however, in its early stages of development (Salekin, Worley, & Grimes, 2010; Wong & Hare, 2002).

The strong collateral support for a developmental view of juvenile sex offending provided by my study and by other research also supports the case for early intervention with young sex offenders.

There is considerable evidence to show that, at early stages of psychological development, there is commonality of developmental precursors linked to a wide range of psychopathology (Keogh, 2002). There is also a wealth of literature about the need for early intervention with offenders generally, yet little is known about the developmental pathway to sexual offending in particular. Consequently, there has been little focus on targeted prevention. Despite this, available data provide support for the idea that children who have been sexually abused are at significant risk of becoming paedophilic sex offenders.

More generally, there is also sufficient evidence to indicate that children who have been subjected to physical and sexual abuse need to be monitored for adverse effects on their capacity for attachment and for the development of clinical characteristics known to be associated with juvenile sex offenders and their sub-groups. Related to this, there are implications for social policy in order to ensure that children who show early signs of psychopathology should be monitored carefully and offered appropriate early intervention by schools and by mental health agencies. Where indicated, such children should be offered therapy to address attachment incapacity at an early age, in particular, perhaps, with attachment theory-informed family psychotherapy, or, at earlier ages, through mother–infant interventions (Keogh, Kourt, Enfield, & Enfield, 2007).

Moreover, the data suggest the need for a set of indicators concerning the development of juvenile sex offending behaviour, which currently do not exist. As early intervention is cost effective and the consequences of sexual offending very serious (Jenkins, 1999), it is incumbent on governments to consider these facts and devote the appropriate resources to schools and child mental health services. This would enable such services to become equipped with specialist practitioners who could assist in detecting children who are likely to be at risk for future sex offending.

In conclusion, as we have looked through a glass darkly into the internal world of the juvenile sex offender, we have seen that his sexualized or violently sexualized behaviour represents a developmental struggle (or resistance) to find secure attachment and love. Consequently, what we glean from our understanding of juvenile sex offenders could shed light on other forms of offending.

REFERENCES

Abel, G. G., Mittleman, M. S., & Becker, J. (1985). Sexual offenders: results of assessment and recommendations for treatment. In: H. Ben-Aron, S. Hucker, & C. Webster (Eds.), *Clinical Criminology: The Assessment and Treatment of Criminal Behavior* (pp. 191–205). Toronto: M & M Graphics.

Abracen, J., Looman, J., & Anderson, D. (2000). Alcohol and drug abuse in sexual and non-sexual violent offenders. *Sexual Abuse: A Journal of Research and Treatment, 12*(4): 263–274.

Abrahamsen, D. (1985). *Confessions of Son of Sam*. New York: Colombia University Press.

Aichorn, A. (1925). *Wayward Youth*. New York: Viking.

Ainsworth, M. D. S. (1967). *Infancy in Uganda: Infant Care and the Growth of Attachment*. Baltimore, MD: Johns Hopkins University Press.

Ainsworth, M. D. S. (1973). The development of infant–mother attachment. In: B. M. Caldwell & H. N. Riccciuti (Eds.), *Review of Child Development Research* (Vol. 3) (pp. 1–94). Chicago, IL: University of Chicago Press

Ainsworth, M. D. S. (1979). Infant–mother attachment. *American Psychologist, 34*: 932–937.

Ainsworth, M. D. S., Blehar, M. C., Waters, E., & Wall, S. (1978). *Patterns of Attachment: A Psychological Study of the Strange Situation*. Hillsdale, NJ: Lawrence Erlbaum.

Akhtar, S. (2009). *Comprehensive Dictionary of Psychoanalysis*. London: Karnac.

Aljazireh, L. (1993). Historical, environmental, and behavioral correlates of sexual offending by male adolescents: a critical review. *Behavioral Sciences and the Law, 11*(4): 423–440.

Allen, J. C., & Fonagy, P. (2006). *Handbook of Mentalization-Based Treatment*. Chichester: Wiley.

Anderson, V. N., Simpson-Taylor, D., & Herrmann, D. J. (2004). Gender, age, and rape supportive attitudes. *Sex Roles, 50*(1): 77–90.

Archer, R. P., Maurish, M., Imhof, E. A., & Piotrowski, C. (1991). Psychological test usage with adolescent clients: 1990 survey findings. *Professional Psychology, Research and Practice, 22*: 247–252.

Arkowitz, H., & Lilienfeld, S. O. (2006). Psychotherapy on trial. *Scientific American Mind, 2*: 42–49.

Aromaeki, A. S., Lindman, R. E., & Eriksson, C. J. P. (2002). Testosterone, sexuality and antisocial personality in rapists and child molesters: a pilot study. *Psychiatry Research, 110*(3): 239–247.

Arrigo, B. A., & Shipley, S. (2001). The confusion over psychopathy (I): Historical considerations. *International Journal of Offender Therapy and Comparative Criminology, 45*(3): 325–344.

Ashkar, P. J. & Kenny, D. T. (2006). Moral reasoning of adolescent male offenders: comparison of sexual and non-sexual offenders. *Criminal Justice and Behaviour, 33*(3): 1–17.

Asmussen, K. (2010). Key facts about child maltreatment. *NSPCC Research Briefing*.

Atkinson, L., & Zuckermann, K. J. (1997). *Attachment and Psychopathology*. New York: Guilford Press.

Auslander, B. A. (1999). An exploratory study investigating variables in relation to juvenile sexual offending. *Dissertation Abstracts Intentional: Section B the Sciences & Engineering, 59*(9B): 5069.

Awad, G. A., & Saunders, E. B. (1991). Male adolescent sexual assaulters: clinical observations. *Journal of Interpersonal Violence, 6*: 446–460.

Bagley, C., Wood, M., & Young, L. (1994). Victim to abuser: mental health and behavior sequels of child sexual abuse in a community survey of young adult males. *Child Abuse and Neglect, 18*(8): 683–697.

Barbaree, H. E., Hudson, S. M., & Seto, M. C. (1993). Sexual assault in society: the role of the juvenile offender. In: H. E. Babaree, S. M. Hudson, & M. C. Seto (Eds.), *The Juvenile Sex Offender* (pp. 1–24). New York: Guilford Press.

Barbaree, H. E., Seto, M. C., Serin, R., Amos, N., & Preston, D. (1994). Comparisons between sexual and nonsexual rapist subtypes: sexual arousal to rape, offense precursors, and offense characteristics. *Criminal Justice and Behavior, 21*(1): 95–114.

Bargh, J. A., & Ferguson, M. L. (2000). Beyond behaviorism: on the automaticity of higher mental processes. *Psychological Bulletin, 126*: 925–945.

Bartels, A., & Zeki, S. (2004). The neural correlates of maternal and romantic love. *NeuroImage, 21*: 1155–1166.

Bartholomew, K. (1990). Avoidance of intimacy: an attachment perspective. *Journal of Social and Personal Relationships, 7*: 147–178.

Bartholomew, K., & Horowitz, L. M. (1991). Attachment styles among young adults: a test of a four-category model. *Journal of Personality and Social Psychology, 61*: 226–244.

Bartol, C. R. (2001). Introduction to the special issue, psychopathy and risk assessment. *Criminal Justice and Behavior, 28*(4): 399–401.

Bateman, A., & Fonagy, P. (2009). Randomized control trial of outpatient mentalization based treatment versus structured clinical management for borderline personality disorder. *American Journal of Psychiatry, 166*: 1355–1364.

Batgos, J., & Leadbeater, B. J. (1994). Parental attachment, peer relations and dysphoria in adolescence. In: M. J. Sperling & W. H. Berman (Eds.), *Attachment in Adults: Clinical and Developmental Perspectives* (pp. 155–178). New York: Guilford Press.

Beck, S. (1943). The Rorschach test in psychopathology. *Journal of Consulting Psychology, 7*: 103–111.

Becker, J. V. (1998). What we know about the characteristics and treatment of adolescents who have committed sexual offences. *Child Maltreatment, 3*(4): 317–330.

Becker, J. V., & Able, G. (1985). Methodological issues in evaluating and treating adolescent sexual offenders. In: E. Otey & G. Ryan (Eds.), *Adolescent Sex Offenders: Issues in Research and Treatment* (pp. 109–129). Rockville, MD: Department of Health and Human Services.

Becker, J. V., Cunningham-Rathner, J., & Kaplan, M. (1986). Adolescent sex offenders: demographics, criminal and sexual histories, and recommendations for reducing future offenses. *Journal of Interpersonal Violence, 1*(4): 431–445.

Becker, J. V., Harris, C., & Sales, B. D. (1993). Juveniles who commit sexual offenses: a critical review of research. In: G. C. Nagoyama, R. Hall, J. Hirschman, J. R. Graham, & N. S. Zaragaza. (Eds.), *Sexual Aggression: Issues in Etiology, Assessment, Treatment, and Policy* (pp. 215–228). Pennsylvania, PA: Taylor & Francis.

Becker, J. V., Kaplan, M. S., Cunningham-Rathner, J., & Kavoussi, R. (1986). Characteristics of adolescent incest perpetrators: preliminary findings. *Journal of Family Violence, 1*: 85–97.

Beech, A. R., & Mitchell, I. J. (2005). A neurobiological perspective on attachment problems in sexual offenders and the role of selective serotonin re-uptake inhibitors in the treatment of such problems. *Clinical Psychology Review, 25*: 153–182.

Belanger, N., & Earls, C. (1996). Sex offender recidivism. *Forum on Corrections Research, 8*(2): 22–24.

Belcher, P. (1995). A comparison of male adolescent sex offenders using the Rorschach. Unpublished Doctoral dissertation, Massachusetts.

Belsky, J., Steinberg, L., & Draper, P. (1991). Childhood experiences, interpersonal development and reproductive strategy: an evolutionary theory of socailization. *Child Development, 62*: 647–670.

Ben-Porath, Y. S., Graham, J. R., Hall, C. N., Hirschamn, R. D., & Zaragoza, M. S. (1995). *Forensic Applications of the MMPI-2*. London: Sage.

Bengis, S. M. (1997). Comprehensive service delivery with a continuum of care. In: G. Ryan & S. Lane (Eds.), *Juvenile Sex Offending* (pp. 211–218). San Francisco, CA: Jossey Bass.

Benoit, J. L., & Kennedy, W. A. (1992). The abuse history of male adolescent sex offenders. *Journal of Interpersonal Violence, 7*(4): 534–548.

Berner, W., Brownstone, G., & Sluga, W. (1983). The Cyproteronacetat treatment of sexual offenders. *Neurocience & Biobehavioral Reviews, 7*(3): 441–443.

Bernstein, A., Newman, J. P., Wallace, J. F., & Luh, K. E. (2000). Left hemisphere activation and deficient response modulation in psychopaths. *Psychological Science, 11*(5): 414–424.

Bion, W. R. (1962). *Learning from Experience*. London: Heinemann; reprinted in Maresfield Reprints, London: Karnac, 1984.

Bion, W. R. (1967). *Second Thoughts: Selected Papers on Psychoanalysis*. New York: Jason Aronson.

Blackburn, R. (1993). *The Psychology of Criminal Conduct: Theory, Research and Practice*. Chicester: Wiley.

Blair, R. J. R. (2008). The amygdala and ventromedial prefrontal cortex: functional contributions and dysfunctions in psychopathy. *Philosophical Transactions of the Royal Society*. Published online 23 April: rstb. royalsocietypublishing.org.

Blair, R. J. R. (2010). Psychopathy, frustration, and reactive aggression: the role of the ventromedial prefrontal cortex. *British Journal of Psychology, 101*(3): 383–399.

Blatt, S. J., Auerbach, J. S., & Levy, K. N. (1997). Mental representations in personality development, psychopathology and the therapeutic process. *Review of General Psychiatry*, *1*(4): 351–374.

Blos, P. (1967). The second individuation process of adolescence. *The Psychoanalytic Study of the Child*, *22*: 162–186.

Boris, N. W., Wheeler, E. E., Heller, S. S., & Zeanah, C. Z. (2000). Attachment and developmental psychopathology: a case study. *Psychiatry*, *63*: 74–83.

Bowlby, J. (1944). *Forty-four Juvenile Thieves: Their Character and Their Home Life*. London: Balliere, Tyndall and Cox.

Bowlby, J. (1958). The nature of the child's tie to his mother. *International Journal of Psychoanalysis*. *XXXIX*: 1–23.

Bowlby, J. (1959). Separation anxiety. *International Journal of Psychoanalysis*, *XLI*: 1–25.

Bowlby, J. (1960). Grief and mourning in infancy and early childhood. *Psychoanalytic Study of the Child*, *VX*: 3–39.

Bowlby, J. (1969). *Attachment*. *Attachment and Loss* (Vol. 1) (2nd edn). New York: Basic Books, 1999.

Bowlby, J. (1973). *Separation: Anxiety & Anger*. *Attachment and Loss* (Vol. 2): (International Psycho-analytical Library, No. 95). London: Hogarth Press.

Bowlby, J. (1980). *Loss: Sadness & Depression*. Attachment and Loss (Vol. 3): (International Psycho-analytical Library, No. 109). London: Hogarth Press.

Bowlby, J. (1988). *A Secure Base: Parent–Child Attachment and Healthy Human Development*. London: Tavistock.

Bradford, J. M. W. (1999). The paraphilias, obsessive compulsive spectrum disorder, and the treatment of sexually deviant behavior. *Psychiatric Quarterly*, *70*: 209–219.

Brannon, J. M., & Troyer, R. (1995). Adolescent sex offenders: investigating adult commitment rates four years later. *International Journal of Offender Therapy and Comparative Criminology*, *39*(4): 317–326.

Bridges, M. R., Wilson, J. S., & Gacono, C. B. (1998). A Rorschach investigation of defensiveness, self perception, interpersonal relations, and affective states in incarcerated pedophiles. *Journal of Personality Assessment*, *70*(2): 365–385.

Britton, R. (1989). The missing link: parental sexuality in the Oedipus complex. In: J. Steiner, M. Feldman, & E. O'Shaughnessy (Eds.), *The Oedipus Complex Today* (pp. 83–103.). London: Karnac, 2005.

Britton, R. (2004). Narcissistic disorders in clinical practice. *Journal of Analytical Psychology*, *49*: 477–490.

Brown, S. L., & Forth, A. E. (1997). Psychopathy and sexual assault: static risk factors, emotional precursors, and rapist subtypes. *Journal of Consulting and Clinical Psychology, 65*(5): 848–857.

Buckholtz, J. W., Treadway, M. T., Cowan, R. L., Woodward, N. D., Benning, S. D., Li, R., Ansari, M. S., Baldwin, R. M., Schwartzman, A. N., Shelby, E. S., Smith, C. E., Kessler, R. M., & Zald, D. H. (2010). Mesolimbic dopamine reward system hyperactivity in individuals with psychopathic traits. *Nature/Neuroscience, 13*(40): 419–421.

Burgess, A. W., Hartman, C. R., McCormack, A., & Grant, C. A. (1988). Child victim to juvenile victimizer: treatment implications. *International Journal of Family Psychiatry, 9*(4): 403–416.

Burk, L. R., & Burkhart, B. R. (2003). Disorganized attachment as a diathesis for sexual deviance developmental experience and the motivation for sex offending. *Aggression and Violent Behavior, 52*: 901–907.

Burns, B., & Viglione, D. J. Jr. (1996). The Rorschach human experience variable, interpersonal relatedness, and object representation in nonpatients. *Psychological Assessment, 8*(1): 92–99.

Burton, D. L. (2000). Were adolescent sexual offenders children with sexual behavior problems? *Sexual Abuse: A Journal of Research and Treatment, 12*(1): 37–48.

Burton, D. L., Miller, D. L., & Shill, C. T. (2002). A social learning theory comparison of victimization of adolescent sexual offenders and nonsexual offending male delinquents. *Child Abuse & Neglect, 26*: 893–907.

Butcher, J. N., Williams, C. L., Graham, J. R., Archer, R. P., Tellegen, A., Ben-Porath, Y. S., & Kaemer, B. (1992). *Minnesota Mutiphasic Personality Inventory-Adolescent (MMPI-A): Manual for Administration, Scoring and Interpretation*. Minneapolis, MN: University of Minnesota Press.

Butts, J. A., & Snyder, H. N. (1997). The youngest delinquents: offenders under age 15. *Juvenile Justice Bulletin*, 1–11.

Campbell, D. (2010). Guns, gangs and debt: a response to the absent father. A paper given at the Australian Psychoanalytical Society's Open Day, entitled "Through a glass darkly: reverberations of early trauma: shame, perversion and violence", 31 July, Sydney, Australia.

Capote, T. (2000). *In Cold Blood*. New Brunswick, NJ: Transaction Publishers.

Caputo, A. A., Frick, P. J., & Brodsky, S. L. (1999). Family violence and juvenile sex offending: the potential mediating role of psychopathic traits and negative attitudes towards women. *Criminal Justice and Behavior, 26*(3): 338–356.

Carlson, E., & Sroufe, L. A. (1995). The contribution of attachment theory to developmental psychopathology. In: D. Cicchetti & D. Cohen (Eds.), *Developmental Processes and Psychoapthology Vol.1: Theoretical Perspectives and Methodological Approaches* (pp. 581–617) New York: Cambridge University Press.

Carlson, V., Cicchetti, D., Barnett, D., & Braunwald, K. (1989). Disorganised/dissociated attachment in maltreated infants. *Developmental Psychiatry, 25*(4): 525–531.

Carpenter, D. R., Peed, S. F., & Eastman, B. (1995). Personality characteristics of adolescent sexual offenders: a pilot study. *Sexual Abuse: A Journal of Research and Treatment, 7*(3): 195–203.

Carter, C. S. (1998). Neuroendocrine perspectives on social attachment and love. *Psychneuroendocrinology, 23*: 779–818.

Cassidy, J., & Kobak, R. (1988). Avoidance and its relationship with other defensive processes. In: J. Belsky & T. Nezworski (Eds.), *Clinical Implications of Attachment* (pp. 330–322). Hillsdale, NJ: Lawrence Erlbaum.

Chandler, M., & Moran, T. (1990). Psychopathy and moral development: a comparative study of delinquent and non-delinquent youth. *Development & Psychopathology, 2*(3): 227–246.

Chaouloff, F. (2000). Serotonin, stress and corticoids. *Journal of Psychopharmacology, 14*: 139–151.

Chasseguet-Smirgel, J. (1983). Perversion and the universal law. *International Review of Psychoanalysis, 10*: 293–301.

Chorn, R., & Parekh, A. (1997). Adolescent sex offenders: a self-psychological perspective. *American Journal of Psychiatry, 51*: 210–228.

Christian, R. E., Frick, P. J., Hill, N. L., Tyler, L., & Frazer, D. R. (1997). Psychopathy and conduct problems in children: implications for subtyping children with conduct problems. *Journal of the American Academy of Child and Adolescent Psychiatry, 36*(4): 437–443.

Cleckly, H. (1941). *The Mask of Sanity* (5th edn), St Louis, MO: Mosby, 1976.

Clum, G. A., Calhoun, K. S., & Kimerly, R. (2000). Associations among symptoms of depression and post-traumatic stress disorder and self-reported health in sexually assaulted women. *Journal of Nervous and Mental Diseases, 188*: 671–678.

Cohan, R. (1998). A comparison of sex offenders against minors and rapists of adults on selected Rorschach variables. Unpublished Doctoral dissertation, The Wright Institute.

Collins, N. L., & Read, S. J. (1999). Adult attachment, working models and relationship quality in dating couples. *Journal of Personality and Social Psychology, 50*: 345–362.

Comrey, A. L. (1958). A factor analysis of items on the F scale of the MMPI. *Educational and Psychological Measurement, 18*: 612–632.

Cooke, D. J., Forth, A. E., & Hare, R. D. (1998). *Psychopathy: Theory, Research and Implications for Society.* Dordrect: Kluwer.

Cooper, C. L., Murphy, W. D., & Haynes, M. R. (1996). Characteristics of abused and non-abused adolescent sexual offenders. *Sexual Abuse: A Journal of Research and Treatment, 8*: 105–119.

Cortoni, F., & Marshall, W. L. (1998). The relationship between attachment and coping in sexual offenders. Paper presented to the ATSA Research and Treatment Conference. Vancouver.

Cowan, P. A., Cohn, D. A., Pape, E., Cowan, C., & Pearson, J. L. (1996). Parents' attachment histories and children's externalizing and internalizing behaviors: exploring family systems models of linkage. *Journal of Consulting and Clinical Psychology, 64*(1): 53–63.

Craik, K. (1943). *The Nature of Explanation.* Cambridge: Cambridge University Press, 1967.

Crittenden, P. M. (1995). Attachment and risk for psychopathology: the early years. *Journal of Developmental and Behavioral Pediatrics: Supplemental Issue on Developmental Delay and Psychopathology in Young Children. 16*: S12–16.

Crittenden, P. M. (1997a). Patterns of attachment and sexuality: risk of dysfunction versus oppourtunity for creative integration. In: L. Atkinson & K. J. Zuckerman (Eds.), *Attachment and Psychopathology* (pp. 47–93). New York: Guilford Press.

Crittenden, P. M. (1997b). The effect of early relationship experiences on relationships in adulthood. In: S. Duck (Ed.), *Handbook of Personal Relationships* (pp. 99–119). Chichester: Wiley.

Crittenden, P. M. (2002). Attachment theory, information processing and psychiatric disorder. *World Psychiatry, 1*(2): 72–75.

Crittenden, P. M., & Claussen, A. H. (2000). *The Organization of Attachment Relationships: Maturation, Culture, and Context.* New York: Cambridge University Press.

Csersevits, M. (2000). A comparative study of juvenile sex offenders, juvenile delinquents and juvenile dependents using the Rorschach inkblot test. Unpublished Doctoral thesis, Temple University.

Cummings, E. M., & Cicchetti, D. (1990). Attachment, depression and the transmission of depression. In: M. Greenberg, D. Cichetti, & E. M. Cummings (Eds.), *Attachment in the Preschool Years* (pp. 339–372). Chicago, IL: University of Chicago Press.

Daleiden, E. L., Kaufman, K. L., Hilliker, D. R., & O'Neil, J. N. (1998). The sexual histories and fantasies of youthful males: a comparison of sexual offending, nonsexual offending and non-offending groups. *Sexual Abuse: A Journal of Research and Treatment, 10*(3): 195–209.

Dallam, S. J., Gleaves, D. H., Cepeda-Benito, A., Silberg, J. K., Kraemer, H. C., & Spiegal, D. (2001). The effects of child sexual abuse: comment on Rind, Tromovitch and Bauserman. *Psychological Bulletin, 127*(6): 715–733.

Dalton, J. E. (1996). Juvenile male sex offenders: mean scores on the BASC self-report of personality. *Psychological Reports, 79*: 634–639.

Davis, G. E., & Leitenberg, H. (1987). Adolescent sex offenders. *Psychological Bulletin, 101*: 417–427.

De Masi, F. (2003). *The Sadomasochistic Perversion: The Entity and the Theories.* London: Karnac.

Deisher, R. W., Wenet, G. A., Paperny, D. M., Clark, T. F., & Fehrenbach, P. A. (1982). Adolescent sexual offense behavior: the role of the physician. *Journal of Adolescent Health Care, 2*: 279–286.

Del Carmen, R., & Huffman, L. (1996). Epilogue: bridging the gap between research on attachment and psychopathology. *Journal of Consulting and Clinical Psychology, 64*(2): 291–294.

Diamond, D., & Blatt, S. J. (1994). Internal working models and the representational world in attachment and psychoanalytic theories. In: M. B. Sperling & W. H. Berman (Eds.), *Attachment in Adults: Clinical and Developmental Perspectives* (pp. 72–97). New York: Guilford Press.

Diamond, D., Blatt, S. J. & Lichtenberg, J. D. (Eds.) (2007). *Attachment and Sexuality.* Psychoanalytic Inquiry Book Series, Vol. 21. New York: Analytic Press.

Dickinson, L. M., deGruy, F. V., Dickinson, W. P., & Candib, L. M. (1999). Health-related quality of life and symptom profile of female survivors of sexual abuse. *Archives of Family Medicine, 8*(1): 35–43.

Doidge, N. (2007). *The Brain That Changes Itself.* Melbourne: Scribe.

Dolan, M., Holloway, J., Bailey, S., & Kroll, L. (1996). The psychosocial characteristics of juvenile sexual offenders referred to an adolescent forensic service in the UK. *Medicine, Science and Law, 36*(4): 343–352.

Dolan, M. C. (1994). Psychopathy – a neurobiological perspective. *British Journal of Psychiatry, 165*: 151–159.

Dolan, M. C., & Anderson, I. M. (2003). The relationship between serotonergic function and the Psychopathy Checklist: Screening Version. *British Journal of Psychiatry, 17*(2): 216–222.

Dolan, M. C., & Doyle, M. (2000). Violent risk prediction: clinical and actuarial measures and the role of the Psychopathy Checklist. *British Journal of Psychiatry, 177*(4): 303–311.

Dolan, M. C., Anderson, I. M., & Deakin, J. F. W. (2001). Relationship between 5-HT function and impulsivity and aggression in male offenders with personality disorders. *British Journal of Psychiatry, 178*: 352–359.

Doren, D. M. (1987). *Understanding and Treating the Psychopath*. New York: John Wiley.

Dorr, D. (1998). Psychopathy in the pedophile. In: T. Millon, E. Simmons, M. Birket-Smith, & R. D. Davis (Eds.), *Psychopathy: Antisocial, Criminal and Violent Behavior* (pp. 304–320). New York: Guilford Press, 2003.

du Vigneaud, V., Ressler, C., Swan, J. M., Roberts, C. W., Katsoyannis, P. G., & Gordon, S. (1953). The synthesis of an octapeptide amide with the hormonal activity of oxytocin. *Journal of the American Chemistry Society, 75*(19): 4879–4888.

Durham, R. C., Chambers, J. A., Power, K. G., Sharp, D. M., Macdonald, R. R., Major, K. A., Dow, M. G., & Gumley, A. L. (2005). Long term outcome of cognitive behaviour therapy clinical trials in central Scotland. *Health Technology and Assessment, 9*: 1–174.

Dutton, D. G., & Hart, S. D. (1992). Evidence for long term, specific effects of childhood abuse and neglect on criminal behaviour in men. *International Journal of Offender Therapy and Comparative Criminology, 36*: 129–137.

Edens, J. F., Skeem, J. L., Cruise, K. R., & Cuffman, E. (2001). Assessment of 'juvenile psychopathy' and its association with violence: a critical review. *Behavioral Sciences and the Law, 19*: 53–80.

Egeland, B., & Sroufe, L. A. (1981). Attachment and early maltreatment. *Child Development, 52*: 44–52.

Elicker, J., Englund, M., & Sroufe, L. A. (1992). Predicting peer competence and peer relationships in childhood from early parent–child relationships. In: R. Parker & G. Ladd (Eds.), *Family–Peer Relationships: Modes of Linkage* (pp. 77–139). Hillsdale, NJ: Lawrence Erlbaum.

Ellis, C. D. (2002). Male rape: the silent victims. *Collegian, 9*(4): 34–39.

Enfield, C. (2011). Personal communication concerning professional contact with John Bowlby.

Epperson, D. L., Ralston, C. A., Fowers, D., DeWitt, J., & Gore, K. S. (2005). Actuarial risk assessment with juveniles who offend sexually: development of the Juvenile Sexual Offense Recidivism Risk Assessment Tool-II (JSORRAT-II). In: D. Prescott (Ed.), *Risk Assessment of Youth Who Have Sexually Abused: Theory, Controversy, and Emerging Strategies* (pp. 115–169). Oklahoma City, OK: Woods & Barnes.

Epps, K. (2000). Adolescent sex offenders. Unpublished doctoral dissertation, University of Birmingham.

Erikson, E. H. (1968). *Identity: Youth and Crisis*. New York: Norton.

Etherington, R. (1993). Diagnostic and personality differences of juvenile sex offenders, non-sex offenders and non-offenders (Doctoral dissertation) California School of Professional Psychology) *Dissertation Abstracts International, 54(4-B)*: 2195, (UMI No. 9324334).

Exner, J. E. (2003). *The Rorschach: A Comprehensive System* (4th edn). New York: Wiley.

Exner, J. E., & Erdberg, P. (2003). *The Rorschach—A Comprehensive System. Volume 2 Advanced Interpretation* (3rd edn). Hoboken, NJ: Wiley.

Exner, J. E., & Weiner, I. B. (1995). *Assessment of Children and Adolescents* (2nd edn) (Vol. 3). New York: Wiley.

Fairbairn, W. R. D. (1944). Endopychic structure considered in terms of object relationship. In: *Psychoanalytic Studies of the Personality* (pp. 82–136). London: Routledge & Kegan Paul, 1952.

Fairbairn, W. R. D. (1952). *Psychoanalytic Studies of the Personality*. London: Routledge and Kegan Paul, 1981.

Fairbairn, W. R. D., Scharff, D. E., & Birtles, E. F. (1994). *From Instinct to Self: Selected Papers of W. R. D. Fairbairn*. Northvale, NJ: Jason Aronson.

Farrington, D. P. (2000). Psychosocial predictors of adult antisocial personality and adult convictions. *Behavioral Sciences and the Law, 18*: 605–622.

Feeney, J., & Noller, P. (1990). Attachment style as a predictor of adult romantic relationships. *Journal of Personality and Social Psychology, 58*: 281–291.

Fehrenbach, P. A., Smith, W., Monastersky, C., & Deisher, R. W. (1986). Adolescent sexual offenders: Offender and offense characteristics. *American Journal of Orthopsychiatry, 56*: 225–233.

Felthous, A. R., & Sass, H. (2010). *International Handbook on Psychopathic Disorders and the Law*. New York: John Wiley.

Ferreira, V., Carvalho, E., Santos, R., Peralta, P., & Carvalho, M. (2008). T06-P-05 Attachment and sexual compulsivity in sexually active adults: associations with age of first intercourse, number of partners and short-term relations. *Sexologies, 17(S1)*: S99. (Abstracts from the 9th Congress of the European Federation of Sexology).

Ferro, A. (2005). *Seeds of Illness, Seeds of Recovery: The Genesis of Suffering and the Role of Psychoanalysis*. New York: Brunner-Routledge.

Finkelhor, D. (1979). What's wrong with sex between adults and children? Ethics and the problem of sexual abuse. *American Journal of Orthopsychiatry, 49(4)*: 692–698.

Finkelhor, D. (1984). *Child Sexual Abuse: New Theory and Research*. New York: Free Press.

Finkelhor, D., & Dziuba-Leatherman, J. (1994). Victimization of children. *American Psychologist, 49*: 173–183.

Firestone, P., Bradford, M. B., Greenberg, D. M., Larose, M., & Curry, S. (1998). Homicidal and non-homicidal child molesters: psychological, phallometric, and criminal features. *Sexual Abuse: A Journal of Research and Treatment, 10*(4): 305–323.

Flatley, J., Kershaw, C., Smith, K., Chaplin, R., & Moon, D. (2010). *Crime in England and Wales 2009/2010: Findings from the British Crime Survey and Police Recorded Crime*. Home Office Statistical Bulletin, London: Home Office (www.homeoffice.gov.uk/rds).

Fonagy, P. (1996). Prevention: the appropriate target of infant psychotherapy. Paper presented to the Sixth World Congress of the World Association for Infant Mental Health, Tampere, Finland.

Fonagy, P. (2001). *Attachment Theory and Psychoanalysis*. New York: Other Press.

Fonagy, P. (2010). Mentalization-based treatment for borderline personality disorder. A pre-conference workshop presented as part of the *Freud in Asia Conference*, October.

Fonagy, P., & Bateman, A. W. (2008). Comorbid antisocial and borderline personality disorder: mentalization-based treatment. *Journal of Clinical Psychology, 64*: 181–194.

Fonagy, P., & Kachele, H. (2009). Psychoanalysis and other long term psychotherapies. In: M. G. Gelder J. J. Lopez-Obor, & N. Andreasen (Eds.), *New Oxford Textbook of Psychiatry* (2nd edn) Vol. 2 (pp. 1337–1349). Oxford: Oxford University Press.

Fonagy, P., & Luyten, P. (2009). A developmental, mentalization-based approach to the understanding and treatment of borderline personality disorder. *Development and Psychopathology, 21*: 1355–1381.

Fonagy, P., & Target, M. (1997). Attachment and reflective function: Their role in self-organization. *Development & Psychopathology, 9*(4): 679–700.

Fonagy, P., Gergely, G., Jurist, E. L., & Target, M. (2004). *Affect Regulation, Mentalization, and the Development of the Self*. London: Karnac.

Fonagy, P., Leigh, T., Steele, M., Steele, H., Kennedy, R., Mattoon, G., Target, M., & Gerber, A. (1996). The role of attachment status, psychiatric classification and response to psychotherapy. *Journal of Consulting and Clinical Psychology, 64*: 22–31.

Fonagy, P., Roth, A., & Higgitt, A. (2005). The outcome of psychodynamic psychotherapy for psychological disorders. *Clinical Neuroscience Research Special issue: Research in Psychoanalysis and Psychodynamics, 4*: 367–377.

Fonagy, P., Target, M., Steele, M., & Steele, H. (1997). The development of violence and crime as it relates to security of attachment. In: J. D.

Osofsky (Ed.), *Children in a Violent Society, Vol. XIV* (pp. 338–00), New York: Guilford Press.

Fonagy, P., Target, M., Steele, M., Steele, H., Leigh, T., Levinson, A., & Kennedy, R. (1997). Morality, disruptive behaviour, borderline personality disorder, crime and their relationship to security of attachment. In: L. Atkinson & K. J. Zuckerman (Eds.), *Attachment and Psychopathology, Vol. VIII* (pp. 328–338). New York: Guilford Press.

Ford, M. A., & Linney, J. A. (1995). Comparative analysis of juvenile sex offenders, violent nonsexual offenders and status offenders. *Journal of Interpersonal Violence, 10*(1): 1–56.

Forth, A. E., Hart, S. D., & Hare, R. D. (1990). Assessment of psychopathy in male young offenders. *Psychological Assessment: A Journal of Consulting and Clinical Psychology, 2*: 342–344.

Forth, A. E., Kosson, D. S., & Hare, R. D. (2003). *The Psychopathy Checklist: Youth Version Manual.* Toronto, Ontario, Canada: Multi-Health Systems.

Freeman, K. A., Dexter-Mazza, E. T., & Hoffman, K. C. (2005). Comparing personality characteristics of juvenile sex offenders and non-sex offending delinquent peers: a preliminary investigation. *Sexual Abuse: A Journal of Research and Treatment, 17*: 3–17.

Freidrich, W., & Lueke, W. (1988). Young school age sexually aggressive children. *Professional Psychology: Research and Practice, 19*: 155–164.

Freud, A. (1949). The analytic treatment of major criminals: therapeutic results and technical problems. In: *Searchlights on Delinquency,* K. Eissler (Ed.) (pp. 174–189). New York: International Universities Press.

Freud, S. (1905d). *Three Essays on the Theory of Sexuality. S.E., 7*: 135–243. London: Hogarth.

Freud, S. (1917e). Mourning and melancholia. *S.E., 17*: 239–258. London: Hogarth.

Freud, S. (1924c). The economic problem of masochism. *S.E., 19*: 157–170. London: Hogarth.

Freud, S. (1928b). Dostoevsky and parricide. *S.E., 21*: 175–196. London: Hogarth.

Freud, S. (1950 [1895]). *Project for a Scientific Psychology. S.E., 1*: 283–397. London: Hogarth.

Frith, C. D. (2007). The social brain. *Philosophical Transactions of the Royal Society of Biology, 362*(1480): 671–678.

Fromm, E. (1964). *The Heart of Man: Its Genius for Good and Evil.* New York: Harper and Row.

Furr, K. (1994). Prediction of sexual or violent recidivism among sexual offenders: a comparison of prediction instruments. *Annals of Sexual Research, 6*: 271–286.

Gacono, C. B., & Meloy, J. R. (1991). A Rorschach investigation of attachment and anxiety in antisocial personality disorder. *Journal of Nervous and Mental Diseases, 179*(9): 546–552.

Gacono, C. B., & Meloy, J. R. (1994). *The Rorschach Assessment of Aggressive and Psychopathic Personalities.* Hillsdale, NJ: Lawrence Erlbaum.

Gacono, C. B., Meloy, J. R., & Berg, J. L. (1992). Object relations, defensive operations and affective states in narcissistic, borderline and antisocial personality disorder. *Journal of Personality Assessment, 59*(1): 32–49.

Gacono, C. B., Meloy, J. R., & Bridges, M. R. (2000). A Rorschach comparison of psychopaths, sexual homicide perpetrators, and non-violent pedophiles: where angels fear to tread. *Journal of Clinical Psychology, 56*(6): 757–777.

Gacono, C. B., Meloy, J. R., & Heaven, T. R. (1991). A Rorschach investigation of narcissism and hysteria in antisocial personality disorder. *Journal of Mental and Nervous Disease, 179*(9): 546–552.

Gal, M., & Hoge, R. D. (1999). A profile of the adolescent sex offender. *Forum on Correctional Research, 11:* 7–11.

Gallagher, H. L., & Frith, C. D. (2003). Functional imaging of 'theory of mind'. *Trends in Cognitive Science, 7*(2): 77–83.

Galton, F. (1874). *English Men of Science: Their Nature and Nurture.* London: Frank Cass.

Ganellen, R. J. (2001). Weighing evidence for the Rorschach's validity: a response to Wood et al (1999). Special series: More data on the current Rorschach controversy. *Journal of Personality Assessment, 77*(1): 1–15.

George, C., Kaplan, N., & Main, M. (1984). Adult Attachment Interview protocol. Unpublished manuscript, University of California at Berkeley.

Gerber, A. J., Koscis, J. H., Milrod, B. L., Roose, S. P., Barber, J. B., Thase, M. E., Perkins, P., & Leon, A. C. (2011). A quality based review of randomized controlled trials of psychodynamic psychotherapy. *American Journal of Psychiatry, 168:* 19–28.

Gillespie, W. H. (1956). The general theory of sexual perversion *International Journal of Psychoanalysis, 37:* 396–403.

Giotakos, O., Markianos, M., Vaidakis, N., & Christodoulou, N. (2004). Sex hormones and biogenic amine turnover of sex offenders in relation to their temperament and character dimensions. *Psychiatry Research, 127*(3): 185–193.

Glaser, D. (2000). Child abuse and neglect and the brain: a review. *Journal of Child Psychology and Psychiatry, 41*(1): 97–116.

Glasser, M. (1998). On violence: a preliminary communication. *International Journal of Psychoanalysis, 79:* 887–902.

Glover, E. (1960). *The Roots of Crime*. London: Imago Publishing Company.

Goldberg, S., Gotowiec, A., & Simmons, R. J. (1995). Infant–mother attachment and behavior problems in healthy and chronically ill pre-schoolers. *Development & Psychopathology, 7*: 267–282.

Goodrow, K. K., & Lim, M. G. (1998). Attachment theory applied to juvenile sex offending. *Journal of Offender Rehabilitation, 27*(1/2): 149–165.

Gottfredson, S. D., & Moriarty, L. J. (2006). Clinical versus actuarial judgments in criminal justice decisions: should one replace the other? *Federal Probation, 70*(2): 15–18.

Graham, J. R. (1993). *MMPI-2: Assessing Personality and Psychopathology*. New York: Oxford University Press.

Graves, R. B., Openshaw, D. K., Ascione, F. R., & Ericksen, S. L. (1996). Demographic and parental characteristics of youthful sexual offenders. *International Journal of Offender Therapy & Comparative Criminology, 40*(4): 300–317.

Gray, A., Pithers, W. D., Busconi, A., & Houchens, P. (1999). Developmental and etiological characteristics of children with sexual behavioral problems: treatment implications. *Child Abuse and Neglect, 23*(6): 601–621.

Greenberg, M. T. (1999). Attachment and psychopathology in childhood. In: J. Cassidy and P. Shaver (Eds.), *Handbook of Attachment :Theory, Research and Clinical Applications*, pp. 469–496. New York: Guilford Press.

Gregory, K. D. (1998). Treatment impact on recidivism: a comparison of juvenile sex offenders and juvenile violent offenders. Unpublished Masters thesis, University of South Carolina.

Gretton, H., McBride, M., Hare, R. D., O'Shaughnessy, R., & Kumka, G. (2001). Psychopathy and recidivism in adolescent sex offenders. *Criminal Justice and Behavior, 28*(4): 427–449.

Gross, F. L. (1987). *Introducing Erik Erikson: An Invitation to his Thinking*. Lanham, MD: University Press of America.

Gross, S., Stasch, M., Schmal, H., Hillenbrand, E., & Cierpka, M. (2007). Changes in the mental representations of relational behavior in depressive patients. *Psychotherapy Research, 17*(5): 522–534.

Grossman, K. E., & Grossman, K. (1991). Attachment quality as an organizer of emotional and behavioral responses in a longitudinal perspective. In: C. M. Parkes, J. Stevenson-Hinde, & J. Marris (Eds.), *Attachment Across the Life Cycle* (pp. 93–114). New York: Routledge.

Groth, A. N. (1977). The adolescent sex offender and his prey. *International Journal of Offender Therapy & Comparative Criminology, 21*: 249–254.

Groth, A. N. (1982). Undetected recidivism in rapists and child molesters. *Crime and Delinquency, 28*: 450–458.

Groth, N. A., & Loredo, C. (1981). Juvenile sex offenders: guidelines for assessment. *International Journal of Offender Therapy & Comparative Criminology, 25*: 31–39.

Grotstein, J. (1982). Newer perspectives in object relations theory. *Contemporary Psychoanalysis, 18*: 43–91.

Haapasalo, J., & Kankkonen, M. (1997). Self reported childhood abuse among sex and violent offenders. *Archives of Sexual Behavior, 26*(4): 343–461.

Hagan, M. P., King, R. P., & Patros, R. L. (1994). Recidivism among adolescent perpetrators of sexual assault against children. *Journal of Offender Rehabilitation, 21*(1–2): 127–137.

Hanson, R. K., & Bussière, M. T. (1998). Predicting relapse: a meta-analysis of sexual offender recidivism studies. *Journal of Clinical and Consulting Psychology, 66*: 348–362.

Hare, R. D. (1991). *The Hare Psychopathy Checklist—Revised.* Toronto, Ontario: Multi-Health Systems.

Hare, R. D. (1996). Psychopathy: a clinical construct whose time has come. *Criminal Justice and Behavior, 23*: 25–54.

Hare, R. D. (1998a). Psychopaths and their nature: implications for the mental health and criminal justice systems. In: T. Millon & E. Simonsen (Eds.), *Psychopathy: Antisocial, Criminal, and Violent Behavior* (pp. 188–212). New York: Guilford Press.

Hare, R. D. (1998b). Psychopathy, affect, and behaviour. In: D. Cooke, A. Forth, & R. D. Hare (Eds.), *Psychopathy: Theory, Research, and Implications for Society* (pp. 105–137). Dordrecht: Kluwer.

Hare, R. D. (1998c). The Hare PCL-R: some issues concerning its use and misuse. *Legal and Criminological Psychology, 3*: 99–119.

Hare, R. D. (1999). Psychopathy as a risk factor for violence. *Psychiatric Quarterly, 70*(3): 181–197.

Harris, A. J. R., & Forth, A. E. (1998). Psychopathic sexual deviants: the intersection of Hare's conception of psychopathy and measures of sexual deviance. *Canadian Psychology, 39*(2a): 132.

Harris, G. T., & Rice, M. E. (1996). Sex offenders: cross-validation of actuarial predictions of recidivism and the interaction of psychopathy and sexual deviance. *International Journal of Psychology, 31*(3–4): 3074–3084.

Hastings, T., Anderson, S. J., & Hemphill, P. (1997). Comparisons of daily stress, coping, problem solving and cognitive distortions in adolescent sex offenders and conduct disordered youth. *Sexual Abuse: A Journal of Research and Treatment, 9*(1): 29–42.

Hathaway, S. R., & Monachesi, E. D. (1957). The personalities of pre-delinquent boys. *Journal of Criminal Law,Criminology, and Police Science, 48*: 149–163.

Hazan, C., & Shaver, P. R. (1987). Romantic love conceptualized as an attachment process. *Journal of Personality and Social Psychology, 52*: 511–524.

Heim, C., Newport, D. J., Heit, S., Graham, Y. P., Wilcox, M., Bonsall, R., Miller, A. H., & Nemeroff, C. B. (2000). Pituitary–adrenal and autonomic responses to stress in women after sexual and physical abuse in childhood. *American Journal of Medicine, 284*(5): 592–597.

Heim, C., Newport, D. J., Wagner, D., Wilcox, M. M., Miller, A. H., & Nemeroff, C. B. (2002). The role of early adverse experience and adulthood stress in the prediction of neuroendocrine stress in women: a multiple regression analysis. *Depression and Anxiety, 15*: 117–125.

Helmeke, C., Seidel, K., Poeggel, G., Bredy, T. W., Abraham, A., & Braun, K., (2009). Paternal deprivation during infancy results in dendrite and time specific changes of dendrite development and spine formation in the orbitofrontal cortex of the biparental rodent *Octodon degus*. *Neuroscience, 163*(3): 790–798.

Henggeler, S. W., & Borduin, C. M. (1995). Multisysytemic treatment of serious juvenile offenders and their families. In: I. M. Schwartz & P. Au Clair (Eds.), *Home-Based Services for Troubled Children. Child, Youth and Family Services* (pp. 113–130). Lincoln, NE: University of Nebraska Press.

Henggeler, S. W., Schoenwald, S. K., Borduin, C. M., Rowland, M. D., & Cunningham, P. B. (1998). *Multisystemic Treatment of Antisocial Behaviour in Children and Adolescents*. New York: Guilford Press.

Hent, J. P. M., Harte, J. M., & Weenink, A. G. M. (1999). Using the Rorschach in forensic psychological assessment. Paper presented at the XVIth International Rorschach Society World Congress, Amsterdam, July.

Herkov, M. J., Gynther, M. D., Thomas, S., & Myers, W. C. (1996). MMPI differences among adolescent inpatients, rapists, sodomists and sexual abusers. *Journal of Personality Assessment, 66*(1): 81–90.

Herpetz, S. C., & Saas, H. (2000). Emotional deficiency and psychopathy. *Behavioral Sciences and the Law, 18*: 567–580.

Hertsgaard, L., Gunnar, M., Erickson, M. F., & Nachmias, M. (1995). Adrenocortical responses to the strange situation in infants with disorganized attachment relationships. *Child Development, 66*: 1100–1106.

Hertz, M. (1941). Evaluation of the Rorschach method and its application to normal childhood and adolescence. *Character and Personality, 10*: 151–162.

Hervé, H., & Yuille, J. C. (2007). *The Psychopath: Theory, Research and Practice.* Mahwah, NJ: Lawrence Erlbaum.

Hiller, J., Rosenthal, R., Bornstein, R., Berry, D., & Brunell-Neuleib, S. (1999). A comparative meta-analysis of Rorschach and MMPI validity. *Psychological Assessment, 11*: 278–296.

Hilton, M. R., & Mezey, G. C. (1996). Victims and perpetrators of child sexual abuse. *British Journal of Psychiatry, 169*: 408–421.

Hindy, C. G., Schwartz, J. C., & Brodsky, A. (1989). *If This Is Love, Why Do I Feel so Insecure?* New York: Atlantic Monthly Press.

Hinshelwood, R. (1999). The difficult patient. *British Journal of Psychiatry, 174*: 187–190.

Hodges, J., Lanyado, M., & Andreou, C. (1994). Sexuality and violence: preliminary clinical hypotheses from psychotherapeutic assessments in a research programme on young sexual offenders. *Journal of Child Psychotherapy, 20*(3): 283–309.

Hoge, R. D., & Andrews, D. A. (1994). *The Youth Level of Service/Case Management Inventory and Manual.* Ottawa, Canada: Carleton University, Department of Psychology.

Hoge, R. D., & Andrews, D. A. (1996). *Assessing the Youthful Offender: Issues and Techniques.* New York: Plenum Press.

Holmes, J. (1993). *John Bowlby and Attachment Theory.* London: Routledge.

Holt, S. E., Meloy, J. R., & Strack, S. (1999). Sadism and psychopathy in violent and sexually violent offenders. *Journal of the American Academy of Psychiatry and the Law, 27*(1): 23–32.

Hsu, L. K. G., & Starzynski, J. (1990). Adolescent rapists and adolescent child sexual assaulters. *International Journal of Offender Therapy and Comparative Criminology, 34*(1): 23–30.

Hubbs-Tait, L., Hughes, K. P., Culp, A. M., Osofsky, J. D., Hann, D. M., Eberhart-Wright, A., & Ware, L. M. (1996). Children of adolescent mothers: attachment representation, maternal depression and later behavioral problems. *American Journal of Orthopsychiatry, 66*: 416–426.

Hudson, S. M., & Ward, T. (1997). Intimacy, loneliness and attachment style in sexual offenders. *Journal of Interpersonal Violence, 12*: 323–339.

Hughes, S. A., DeVille, C., Chalhoub, M., & Romboletti, R. (1992). The Rorschach human anatomy response: predicting sexual offending behavior in juveniles. *The Journal of Psychiatry and Law, 20*(3): 313–333.

Hull, E. M., Muschamp, J. W., & Sato, S. (2004). Dopamine and serotonin: influences on male sexual behavior. *Physiology and Behavior, 83*: 291–307.

Hunter, J. A. (2000). *Understanding Juvenile Sex Offenders: Research Findings and Guidelines for Effective Management and Treatment* (Juvenile Justice Fact Sheet). Charlottsville, VA: Institute of Law, Psychiatry, and Public Policy, University of Virginia.

Hunter, J. A., & Figueredo, A. J. (2000). The influence of personality and history of sexual victimization in the prediction of juvenile perpetrated child molestation. *Behavior Modification, 29*(2): 259–281.

Hyatt-Williams, A. (1998). *Cruelty, Violence, and Murder: Understanding the Criminal Mind.* London: Karnac.

Insel, T. R., & Winslow, J. T. (1998). Serotonin and neuropeptides in affiliative behaviours. *Biological Psychiatry, 44*: 207–219.

Insel, T. R., & Winslow, J. T. (2004). The neurobiology of social attachment. In: D. S. Charney & E. J. Nestler (Eds.), *Neurobiology of Mental Illness* (2nd edn) (pp. 880–890). Oxford: Oxford University Press.

Insel, T. R., & Young, L. J. (2001). The neurobiology of attachment. *Nature Reviews/Neuroscience, 2*: 129–136.

Iwasa, K., & Ogawa, T. (2010). The relationship between texture response on the Rorschach and adult attachment. *Rorschachiana. Journal of the International Rorschach Society, 31*: 4–22.

Jacobs, W. R., Kennedy, W. A., & Mayer, J. B. (1997). Juvenile delinquents: a between group comparison study of sexual and non-sexual offenders. *Sexual Abuse: A Journal of Research and Treatment, 9*: 201–217.

Jay, V. (2002). Pierre Paul Broca. *Archives of Pathology & Laboratory Medicine, 126*: 250–251.

Jenkins, S. (1999). An argument for early and appropriate intervention with juvenile sex offenders. *Psychiatry, Psychology and Law, 6*(1): 79–91.

Johnson, G. M., & Knight, R. A. (2000). Developmental antecedents of sexual coercion in juvenile sex offenders. *Sexual Abuse: A Journal of Research and Treatment, 12*(3): 165–178.

Jonson-Reid, M., & Way, I. (2001). Adolescent sexual offenders: incidence of childhood maltreatment, serious emotional disturbance and prior offences. *American Journal of Orthopsychiatry, 71*(1): 120–130.

Kahn, T. J., & Chambers, H. J. (1991). Assessing reoffense risk with juvenile sex offenders. *Child Welfare, LXX*(3): 333–345.

Kahn, T. J., & Lafond, M. A. (1988). Treatment of the adolescent sexual offender. *Child and Adolescent Social Work, 5*: 135–148.

Karlsson, H., Hirvonen, J., Kalander, J., Markkula, J., Rasi-Hakala, H., Salminen, J. K., Någren, K., Aalto, S., & Hietala, J. (2010). Research letter: Psychotherapy increases brain serotonin 5-HT$_{1A}$ receptors in patients with major depressive disorder. *Psychological Medicine, 40*: 523–528.

Karnolz-Langdon, H. (2011). *A Graphite Drawing of the Limbic System.* Sydney: Helena Karnolz Designs Pty Ltd.

Katz, R. C. (1990). Psychological adjustment in adolescent child molesters. *Child Abuse and Neglect, 14*: 567–575.

Kavoussi, R. J., Kaplan, M., & Becker, J. V. (1988). Psychiatric diagnoses in adolescent sex offenders. *Journal of the American Academy of Child and Adolescent Psychiatry, 27*(2): 241–243.

Kear-Colwell, J., & Sawle, G. A. (2001). Coping strategies and attachment in pedophiles: implications for treatment. *International Journal of Offender Therapy & Comparative Criminology, 45*(2): 171–182.

Kempton, T., & Forehand, R. (1992). Juvenile sex offenders: similar to or different from, other incarcerated delinquent offenders. *Behavior Research and Therapy, 30*(5): 533–536.

Kenny, D. T. (2011). Drugs not the answer for modern problems. *Sydney Morning Herald (Society and Culture)*, 14 March.

Kenny, D. T., Keogh, T., & Seidler, K. (2001). Predictors of recidivism in Australian juvenile sex offenders: implications for treatment. *Sexual Abuse: A Journal of Research and Treatment, 13*(2): 131–148.

Kenny, D. T., Keogh, T., Seidler, K., & Blaszczynski, A. (2000). Offence and clinical characteristics of Australian juvenile sex offenders. *Psychiatry, Psychology and the Law: An Interdisciplinary Journal of the Australian and New Zealand Association of Psychiatry, Psychology and the Law, 7*(2): 212–226.

Keogh, T. (2002). Juvenile recidivism: new and surprising possibilities for mental health promotion and prevention. In: L. Rowling, G. Martin, & L. Walker (Eds.), *Mental Health Promotion and Young People: Concepts and Practice* (pp. 230–244). Sydney: McGraw Hill.

Keogh, T. (2004). Psychopathy and capacity for attachment amongst juvenile sex offenders. Unpublished Doctoral dissertation. The Hesburgh Private Collection, The Hesburgh Library, University of Notre Dame, South Bend, Indiana.

Keogh, T., & Hayes, S. (2003). The diagnostic role of capacity for attachment and level of psychopathy with juvenile sex offenders. Presentation given at the Centenary Institute (Faculty of Medicine), Research in Progress Program (No. 3/2003) University of Sydney.

Keogh, T., Howard, M., Chappell, D., & Hooke, M. T. (2010). Malignant narcissism: territory too far for psychoanalysis? Panel presentation at the Australian Psychoanalytical Society's Open Day, entitled "Through a glass darkly: reverberations of early trauma: shame, perversion and violence", 31 July, Sydney, Australia.

Keogh, T., Kourt, M., Enfield, C., & Enfield, S. (2007). Psychopathology and therapeutic style: integrating object relations theory and attachment theory in working with borderline families. In: M. Ludlam & V. Nyberg (Eds.), *Couples Attachments: Theoretical and Clinical Studies* (pp. 239–242). London: Karnac.

Keogh, T., Quilty, S., Butler, A., Penglase, J., McFarlane, K., & Murray, J. (2004). Time spent in care, recidivism and mental health in an Australian inmate population: more evidence in favour of attachment theory (unpublished report). University of Sydney.

Kernberg, O. F. (1980). *Internal World and External Reality*. New York: Jason Aronson.

Kernberg, O. F. (1984). *Severe Personality Disorders: Psychotherapeutic Strategies*. New Haven, CT: Yale University Press.

Kernberg, O. F. (1995). *Love Relations: Normality and Pathology*. New Haven, CT: Yale University Press.

Kernberg, O. F. (2004). *Aggressivity, Narcissism, and Self-Destructiveness in the Psychotherapeutic Relationship: New Developments in the Psychopathology and Psychotherapy of Severe Personality Disorders*. New Haven, CT: Yale University Press.

Keverne, E. B., & Curley, J. P. (2004). Vasopressin, oxytocin, and social behavior. *Current Opinion in Neurobiology, 14*: 777–783.

Kiehl, K. A., Smith, A. M., Hare, R. D., Mendrek, A., Forster, B. B., Brink, J., & Liddle, P. F. (2001). Limbic abnormalities in affective processing by criminal psychopaths as revealed by functional magnetic resonance. *Biological Psychiatry, 50*(9): 677–684.

King, J. A., Mandansky, D., King, S., Fletcher, K. E., & Brewer, J. (2001). Early sexual abuse and low cortisol. *Psychiatry and Clinical Neurosciences, 55*(1): 71–74.

Kjaer, T. W., Bertelsen, C., Piccini, P., Brooks, D., Alving, J., & Lou, H. C. (2002). Increased dopamine tone during meditation-induced change of consciousness. *Brain Research/Cognitive Brain Research, 13*(2): 255–259.

Klein, M. (1932). *The Psycho-Analysis of Children*. London: Hogarth Press.

Klein, M. (1946). Notes on some schizoid mechanisms. *International Journal of Psychoanalysis, 27*: 99–110.

Klein, M. (1952). The origins of transference. In: *Envy and Gratitude and Other Works: 1946–1963. Volume III, The Writings of Melanie Klein.* London: Hogarth Press and the Institute of Psychoanalysis, 1975.

Klein, M. (1957). Envy and gratitude. In: *Envy and Gratitude and Other Works: 1946–1963. Volume III, The Writings of Melanie Klein.* London: Hogarth Press and the Institute of Psychoanalysis, 1975.

Klein, M. (2002). *Love, Guilt and Reparation: And Other Works 1921–1945.* New York: Free Press.

Knight, R., & Prentky, R. (1993). Exploring characteristics for classifying juvenile sex offenders. In: H. E. Barbaree, W. L. Marshall, & S. M. Hudson (Eds.), *The Juvenile Sex Offender* (pp. 243–263). New York: Guilford Press.

Knet, P., Lindfors, O., & Laaksonen, M. A. (2008). The effectiveness of psychoanalysis and long- and short-term psychotherapy on psychiatric symptoms during a five-year follow-up: a quasi-experimental study. *European Psychiatry, 23(Supplement 2, April)*: S255–S256.

Knop, J., Jensen, P., & Mortensen, E. (2003). Comorbidity of alcoholism and psychopathy. In: T. Millon, E. Simonsen, M. Birket-Smith, & R. D. Davis (Eds.), *Psychopathy: Antisocial, Criminal and Violent Behavior* (pp. 359–371). New York: Guilford Press.

Kobayashi, J., Sales, B. D., Becker, J. V., & Figuerado, A. J. (1995). Perceived parental deviance, parent–child bonding, child abuse and child sexual aggression. *Sexual Abuse: Journal of Research and Treatment, 7*(1): 25–44.

Kohut, H. (1977). *The Restoration of the Self.* New York: International Universities Press.

Korosi, A., & Baram, T. Z. (2008). The central corticotrophin releasing factor system during development and childhood. *European Journal of Pharmacology, 583*: 204–214.

Krafft-Ebing, R. (1886). *Psychopathia Sexualis: A Medico Forensic Study.* New York: Putnam, 1965.

Krauth, A. A. (1997). A comparative study of male juvenile sex offenders. Unpublished Doctoral dissertation, University of Texas, Dallas.

Kroger, J. (1989). *Identity in Adolescence: The Balance Between Self and Other.* London: Routledge.

Kruger, T. H. C., Hartmann, U., & Schedlowski, M. (2005). Prolactinergic and dopaminergic mechanisms underlying sexual arousal and orgasm in humans. *World Journal of Urology, 23*: 130–138.

Kumari, V. (2006). Do psychotherapies produce neurobiological effects? *Acta Neurosychiatrica, 18*(2): 61–70.

Laakso, M. P., Vaurio, O., Koivisto, E., Salainen, L., Eronen, M., Aronen, H. J., Hakola, P., Repo, E., Soininen, H., & Tiihonen, J. (2001). Psychopathy and the hippocampus. *Behavioural Brain Research, 118*(2): 187–193.

Lakey, J. F. (1992). Myth, information and bizarre beliefs of male juvenile sex offenders. *Journal of Addictions and Offender Counseling, 13*(1): 2–10.

Lakey, J. F. (1994). The profile and treatment of adolescent male sex offenders. *Adolescence, 29*(116): 755–761.

Lamb, W., & Jones, E. (2009). The effectiveness of psychoanalysis and longer-term psychodynamic psychotherapy: a meta-analysis. Paper presented to the American Psychoanalytic Association Annual Meeting.

Lamont, A. (2011). Child abuse and neglect statistics. *Report of the National Child Protection Clearinghouse*. Melbourne, Victoria: Australian Institute for Family Studies.

Lang, R., & Langevin, R. (1996a). The MMPI as a predictor of recidivism in sex offenders: a 25-year follow-up study. Paper presented to the 15th International Conference on Personality Assessment, Melbourne, Australia.

Lang, R., & Langevin, R. (1996b). Forensic utility of the MMPI with sex offenders. Paper presented to the 15th International Conference on Personality Assessment, Melbourne, Australia.

Langevin, R., & Lang, R. (1990). Substance abuse amongst sex offenders. *Annals of Sexual Research, 3*: 397–424.

Langevin, R., Paitich, D., & Russon, A. E. (1985). Are rapists sexually anomalous, aggressive or both? In: R. Langevin (Ed.), *Erotic Preference, Gender Identity and Aggression in Men: New Research Studies* (pp. 13–38). Hillsdale, NJ: Earlbaum.

Långström, N., & Grann, M. (2000). Risk for criminal recidivism among young sex offenders. *Journal of Interpersonal Violence, 15*(8): 855–871.

Långström, N., & Lindblad, F. (2000). Young sex offenders: background, personality, and crime characteristics in a Swedish forensic psychiatric sample. *Nordic Journal of Psychiatry, 54*(2): 113–120.

Leguizamo, A. (2000). Juvenile sex offenders: an object relations approach. Doctoral dissertation, University of Michigan, Ann Arbor.

Leichsenring, F., & Leibing, E. (2007). Psychodynamic psychotherapy: a systematic review of techniques, indications and empirical evidence. *Psychology and Psychotherapy, 80*(2): 217–228.

Leichsenring, F., & Rabung, S. (2008). Effectiveness of long-term psychodynamic psychotherapy: a meta-analysis. *Journal of the American Medical Association, 300*(13): 1551–1565.

Levy, D. M. (1951). Psychopathic behaviour in infants and children. *American Journal of Orthopsychiatry, 21*: 223–272.

Levy, R. A., & Ablon, J. S. (2009). *Handbook of Evidence-Based Psychodynamic Psychotherapy: Bridging the Gap Between Science and Practice.* New York: Humana Press.

Lewis, D. O., Shanock, S. S., & Pincus, J. H. (1981). Juvenile sexual assaulters: psychiatric, neurological, psycho-educational and abuse factors. In: D. O. Lewis (Ed.), *Vulnerabilities to Delinquency* (pp. 89–105). Jamaica, New York: Spectrum.

Lilienfeld, S. O., Wood, J. M., & Howard, N. G. (2000). The scientific status of projective techniques. *Psychological Science in the Public Interest: A Journal of the American Psychological Society, 1*(2): 27–59.

Lindsey, R. E., Carlozzi, A. F., & Ellis, G. T. (2001). Differences in the dispositional empathy of juvenile sex offenders, non-sex-offending delinquent juveniles and non-delinquent juveniles. *Journal of Interpersonal Violence, 16*(6): 510–522.

Liu, D., Diorio, J., Tannebaum, B., Caldji, C., Francis, D., Freedman, A., Sharma, S., Pearson, D., Plotsky, P. M., & Meany, J. M. (1997). Maternal care, hippocampal glucocorticoid receptors and hypothalamic-pituitary-adrenal responses to stress. *Science, 277*: 1659–1662.

Loeber, R., & Hay, D. (1997). Key issues in the development of aggression from childhood to early adulthood. *Annual Review of Psychiatry, 48*: 371–410.

Longo, R. E. (1982). Sexual learning and experience among adolescent sexual offenders. *International Journal of Offender Therapy & Comparative Criminology, 26*: 235–241.

Lorberbaum, J. P., Newman, J. D., Horwitz, A. R., Dubno, J. R., Lydiard, R. B., Hamner, M. B., Bohning, D. E., & George, M. S. (2002). A potential for thalamocingulate circuitry in human maternal behavior. *Biological Psychiatry, 51*: 431–445.

Lorenz, K. Z. (1935). Der Kumpan in der Umelt des Vogels (The companion in the bird's world). *Journal für Ornithologie, 83*: 137–213. (Abbreviated translation published 1937 in *Auk, 54*: 245–273.)

Lorrain, D., Riolo, J., Matuszewich, L., & Hull, E. (1999). Lateral hypothalamic serotonin inhibits nucleus accumbens dopamine: implications for safety. *Journal of Neuroscience, 19*: 7648–7652.

Losada-Paisey, G. (1998). Use of the MMPI-A to assess personality of juvenile male delinquents who are sex offenders and non-sex offenders. *Psychological Reports, 83*: 115–122.

Lotke, E. (1996). Sex offenders: does treatment work? *Corrections Compendium, 21*(5): 1–3.

Lovelace, L., & Gannon, L. (1999). Psychopathy and depression: mutually exclusive constructs? *Journal of Behaviour Therapy and Experimental Psychiatry, 30*(3): 169–176.

Loving, J. L. J., & Russell, W. F. (2000). Selected Rorschach variables of psychopathic juvenile offenders. *Journal of Personality Assessment, 75*(1): 126–142.

Lyons-Ruth, K. (1996). Attachment relationships among children with aggressive behavior problems: the role of disorganized early attachment patterns. *Journal of Consulting and Clinical Psychology, 64*(1): 64–73.

MacLean, P. D. (1990). *The Triune Brain in Evolution.* New York: Plenum.

Magagna, J. (2011). How infant observation informs good clinical practice. Paper given at a shared event between NSWIPP (The NSW Institute of Psychoanalytic Psychotherapy) and CAFPAA (Couple and Family Association of Australia, formerly the NSW Institute of Family Psychotherapy), February, 2011, Sydney, Australia.

Mahler, M., Pine, F., & Bergman, A. (1975). *The Psychological Birth of the Human Infant.* New York: Basic Books.

Main, M., & Hess, E. (1990). Parents unresolved traumatic experiences are related to infant disorganized attachment status: is frightened and/or frightening parental behavior the linking mechanism? In: M. Greenberg, D. Cicchetti, & E. M. Cummings (Eds.), *Attachment in the Preschool Years: Theory, Research and Intervention* (pp. 161–182). Chicago, IL: University of Chicago Press.

Main, M., & Solomon, J. (1990). Procedures for identifying infants as disorganized/disoriented during the Ainsworth Strange Situation. In: M. Greenberg, D. Cicchetti & E. Cummings (Eds.), *Attachment in the Preschool Years: Theory, Research and Intervention* (pp. 121–160). Chicago, IL: University of Chicago Press.

Main, M., Kaplan, N., & Cassidy, J. (1985). Security in infancy, childhood and adulthood: a move to the level of representation. In: I. Bretherton & E. Waters (Eds.), *Growing Points of Attachment Theory and Research* (pp. 66–104). Chicago, IL: University of Chicago Press.

Manocha, K. F., & Mezey, G. (1998). British adolescents who abuse: a descriptive study. *Journal of Forensic Psychiatry, 9*(3): 588–608.

Marsh, A., & Viglione, D. J. (1992). A conceptual validation study of the texture response on the Rorschach. *Journal of Personality Assessment, 58*(3): 571–579.

Marshall, L. A., & Cooke, D. J. (1999). The childhood experience of psychopaths: a retrospective study of familial and societal factors. *Journal of Personality Disorders, 13*(3): 211–225.

Marshall, W. L. (1989). Intimacy, loneliness and sexual offenders. *Behavior Research and Therapy, 27*: 497–503.

Marshall, W. L. (1993). The role of attachments, intimacy, and loneliness in the etiology and maintenance of sexual offending. *Sexual and Marital Therapy, 8*(2): 109–121.

Marshall, W. L. (1996). Assessment, treatment, and theorising about sex offenders: developments of the past 20 years and future directions. *Criminal Justice and Behaviour, 23*(1): 162–199.

Marshall, W. L., Cripps, E., Anderson, D., & Cortoni, F. A. (1999). Self esteem and coping strategies in child molesters. *Journal of Interpersonal Violence, 14*(9): 955–962.

Marshall, W. L., Geris, A. S., & Cortoni, F. A. (2000). Childhood attachments, sexual abuse, and their relationship to adult coping in child molesters. *Sexual Abuse: A Journal of Research and Treatment, 12*(1): 17–26.

Marshall, W. L., Hudson, S. M., & Hodkinson, S. (1993). The importance of attachment bonds in the development of juvenile sex offending. In: H. E. Barbaree, W. L. Marshall, & S. M. Hudson (Eds.), *The Juvenile Sex Offender* (pp. 164–181). New York: Guilford Press.

Masterson, J. F. (Ed.) (2005). *The Personality Disorders Through the Lens of Attachment Theory and the Neurobiologic Development of the Self: A Clinical Integration.* Phoenix, AZ: Zeig, Tucker & Theisen.

Mattlar, C. E. (2004). The Rorschach comprehensive system is reliable and cost-effective. *Rorschachiana: Yearbook of the International Rorschach Society, 26*: 158–186.

McCoy, M. E. (1998). Predictors of recidivism in a population of Canadian sex offenders: psychological, physiological, and offence factors. *Dissertation Abstracts International: Section B: The Sciences and Engineering, 59*(3-B).

McDougall, J. (1995). *The Many Faces of Eros: A Psychoanalytical Exploration of Human Sexuality.* London: Free Association Books.

McDowell, C. J., & Acklin, M. W. (1996). Standardization procedures for calculating Rorschach inter-rater reliability: conceptual and empirical foundations. *Journal of Personality Assessment, 66*: 308–320.

McEntee, B. K. (1999). MMPI-A Personality Psychopathology Five. *Dissertation Abstracts International: Section B: The Sciences and Engineering, 60*(2-B Aug. 0837).

McGauley, G., Adshead, G., & Sarkar, S. P. (2007). Psychotherapy of the psychopathic disorders. In: A. R. Felthous & H. Sass (Eds.), *International Handbook on Psychopathic Disorders* (pp. 449–467). Chichester: John Wiley.

McKinley, J. C., & Hathaway, S. R. (1944). The MMPI: hysteria, hypomania and psychopathic deviate. *Journal of Psychology, 28*: 153–174.

McNulty, J. L., Harkness, A. R., Ben-Porath, Y. S., & Williams, C. L. (1997). Assessing the Personality Psychopathology Five (PSY5) in adolescents: new MMPI-A scales. *Psychological Assessment, 9*(3): 93–99.

McWilliams, N. (1994). *Psychoanalytic Diagnosis: Understanding Personality Structure in the Clinical Process*. New York: Guilford Press.

Meany, M. J. (2001). Maternal care, gene expression and the transmission of individual differences in stress reactivity across generations. *Annual Review of Neurosicence, 24*: 1161–1192.

Meck, W. H. (2006). Neuroanatomical localization of an interanl clock: a functional link between mesolimbic, nigrostriatal, and mesocortical dopaminergic systems. *Brain Research, 1109*(1): 93–107.

Mega, M. S., Cummings, J. L., Salloway, S., & Malloy, P. (1997). The limbic system: an anatomic, phylogenetic and clinical perspective. *Journal of Neuropsychiatry and Clinical Neuroscience, 9*: 315–330.

Meloy, R. (1992). *Violent Attachments*. Northvale, NJ: Jason Aronson.

Meloy, R. (1997). *The Psychopathic Mind*. New York: Basic Books.

Meloy, R., & Shiva, A. (2010). A psychoanalytic view of the psychopath. In: A. R. Felthous & H. Sass (Eds.), *International Handbook on Psychopathic Disorders and the Law* (pp. 335–347). Chichester: John Wiley.

Meltzer, D. (1966). The relation of anal masturbation to projective identification. *International Journal of Psychoanalysis, 47*: 335–342.

Meltzer, D. (1973). On the apprehension of beauty. *Contemporary Psychoanalysis, 9*: 224–229.

Meltzer, D. (1979). *Sexual States of Mind*. Strathtay, Perthshire: Clunie Press.

Meyer, G. J. (1997). Assessing reliability: critical corrections for a critical examination of the Rorschach Comprehensive System. *Psychological Assessment, 67*: 558–578.

Mikulincer, M., & Shaver, P. (2007). A behavioral systems perspective on the psychodynamics of attachment and sexuality. In: D. Diamond, S. J. Blatt, & J. Lichtenberg (Eds.), *Attachment and Sexuality* (pp. 61–78) New York: Analytic Press.

Miller, T. A., Fisher, D. A., & Cohen, M. A. (2001). Costs of juvenile violence: policy implications. *Pediatrics, 107*: 1–7.

Millon, T., Simonsen, E., Birket-Smith, M., & Davis, R. D. (2003). *Psychopathy: Antisocial, Criminal and Violent Behavior*. New York: Guilford Press.

Miner, M. H., & Dwyer, S. M. (1997). The psychosocial development of sex offenders: differences between exhibitionists, child molesters and incest offenders. *International Journal of Offender Therapy and Comparative Criminology*, 41(1): 36–44.

Miner, M. H., Siekert, G. P., & Ackland, M. A. (1997). *Evaluation: Juvenile Sex Offender Treatment Program*. Minneapolis MN: Minnesota Correctional Facility—Sauk Center.

Minzenberg, M. J., & Siever, L. J. (2007). Neurochemistry and pharmacology of psychopathy. In: C. J. Patrick (Ed.), *Handbook of Psychopathy* (pp. 251–277). New York: Guilford Press.

Molnar, B., Bukar, S. L., & Kessler, R. C. (2001). Child sexual abuse and subsequent psychopathology: results from the national co-morbidity survey. *American Journal of Public Health*, 91(5): 753–760.

Moss, E., Rousseau, D., Parent, S., St. Laurent, D., & Saintong, J. (1998). Correlates of attachment at school age: maternal reported stress, mother–child interaction and behavior problems. *Child Development*, 69: 1390–1405.

Murphy, S. (1996). Mental. In: S. Murphy (Ed.), *Collected Chapbooks*. Puhos, Finland, West Hartford, CT: Blue Lion Books, 2008.

Murphy, W. D., Haynes, M. R., & Page, I. J. (1992). Adolescent sex offenders. In: W. O'Donohue & J. H. Greer (Eds.), *The Sexual Abuse of Children: Vol. 1: Theory and research; Vol. 2: Clinical Issues* (pp. 394–429). Hillsdale, NJ: Lawrence Erlbaum.

Myers, W. C., & Monaco, L. (2000). Anger experiences, styles of anger expression, sadistic personality disorder, and psychopathy in juvenile sexual homicide offenders. *Journal of Forensic Sciences*, 45(3): 436–440.

Myers, W. C., Burket, R. C., & Harris, E. H. (1995). Adolescent psychopathy in relation to delinquent behaviors, conduct disorder, and personality disorders. *Journal of Forensic Sciences*, 40(3): 436–440.

Ness, C. M. (2001). Emotional expressiveness and problematic behaviors among male juvenile sex offenders, general offenders, and nonoffenders. (Doctoral dissertation, Western Michigan University). *Dissertation Abstracts International 61(9-B)*: 4966. (UMI No. 9988432).

Newman, J. P., Schmitt, W. A., & Voss, W. D. (1997). The impact of motivationally neutral cues on psychopathic individuals: assessing the generality of the response modulation hypothesis. *Journal of Abnormal Psychology*, 106(4): 563–575.

Novak, M. A., & Harlow, H. F. (1975). Social recovery of monkeys isolated for the first year of life. *Developmental Psychology*, 11: 453–465.

O'Brien, M., & Bera, W. H. (1986). Adolescent sexual offenders: a descriptive typology. *Preventing Sexual Abuse: A Newsletter of the National Family Education Network*, 1, (2–4).

O'Callaghan, D., & Print, B. (1995). Adolescent sexual abusers: research, assessment and treatment. In: T. Morrison, M. Erooga, & R. C. Beckett (Eds.), *Sexual Offending Against Children: Assessment and Treatment of Male Abusers* (pp. 146–178). London: Routledge.

Ogden, T. (1989). *The Primitive Edge of Experience*. London: Karnac.

Ogden, T. (1996). The perverse subject of analysis. *Journal of the American Psychoanalytical Association, 34*: 1121–1146

Ogden, T. (2009). A new reading of the origins of object relations theory. In: L. G. Fiorini, T. Bokanowski, & S. Lewkowicz (Eds.), *On Freud's Mourning and Melancholia* (pp. 123–144). London: Karnac.

Olweus, D. (1979). Stability of aggressive reactive patterns in males: a review. *Psychological Bulletin, 86*: 826–875.

Pai, C.-Y., Huang, J.-M., Chen, K.-H., Yang, C.-H., & Zhang, Z.-W. (2006). Association study of dopamine-related genes in sexual offenders. *Crime and Criminal Justice International, 6*(March): 132–133.

Parkes, C., & Stevenson-Hinde, J. (Eds.) (1982). *The Place of Attachment in Human Behavior*. New York: Basic Books.

Patrick, C. J., Cuthbert, B. N., & Lang, P. J. (1993). Emotion in the criminal psychopath: startle reflex modulation. *Journal of Abnormal Psychology, 102*(1): 82–92.

Perry, W., & Viglione D. J. Jr. (1991). The Ego Impairment Index as a predictor of outcome in melancholic depressed patients treated with tricyclic antidepressants. *Journal of Personality Assessment, 56*(3), 487–501.

Perry, W., Mc Dougall, A., & Viglione, D. J. (1995). A five year follow-up on the temporal stability of the EII. *Journal of Personality Assessment, 64*: 112–118.

Perry, W., Viglione, D. J., & Braff, D. (1992). The Ego Impairment Index and schizophrenia. *Journal of Personality Assessment, 56*, 165–175.

Piaget, J. (1976). Time and the intellectual development of the child. In: *The Child and Reality: Problems of Genetic Psychology* (pp. 1–30). Harmondsworth: Penguin.

Pickering, A. D., & Gray, J. A. (2001). Dopamine, appetitive reinforcement, and the neuropsychology of human learning: an individual differences approach. In: A. Eliasz & A. Angleitner (Eds.), *Advances in Individual Differences Research* (pp. 113–149). Lengerich, Germany: PABST Science.

Pinel, P. (1801). *A Treatise on Insanity*. New York: Hafner, 1962.

Piotrowski, Z. (1957). *Perceptanalysis*. NewYork: Macmillan.

Poeck, K. (1985). The Kluver–Bucy syndrome in man. In: F. Jam (Ed.) *The Handbook of Clinical Neurology* (pp. 257–263), New York: Elsevier.

Polaschek, D. L. L., Hudson, S. M., Ward, T., & Siegert, R. J. (2001). Rapists' offense processes: a preliminary descriptive model. *Journal of Interpersonal Violence, 16*(6): 523–544.

Ponder, J. I. (1999). An investigation of psychopathy in a sample of violent juvenile offenders. *Dissertation Abstracts International: Section B: The Sciences and Engineering, 59*(March): 5150.

Porges, S. W. (2003). Social engagement and attachment: a phylogenetic perspective. Roots of mental illness in children. *Annals of the New York Academy of Sciences, 1008*: 31–47.

Porter, S., Fairweather, D., Drugge, J., Hervé, H., Birt, A., & Boer, D. P. (2000). Profiles of psychopathy in incarcerated sexual offenders. *Criminal Justice and Behavior, 27*(2): 216–233.

Prentky, R., & Righthand, S. (2003). *Juvenile Sex Offender Assessment Protocol-II (J-SOAP-II) Manual.* A publication of the Office of Juvenile Justice and Delinquency Prevention's Juvenile Justice Clearinghouse, USA (NCJ 202316).

Pridmore, S., Chambers, A., & McArthur, M. (2005). Neuroimaging in psychopathy. *Australian and New Zealand Journal of Psychiatry, 39*: 856–865.

Quinn, K. M. (1992). Juvenile sex offenders. In: M. G. Kalogerakis (Ed.), *Handbook of Psychiatric Practice in the Juvenile Court* (pp. 105–109). Washington, DC: American Psychiatric Association.

Rapaport, D., Gill, M., & Schafer, R. (1945.) *Diagnostic Psychological Testing.* Volume I. Chicago, IL: Year Book Publishers.

Reich, W. (1945). *Character Analysis* (2nd edn). New York: Farrar, Straus & Giroux.

Reid, W. H., & Gacono, C. (2000). Treatment of antisocial personality, psychopathy, and other characterologic antisocial syndromes. *Behavioral Sciences and the Law, 18*(5): 647–662.

Reitzel, L. R., & Carbonell, J. L. (2006). The effectiveness of sexual offender treatment for juveniles as measured by recidivism: a meta-analysis. *Sexual Abuse, 18*: 401–421.

Rich, P. (2009). *Juvenile Sex Offenders: A Comprehensive Guide to Risk Evaluation.* Hoboken, NJ: John Wiley.

Richardson, G., Graham, F., Bhate, S. R., & Kelly, T. P. (1996). A British sample of sexually abusive adolescents: abuser and abuse characteristics. *Criminal Behaviour and Mental Health, 5*: 187–208.

Rilke, R. M. (2004). Classic poetry series. Poemhunter.com.

Riviere, J. (1985). The unconcious phantasy of an inner world reflected in examples from literature. In: M. Klein, P. Heiman & R. E. Mioney

Kyrle (Eds.), *New Directions in Psychoananlysis: The Significance of Infant Conflict in the Pattern of Adult Behaviour* (pp. 346–370). London: Karnac.

Rodrigues, S. M., Saslow, L. R., Garcia, N., John, O. P., & Keltner, D. (2009). Oxytocin receptor genetic variation relates to empathy and stress reactivity in humans. *Proceedings of the National Academy of Sciences of the United States of America, 106*(5): 21437–21441.

Rorschach, H. (1921). *Psychodiagnostics*. New York: Grune & Stratton, 1942.

Rosen, L. N., Fontaine, J., Gaskin-Lanlyan, N. D., Price, C., & Bachar, K. J. (2009). *Compendium of Research on Violence Against Women (1993–2009)*. Violence and Victimization Research Division, US National Institute of Justice Report.

Rosenfeld, H. A. (1964). *Psychotic States*. London: Hogarth Press.

Rosenfeld, H. A. (1971). A clinical approach to the psychoanalytic theory of the life and death instincts: an investigation into the aggressive aspects of narcissism. *International Journal of Psychoanalysis, 52*: 169–178.

Rosenfeld, H. A. (1987). *Impasse and Interpretation: Therapeutic and Anti-Therapeutic Factors in the Psychoanalytic Treatment of Psychotic, Borderline, and Neurotic Patients*. New York: New Library of Psychoanalysis, Routledge.

Rosenstein, D. S., & Horowitz, H. A. (1996). Adolescent attachment and psychopathology. *Journal of Consulting and Clinical Psychology, 64*(2): 244–253.

Rothbard, J. C., & Shaver, P. R. (1991). *Attachment Styles and the Quality and Importance of Attachment to Parents*. Buffalo, NY: State University of New York.

Ruszczynski, S. (2010a). The frightened couple. A paper given at the first EFPP Conference of the Section of Couple and Family Psychotherapy: Families in Transformation: A Challenge for Psychoanalytic Psychotherapy, held in May, 2010, Florence, Italy.

Ruszczynski, S. (2010b). Becoming neglected: a perverse relationship to care. *British Journal of Psychotherapy, 26*(1): 22–32.

Ryan, G. (1997). Sexually abusive youth: defining the population. In: G. Ryan & S. Lane (Eds.), *Juvenile Sex Offending: Causes, Consequences and Correction*. San Francisco, CA: Jossey-Bass.

Ryan, G., Leversee, F., & Lane, S. (2010). *Juvenile Sex Offending: Causes, Consequences and Correction*. Hoboken, NJ: Wiley.

Ryan, G., Miyoshi, T. J., Metzner, J., Krugman, R. D., & Fryer, G. E. (1996). Trends in a national sample of sexually abusive youths. *Journal of the American Academy of Child and Adolescent Psychiatry, 35*(1): 17–25.

Salekin, R. T., Worley, C., & Grimes, R. D. (2010). Treatmnet of psychopathy: a review and brief introduction to the mental model approach for psychopathy. *Behavioral Sciences and the Law, 28*(2): 235–266.

Saunders, E., Awad, G., & White, G. (1986). Male adolescent offenders: the offender and the offence. *Canadian Journal of Psychology, 31*: 542–549.

Sawle, G. A., & Kear-Colwell, J. (2001). Adult attachment style and pedophilia: a developmental perspective. *International Journal of Offender Therapy and Comparative Criminology, 45*(1): 32–50.

Schore, A. (2005). Attachment, affect regulation, and the developing right brain: linking developmental neuroscience to pediatrics. *Pediatrics in Review, 26*: 204–211.

Schram, D. D., Milloy, C. D., & Rowe, W. E. (1991). *Juvenile Sex Offenders: A Follow up of Reoffense Behavior*. Washington, DC: Washington State Institute for Public Policy.

Segal, H. (1983). Some clinical implications of Melanie Klein's work— emergence from narcissism. *International Journal of Psychoanalysis, 64*: 269–276.

Seghorn, T. K., Prentky, R. A., & Boucher, R. J. (1987). Childhood sexual abuse in the lives of sexually aggressive offenders. *Journal of the American Academy of Child and Adolescent Psychiatry, 26*: 262–267.

Seidman, B. T., Marshall, W. L., Hudson, S. M., & Robertson, P. J. (1994). An examination of intimacy and loneliness in sex offenders. *Journal of Interpersonal Violence, 9*(4): 518–534.

Serin, R. C., Mailoux, D. L., & Malcolm, P. B. (2001). Psychopathy, deviant sexual arousal and recidivism among sexual offenders. *Journal of Interpersonal Violence, 16*(3): 234–246.

Seto, M. C., & Barbaree, H. E. (1998). Psychopathy, treatment behaviour and sex offender recidivism. *Journal of Interpersonal Violence, 14*(12): 1235–1248.

Seto, M. C., & Lalumière, M. L. (2010). What is so special about male adolescent sex offending? A review and test of explanations through meta-analysis. *Psychological Bulletin, 136*(4): 526–575.

Shaw, D. S., Owens, E. B., Vondra, J. I., Keenan, K., & Winslow, E. B. (1996). Early risk factors and pathways in the development of early disruptive behavior problems. *Development & Psychopathology, 8*: 679–699.

Shedler, J. (2010). The efficacy of psychodynamic psychotherapy. *American Psychologist, 63*(2): 98–109.

Sickmund, M., Snyder, H. N., & Poe-Yamagata, E. (1997). *Juvenile Offenders and Victims: 1997 Update on Violence.* Washington, DC: Office of Juvenile Justice and Delinquency Prevention.

Sinourd, D. J., Hoge, R. D., Andrews, D. A., & Leschied, A. W. (1994). An empirically based typology of male young offenders. *Canadian Journal of Criminology, 36*(4): 447–461.

Sjögren, B., Widström, A. M., Edman, G., & Uvnäs-Moberg, K. (2000). Changes in personality pattern during the first pregnancy and lactation. *Journal of Psychosomatic Obstetrics and Gynaecology, 21*(1): 31–38.

Skeem, J. L., Monahan, J., & Mulvey, E. P. (2002). Psychopathy, treatment involvement and subsequent violence among civil psychiatric patients. *Law and Human Behavior, 26*(6): 577–585.

Skuse, B., Bentovim, A., Hodges, J., Stevenson, J., Andreou, C., Layando, M., New, M., Williams, R., & McMillan, D. (1998). Risk factors for the development of sexually abusive behaviour in sexually victimised adolescent boys: cross-sectional study. *British Medical Journal, 317*: 175–179.

Smallbone, S. W., & Dadds, M. R. (1998). Childhood attachment and adult attachment in incarcerated male sex offenders. *Journal of Interpersonal Violence, 13*(5): 555–573.

Smallbone, S. W., & Dadds, M. R. (2000). Attachment and coercive sexual behavior. *Sexual Abuse: A Journal of Research and Treatment, 12*(1): 3–15.

Smallbone, S. M., & Dadds, M. R. (2001). Further evidence for a relationship between attachment insecurity and coercive sexual behaviour in nonoffenders. *Journal of Interpersonal Violence, 16*(1): 22–35.

Smith, A. M., Gacono, C. B., & Kaufman, L. (1997). A Rorschach comparison of psychopathic ad non-psychopathic conduct disordered adolescents. *Journal of Clinical Psychology, 53*(4): 289–300.

Smith, W. R., Monastersky, C., & Deisher, R. M. (1987). MMPI-based personality types among juvenile sexual offenders. *Journal of Clinical Psychology, 43*(94): 422–430.

Sniffen, C. (2009). *2008 Report: Research on Rape and Violence.* California Coalition Against Sexual Assault (CALCASA) Report.

Snyder, H. N., & Sickmund, M. (1995). *Juvenile Offenders and Victims: A National Report.* Pittsburgh, PA: National Center for Juvenile Justice.

Snyder, H. N., Sickmund, M., & Poe-Yamagata, E. (1996). *Juvenile Offenders and Victims: 1996 Update on Violence.* Washington, DC: Office of Juvenile Justice and Delinquency Prevention.

Soderstrom, H., Blennow, K., Sjodin, A., & Forsman, A. (2003). New evidence for an association between CSF HVA: HIAA ratio and psychopathic traits. *Journal of Neurology, Neurosurgery and Psychiatry*, 74: 918–921.

Spaccarelli, S., Bowden, B., Coatsworth, J. D., & Klim, S. (1997). Psychosocial correlates of male sexual aggression in a chronic delinquent sample. *Criminal Justice and Behavior, 24*(1): 71–95.

Sperling, M. B., & Berman, W. H. (Eds.) (1994). *Attachment in Adults: Clinical and Developmental Perspectives*. New York: Guilford Press.

Sroufe, L. A., Egeland, B., & Kreutzer, T. (1990). The fate of early experience following developmental change: longitudinal approaches to individual adaptation in childhood. *Child Development, 61*: 1363–1373.

Stalenheim, E. G., Erikssson, E., Von Knorring, L., & Wide, L. (1998). Testosterone as a biological marker in psychopathy and alcoholism. *Psychiatry Research, 77*(2): 79–88.

Steinberg, L. (2005). Cognitive and affective development in adolescence. *Trends in Cognitive Science, 9*(2): 69–74.

Stern, D. N. (1985). *The Interpersonal World of the Infant*. New York: HarperCollins, Basic Books.

Stirpe, T., Abracen, J., Stermac, L., & Wilson, R. (2006). Sexual offenders' state of mind regarding childhood attachment: a controlled investigation. *Sexual Abuse: A Journal of Research and Treatment, 18*(3): 289–302.

Stoller, R. (1975). *Perversion: The Erotic Form of Hatred*. Washington, DC: American Psychiatric Press.

Symington, J., & Symington, N. (1996). *The Clinical Thinking of Wilfred Bion*. London: Karnac.

Thornton, D. (2002). Constructing and testing a framework for dynamic risk assessment. *Sexual Abuse: A Journal of Research and Treatment, 14*: 139–154.

Tingle, D., Barnard, G. W., Robbins, L., Newman, G., & Hutchinson, D. (1986). Childhood and adolescent characteristics of pedophiles and rapists. *International Journal of Law and Psychiatry, 9*: 103–116.

Tjaden, P., & Thoennes, N. (2000). *Full Report of the Prevalence, Incidence, and Consequences of Violence Against Women: Findings from the National Violence Against Women Survey*. Washington, DC: National Institute of Justice.

Truscott, D. (1993). Adolescent offenders: comparison for sexual, violent and property offences. *Psychological Reports, 73*: 657–658.

Valliant, P. M., & Antonowicz, D. H. (1992). Rapists, incest offenders and child molesters in treatment: cognitive and social skills training.

International Journal of Offender Therapy & Comparative Criminology, 36: 221–230.

Valliant, P. M., & Bergeron, T. (1997). Personality and criminal profile of adolescent sex offenders and general offenders in comparison to non-offenders. *Psychological Reports, 81:* 483–489.

Van IJzendoorn, M. H., Schuengel, C., & Bakermans-Kranenburg, M. J. (1999). Disorganized attachment in early childhood: meta-analysis of precursors, concomitants and sequelae. *Developmental Psychopathology, 11:* 225–249.

Van Ness, S. R. (1984). Rape as instrumental violence: a study of youth offenders. *Journal of Offender Counseling, Services and Rehabilitation, 13:* 161–170.

Van Wijk, A., Blokland, A. A. J., Duits, N., Vermeiren, R., & Harkink, J. (2007). Relating psychiatric disorders, offender and offence character-istics in a sample of adolescent sex offenders and non-sex offenders. *Criminal Behaviour and Mental Health, 17:* 15–30.

Van Wijk, A., van Horn, J., Bullens, R., Bijleveld, C., & Doreleijers, T. (2005). Juvenile sex offenders: A group on its own? *International Journal of Offender Therapy and Comparative Criminology, 49:* 25–36.

Van Wijk, A., Vermeiren, J., Loeber, R., Hart-Kerkoffs, L., Doreleijers, T., & Bullens, R. (2006). Juvenile sex offenders compared with non-sex offenders: a review of the literature 1995–2005. *Trauma, Violence & Abuse, 7:* 227–243.

Veneziano, C., Veneziano, L., LeGrand, S., & Richards, L. (2004). Neuro-psychological executive functions of adolescent sex offenders and non-sex offenders. *Perceptual and Motor Skills, 98:* 661–674.

Vinogradov, S., Dishotsky, N. I., Doty, A, K., & Tinklenberg, J. R. (1988). Patterns of behavior in adolescent rape. *American Journal of Ortho-psychiatry, 52*(2): 179–187.

Vitale, J. E., & Newman, J. P. (2001). Response preservation in psycho-pathic women. *Journal of Abnormal Psychology, 110*(4): 644–647.

Vizard, E., Monck, E., & Mirsch, P. (1995). Child and adolescent abuse perpetrators: a review of the literature. *Journal of Child Psychology and Psychiatry, 36*(5): 731–756.

Waddell, M. (1998). *Inside Lives: Psychoanalysis and the Growth of Personality.* London: Duckworth.

Wall, J. K. (2011). *Agnosticism: The Battle Against Shameless Ignorance.* Bloomington, IN: iUniverse Books.

Ward, T. & Siegert, R. J. (2002). Towards a comprehensive theory of child sexual abuse: a theory knitting perspective. *Psychology, Crime and Law, 8:* 319–351.

Ward, T., Hudson, S. M., & France, K. G. (1993). Self-reported reasons for offending in child molesters. *Annals of Sex Research, 6*: 139–148.

Ward, T., Hudson, S. M., & Marshall, W. L. (1996). Attachment style in sex offenders: a preliminary study. *Journal of Sex Research, 33*: 17–26.

Ward, T., Hudson, S. M., Marshall, W. L., & Siegert, R. (1995). Attachment style and intimacy deficits in sexual offenders: a theoretical framework. *Sexual Abuse: A Journal of Research and Treatment, 7*(4): 317–335.

Ward, T., Keenan, T., & Hudson, S. M. (2000). Understanding cognitive, affective, and intimacy deficits in sexual offenders: A developmental perspective. *Aggression and Violent Behavior, 5*(1): 41–62.

Weaver, I. C., Cervoni, N., Champagne, F. A., D'Alessio, A. C., Sharma, S., Seckl, J. R., Dymov, S., Szyf, M., & Meany, M. J. (2004). Epigenetic programming by maternal behavior. *Nature Neuroscience, 7*(8): 791–792.

Weigert, E. (1967). Narcissism: benign and malignant forms. In: Robert W. Gibson (Ed.), *Crosscurrents in Psychiatry and Psychoanalysis* (pp. 222–238). Philadelphia, PA: Lippincott.

Weiner, I. B. (1993). Clinical considerations in the conjoint use of the Rorschach and the MMPI. *Journal of Personality Assessment, 60*(1): 148–152.

Weiner, I. B. (1996). Some observations on the validity of the Rorschach Inkblot Method. *Psychological Assessment, 8*(2): 206–213.

Weiner, I. B. (1997). Current status of the Rorschach Inkblot Method. *Journal of Personality Assessment, 68*(1): 5–19.

Weiss, J. M. A. (1985). The nature of psychopathy: treatment, prevention social implications. *Directions in Psychiatry, 25*: 1–6.

Welldon, E. (1992). *Mother, Madonna, Whore: The Idealization and Denigration of Motherhood*. London: Karnac, 2004.

Welldon, E. (1994). Forensic psychotherapy. In: P. A. P. Clarkson, (Ed.), *The Handbook of Psychotherapy* (pp. 1–44.). London: Routledge.

West, M., & Sheldon-Keller, A. (1994). *Patterns of Relating: An Adult Attachment Perspective*. New York: Guilford Press.

Whitaker-Azmitia, P. M. (2001). Serotonin and brain development: role in human developmental diseases. *Brain Research Bulletin, 56*: 479–485.

Widom, C. S. (1989). Does violence beget violence? A critical examination of the literature. *Psychological Bulletin, 106*: 3–28.

Widlocher, D. (Ed.) (2001). *Infantile Sexuality and Attachment*. New York: Other Press.

Williams, A., & Carolyn, L. (1997). Assessing the Personality Psychopathology Five (PSY-5) in Adolescents: New MMPI-A Scales. *Psychological Assessment, 9*(3): 250–259.

Winnicott, D. W. (1945). Primitive emotional development. In: *Collected Papers: Through Paediatrics to Psychoanalysis*, London: Tavistock, 1958

Winnicott, D. W. (1956). Primary maternal preoccupation. In: *Collected Papers: Through Paediatrics to Psychoanalysis*, London: Tavistock, 1958

Winnicott, D. W. (1958). *Collected Papers: Through Paediatrics to Psychoanalysis*. London: Tavistock.

Winnicott, D. W. (1961). Adolescence: struggling through the doldrums. In: D. W. Winnicott (Ed.), *The Family and Individual Development*. London: Tavistock, 1965.

Winslow, J. T., & Insel, T. R. (1993). Effects of central vasopressin administration to infant rats. *European Journal of Pharamacology, 223*: 101–107.

Winslow, J. T., & Insel, T. R. (2002). The social deficits of the oxytocin knockout mouse. *Neuropeptides, 36*: 221–229.

Wong, S., & Hare, R. D. (2002). *Program Guidelines for the Institutional Treatment of Violent Psychopathic Offenders*. Toronto, ON: Multi-Health Systems.

Wood, J. M., Lilienfeld, S. O., Nezworski, M. T., & Garb, H. N. (2001). Coming to grips with negative evidence for the comprehensive system for the Rorschach: a comment on Gacono, Loving and Bornholdt; Ganellen; and Bornstein. *Journal of Personality Assessment, 77*(1): 48–70.

Wood, J. M., Nezworski, M. T., & Garb, H. N. (2003). What's right with the Rorschach? *The Scientific Review of Mental Health Practice, 2*(2): 1–8.

Wood, J. M., Nezworski, M. T., & Stejskal, W. J. (1996). The Comprehensive System for the Rorschach: a critical examination. *Psychological Science, 7*: 3–10.

Wood, J. M., Nezworski, M. T., Stejskal, W. J., Garven, S., & West, S. G. (1999). Methodological issues in evaluating Rorschach validity: a comment on Burns & Viglione (1996), Weiner (1996) and Ganellen (1996). *Assessment, 6*: 115–120.

Worling, J. R. (1995). Sexual abuse histories of adolescent male sex offenders: differences on the basis of age and gender of their victims. *Journal of Abnormal Psychology, 104*(4): 610–613.

Worling, J. R., & Curwen, T. (2001). Estimate of Risk of Adolescent Sexual Offense Recidivism (ERASOR; Version. 2.0) In: M. C. Calder (Ed.), *Juveniles and Children Who Sexually Abuse: Frameworks for Assessment* (pp. 372–397). Lyme Regis: Russell House.

Young, L. J. (2002). The neurobiology of social recognition, approach and avoidance. *Biological Psychiatry. 51:* 18–26.

Zakireh, B., Ronis, S. T., & Knight, R. A. (2008). Individual beliefs, attitudes and victimization histories of male juvenile sex offenders. *Sexual Abuse: A Journal of Research and Treatment, 20:* 323–351.

Zeanah, C. H. E. (1993). *Handbook of Infant Mental Health.* New York: Guilford Press.

Zgourides, G., Monto, M., & Harris, R. (1997). Correlates of adolescent male sexual offense: Prior adult sexual contact, sexual attitudes, and use of sexually explicit materials. *International Journal of Offender Therapy and Comparative Criminology, 41*(3): 272–283.

INDEX

Aalto, S., 76, 196
Abel, G. G., 5, 177
Able, G., 4, 179
Ablon, J. S., 158, 169, 200
Abracen, J., 14, 36–37, 177, 210
Abraham, A., 75, 193
Abrahamsen, D., 60, 177
abuse
  alcohol, 10, 13–14, 37, 44, 47, 64, 100,
    143–144
  drug, 10, 13–14, 44, 46, 64, 86, 100,
    143–144
  physical, 11, 14–15, 37, 89
  sexual, 5–7, 10–11, 15–16, 38, 40, 50,
    64, 88–89, 114, 143, 147, 151, 175
  substance, 6, 14, 44, 50, 120, 125
Ackland, M. A., 13, 204
Acklin, M. W., 130, 202
Adshead, G., 138, 202
aggression, xi–xii, xvi, 13–14, 25, 31, 33,
  35, 40, 44, 47, 54–55, 57, 59, 63–64,
  66, 68–69, 83, 85, 87, 96, 99–100,
  104–106, 111, 113, 116, 120, 129,
  145–146, 149–150, 164–165 *see also*:
  narcissism
  sexual, 10, 34, 78, 89, 143
Aichorn, A., 55, 177
Ainsworth, M. D. S., xxiv, 21, 23–24,
  177
Akhtar, S., 53–54, 178
Aljazireh, L., 11–12, 14, 41, 178
Allen, J. C., 159, 178
Alving, J., 76, 197
American Psychological Association,
  134–135, 137
Amos, N., 49, 178–179
amygdala, 46, 74, 77, 79–80, 152, 161
Anderson, D., 14, 93, 111, 177, 202
Anderson, I. M., 83, 88, 185–186
Anderson, S. J., 13, 15, 192
Anderson, V. N., 4, 178
Andreou, C., 16, 113, 194, 209
Andrews, D. A., 4, 125, 194, 209
Ansari, M. S., 85, 182

Antonowicz, D. H., 5, 210–211
anxiety, xvii, xxii–xxiii, 6, 11, 27–29, 34,
  37, 44, 46, 49, 59, 61–62, 83–84, 111,
  142, 145–146, 154
Archer, R. P., 127–129, 178, 182
Arkowitz, H., 158, 178
Aromaeki, A. S., 47, 178
Aronen, H. J., 46, 199
Arrigo, B. A., 45, 178
Ascione, F. R., 4, 10, 191
Ashkar, P. J., 11, 178
Asmussen, K., 6, 178
Atkinson, L., 11, 110, 178
attachment
  adult, 22, 26–29, 31–32, 34, 36–39, 89,
    113, 117, 143, 155, 161, 183
  behaviour, xxiv, xxviii, 25, 32, 75, 79,
    81, 110
  capacity for, xix, xxix, 7–8, 11, 14, 31,
    36–37, 41, 43, 59, 70, 94–96, 98,
    101–102, 107–111, 116–118, 123,
    126, 133, 138, 143, 155, 157–158,
    162, 172–175
  figure(s), xvii, 22, 32, 153, 160, 162
  hunger, xxviii, 34–35, 38–39, 114, 149,
    161, 167
  insecure, xxiv–xxv, xxviii, 14, 30,
    32–33, 37–38, 74, 81, 87–89, 110,
    114
  needs, xxix, 17, 36, 39–40, 113
  patterns, 30–32, 36, 38, 88, 114
  relationship(s), xxi, 26, 59, 162
  secure, xxiv, xxvii, 21, 23–24, 27,
    29–32, 34, 38–40, 78, 82, 89, 154,
    171–172, 175
  theory, xxiv–xxvi, xxviii, 23–24, 29,
    32, 37, 48, 58, 75, 88, 120, 132,
    158, 159–160, 174–175
Auerbach, J. S., xxv, 181
Auslander, B. A., 49, 178
Awad, G. A., 7, 10–12, 16, 178, 208

Bachar, K. J., 5–6, 207
Bagley, C., 15, 178

Bailey, S., 4–5, 9–10, 12–13, 112, 185
Bakermans-Kranenburg, M. J., 78, 211
Baldwin, R. M., 85, 182
Baram, T. Z., 74, 198
Barbaree, H. E., 3, 49–50, 178–179, 208
Barber, J. B., 169, 190
Bargh, J. A., 77, 179
Barnard, G. W., 16, 37, 210
Barnett, D., 24, 183
Bartels, A., 86, 179
Bartholomew, K., 21, 26, 29, 113, 179
Bartol, C. R., 49, 179
Bateman, A. W., 58, 160, 179, 188
Batgos, J., 31, 179
Beck, S., 130, 179
Becker, J. V., 3–5, 7, 10–12, 15, 112, 115–117, 120, 177, 179–180, 196, 198
Beech, A. R., 81, 83, 180
behaviour *see also*: attachment
    antisocial, 4, 7, 12–14, 44, 48, 54, 56, 84, 89, 103, 144
    sexual, xvii, xxiv, xxviii, 4, 13, 31–32, 35, 45, 67, 70–71, 73–76, 79, 81–86, 88–90, 94, 150–151, 155, 172–173
    violent, xvii, xxvi, 32, 44, 49, 59, 83, 85, 120, 144
Belanger, N., 5, 180
Belcher, P., 13, 180
Belsky, J., 110, 180
Bengis, S. M., 12, 180
Benning, S. D., 85, 182
Benoit, J. L., 14, 180
Ben-Porath, Y. S., 100, 103, 128–130, 180, 182, 203
Bentovim, A., 16, 209
Bera, W. H., 4, 113, 117, 120, 204
Berg, J. L., 60, 102, 190
Bergeron, T., 12, 211
Bergman, A., 57, 201
Berman, W. H., 14, 22, 29, 31, 58, 110, 210
Berner, W., 87, 180
Bernstein, A., 46, 180
Berry, D., 136, 194
Bertelsen, C., 76, 197
Bertin, C., xxi, xiv
Bhate, S. R., 14, 206
Bijleveld, C., 10–11, 115, 211
Bion, W. R., 56, 61, 180

Birket-Smith, M., 45, 49, 203
Birt, A., 51, 112, 116, 206
Birtles, E. F., 154, 187
Blackburn, R., 49, 180
Blair, R. J. R., 46, 83, 180
Blaszczynski, A., 4, 6–7, 9–11, 115, 196
Blatt, S. J., xxi, xxv, 21, 26, 173, 181, 185
Blehar, M. C., xxiv, 21, 23–24, 177
Blennow, K., 83, 210
Blokland, A. A. J., 11, 13, 211
Blos, P., 63, 112, 153, 181
Boer, D. P., 51, 112, 116, 206
Bohning, D. E., 80, 200
Bonsall, R., 75, 193
Borduin, C. M., 158, 193
Boris, N. W., 31, 181
Bornstein, R., 136, 194
Boucher, R. J., 15–16, 208
Bowden, B., 17, 210
Bowlby, J., xxiv, 21–24, 30, 32, 43, 58, 111–112, 173, 181
Bradford, J. M. W., 83, 181
Bradford, M. B., 50, 188
Braff, D., 132, 205
Brannon, J. M., 5, 181
Braun, K., 75, 193
Braunwald, K., 24, 183
Bredy, T. W., 75, 193
Brewer, J., 6, 197
Bridges, M. R., 37, 114, 133, 149, 181, 190
Brink, J., 46, 197
Britton, R., xxiii, 35, 60, 62, 181
Brodsky, A., 32, 194
Brodsky, S. L., 14, 182
Brooks, D., 76, 197
Brown, S. L., 49, 182
Brownstone, G., 87, 180
Brunell-Neuleib, S., 136, 194
Buckholtz, J. W., 85, 182
Bukar, S. L., 6, 204
Bullens, R., 9–11, 115, 211
Burgess, A. W., 15, 182
Burk, L. R., 36, 182
Burket, R. C., 44, 204
Burkhart, B. R., 36, 182
Burns, B., 99, 132, 182
Burton, D. L., 4–5, 9–10, 14, 16, 182
Busconi, A., 5, 191
Bussière, M. T., 12, 49–50, 116, 192
Butcher, J. N., 128–129, 182

Butler, A., 10, 197
Butts, J. A., 5, 182

Caldji, C., 74, 200
Calhoun, K. S., 6, 183
Campbell, D., 61, 66, 170, 182
Candib, L. M., 6, 185
Capote, T., 56, 182
Caputo, A. A., 14, 182
Carbonell, J. L., 158, 206
care-giver(s), xxiv, 22–26, 30, 57, 119,
     160, 162–163, 166, 171
Carlozzi, A. F., 12, 110, 200
Carlson, E., 31, 110, 182
Carlson, V., 24, 183
Carolyn, L., 129, 213
Carpenter, D. R., 11, 115, 183
Carter, C. S., 76, 80, 183
Carvalho, E., 31, 187
Carvalho, M., 31, 187
case studies/vignettes
     Aaron, 143–147, 150–152
     Mario, 63–66
     Paulie, 147–152
Cassidy, J., 22, 26, 34, 183, 201
Cepeda-Benito, A., 6, 185
Cervoni, N., 74, 212
Chalhoub, M., 13, 194
Chambers, A., 46, 85, 206
Chambers, H. J., 13, 195
Chambers, J. A., 158, 186
Champagne, F. A., 74, 212
Chandler, M., 46, 183
Chaouloff, F., 82–83, 183
Chaplin, R., 5, 188
Chappell, D., 62, 197
Chasseguet-Smirgel, J., 68, 183
Chen, K.-H., 85, 205
child molester(s), 5, 12–17, 37–39, 50,
     67, 71, 93–95, 98, 101–106, 108,
     112–114, 116, 118, 173
Chorn, R., 112, 183
Christian, R. E., 17, 44, 183
Christodoulou, N., 47, 87, 190
Cicchetti, D., 24, 31, 183–184
Cierpka, M., 160, 191
Clark, T. F., 5, 185
Claussen, A. H., 39, 184
Cleckly, H., 43, 45, 137, 183
Clum, G. A., 6, 183
Coatsworth, J. D., 17, 210

Cohan, R., 13, 183
Cohen, M. A., 6, 203
Cohn, D. A., 32, 184
Collins, N. L., 32, 183
comprehensive system (CS), 97, 130,
     134–135
Comrey, A. L., 102, 184
conduct disorder (CD), 12, 48, 59, 65, 96,
     101, 106, 108, 110, 112, 115, 120, 128,
     133–134, 144–146, 154
containment, xi, xvii, xxi, 33–34, 40,
     57–58, 60–64, 66, 142, 146, 151, 162
Cooke, D. J., 48–49, 184, 201
Cooper, C. L., 6–7, 16, 184
co-operative response (COP), 99, 106,
     145
Cortoni, F. A., 11, 36, 50, 93, 111, 120,
     184, 202
Cowan, C., 32, 184
Cowan, P. A., 32, 184
Cowan, R. L., 85, 182
Craik, K., xxiv, 184
Cripps, E., 93, 111, 202
Crittenden, P. M., 8, 12, 31, 35–36,
     38–40, 75, 78, 111, 114, 184
Cruise, K. R., 49, 186
Csersevits, M., 13, 106, 184
Cuffman, E., 49, 186
Culp, A. M., 14, 194
Cummings, E. M., 31, 184
Cummings, J. L., 80, 203
Cunningham, P. B., 158, 193
Cunningham-Rathner, J., 12, 15, 115,
     179–180
Curley, J. P., 81, 197
Curry, S., 50, 188
Curwen, T., 125, 213
Cuthbert, B. N., 47, 205

D'Alessio, A. C., 74, 212
Dadds, M. R., 32, 36, 38, 209
Daleiden, E. L., 10, 184–185
Dallam, S. J., 6, 185
Dalton, J. E., 11, 185
Davis, G. E., 3–4, 10–11, 185
Davis, R. D., 45, 49, 203
De Masi, F., 62, 68–71, 112–113, 185
Deakin, J. F. W., 83, 185
deGruy, F. V., 6, 185
Deisher, R. W., 5, 11–12, 14, 16, 185, 187,
     209

Del Carmen, R., 31, 185
delinquency, xiii, xvi, 12–13, 45, 48,
    100–101, 103, 128, 136, 145
deMause, L., xi, xiv
depression, xxii–xxiii, 6, 31, 46, 76, 80,
    100–101, 103, 115, 128, 132, 148–149
DeVille, C., 13, 194
DeWitt, J., 124–125, 186
Dexter-Mazza, E. T., 149, 189
Diamond, D., xxi, 21, 26, 173, 185
Dickinson, L. M., 6, 185
Dickinson, W. P., 6, 185
Diorio, J., 74, 200
Dishotsky, N. I., 10, 13, 211
Doidge, N., xxvii, 76, 160, 185
Dolan, M., 4–5, 9–10, 12–13, 112, 185
Dolan, M. C., 49, 82–83, 88, 185–186
Doreleijers, T., 9–11, 115, 211
Doren, D. M., 45, 186
Dorr, D., 49, 186
Doty, A, K., 10, 13, 211
Dow, M. G., 158, 186
Doyle, M., 49, 185
Draper, P., 110, 180
Drugge, J., 51, 112, 116, 206
du Vigneaud, V., 81, 186
Dubno, J. R., 80, 200
Duits, N., 11, 13, 211
Durham, R. C., 158, 186
Dutton, D. G., 6, 186
Dwyer, S. M., 11, 203–204
Dymov, S., 74, 212
Dziuba-Leatherman, J., 15, 187

Earls, C., 5, 180
Eastman, B., 11, 115, 183
Eberhart-Wright, A., 14, 194
Edens, J. F., 49, 186
Edman, G., 81, 209
Egeland, B., 30–31, 186, 210
ego, xx–xxii, 54–55, 69, 132, 168
    -centric, 44, 59, 145, 150
Elicker, J., 31, 186
Ellis, C. D., 6, 186
Ellis, G. T., 12, 110, 200
Enfield, C., 24, 175, 186, 197
Enfield, S., 175, 197
Englund, M., 31, 186
epigenetic(s), xxv, xxvii–xxviii, 30, 48,
    73–75, 78, 89–90, 119, 172
Epperson, D. L., 124–125, 186

Epps, K., 10–11, 186
Erdberg, P., 145, 149, 187
Ericksen, S. L., 4, 10, 191
Erickson, M. F., 78, 193
Erikson, E. H., 153, 186
Eriksson, C. J. P., 47, 178
Eriksson, E., 47, 210
Eronen, M., 46, 199
Etherington, R., 15, 187
Exner, J. E., 97, 130–131, 134, 145, 149,
    187

Fairbairn, W. R. D., xx–xxi, 154, 187
Fairweather, D., 51, 112, 116, 206
fake scale (F), 102, 128
fantasy, 13, 34, 60, 62, 86, 147–148, 150,
    152, 154–155, 164–165, 169
    masturbation, 40, 86, 94, 148, 151
    sexual, 11, 40–41, 68, 113, 115, 120,
        147, 151–152, 154
Farrington, D. P., 48, 187
Federn, E., xii, xiv
Feeney, J., 32, 187
Fehrenbach, P. A., 5, 11–12, 14, 16, 185,
    187
Felthous, A. R., 44–45, 187
Ferguson, M. L., 77, 179
Ferreira, V., 31, 187
Ferro, A., 53, 187
Figuerado, A. J., 5–7, 10, 16, 195, 198
Finkelhor, D., 5, 15, 187
Firestone, P., 50, 188
Fisher, D. A., 6, 203
Flatley, J., 5, 188
Fletcher, K. E., 6, 197
Fonagy, P., 15, 21, 24, 30, 32–33, 36, 40,
    58–59, 65, 110–111, 117–118, 138,
    151, 153, 158–160, 162–165, 173,
    178–179, 188–189
Fontaine, J., 5–6, 207
Ford, M. A., 7, 11, 13, 189
Forehand, R., 116, 196
Forsman, A., 83, 210
Forster, B. B., 46, 197
Forth, A. E., 49–50, 139, 182, 184, 189,
    192
Fowers, D., 124–125, 186
France, K. G., 38, 212
Francis, D., 74, 200
Frazer, D. R., 17, 44, 183
Freedman, A., 74, 200

Freeman, K. A., 149, 189
Freidrich, W., 15, 189
Freud, A., 55, 189
Freud, S., xii–xiii, xx–xxii, 21, 23, 55, 68, 189
Frick, P. J., 14, 17, 44, 182–183
Frith, C. D., 77, 161, 189–190
Fromm, E., 53, 189
Fryer, G. E., 3, 6, 10, 15, 94, 114, 207
Furr, K., 46, 49, 189

Gacono, C. B., 8, 11–12, 37–38, 47, 49, 57, 59–60, 98, 102, 106, 114, 116–117, 130, 133–134, 145, 149, 181, 190, 206, 209
Gal, M., 17, 36, 190
Gallagher, H. L., 161, 190
Galton, F., 73, 190
Ganellen, R. J., 135–136, 190
Gannon, L., 46, 201
Garb, H. N., 134–135, 213
Garcia, N., 81, 207
Garven, S., 136, 213
Gaskin-Lanlyan, N. D., 5–6, 207
George, C., 26, 190
George, M. S., 80, 200
Gerber, A. J., 32, 117, 169, 188, 190
Gergely, G., 33, 40, 151, 153, 162–164, 188
Geris, A. S., 93, 120, 202
Gill, M., 130, 206
Gillespie, W. H., 68, 190
Giotakos, O., 47, 87, 190
Glaser, D., 6, 190
Glasser, M., xiii, xvii, 190
Gleaves, D. H., 6, 185
Glover, E., xiii, xvii, 191
Goldberg, S., 14, 191
Goodrow, K. K., 7–8, 40, 191
Gordon, S., 81, 186
Gore, K. S., 124–125, 186
Gotowiec, A., 14, 191
Gottfredson, S. D., 125, 191
Graham, F., 14, 206
Graham, J. R., 100, 103, 128–129, 180, 182, 191
Graham, Y. P., 75, 193
Grann, M., 5, 199
Grant, C. A., 15, 182
Graves, R. B., 4, 10, 191
Gray, A., 5, 191

Gray, J. A., 84–85, 205
Greenberg, D. M., 50, 188
Greenberg, M. T., 31, 191
Gregory, K. D., 7, 191
Gretton, H., 44, 191
Grimes, R. D., 119, 138, 174, 208
Gross, F. L., 153, 191
Gross, S., 160, 191
Grossman, K. E., 31, 191
Groth, A. N., 4–5, 11–12, 191–192
Groth, N. A., 11, 192
Grotstein, J., 57, 192
Gumley, A. L., 158, 186
Gunnar, M., 78, 193
Gynther, M. D., 4, 12, 115, 117, 193

Haapasalo, J., 15, 192
Hagan, M. P., 5, 192
Hakola, P., 46, 199
Hall, C. N., 100, 103, 180
Hamner, M. B., 80, 200
Hann, D. M., 14, 194
Hanson, R. K., 12, 49–50, 116, 192
Hare, R. D., 13, 43–47, 49, 101, 118, 136–137, 139, 174, 184, 189, 191–192, 197, 213
Hare Psychopathy Checklist (Revised) (PCL(-R)), 44–45, 47, 49–50, 54, 58–59, 65, 83, 88, 95–97, 101, 105, 107–108, 126–127, 133, 136–137, 139, 144–145, 149–150
Harkink, J., 11, 13, 211
Harkness, A. R., 129–130, 203
Harlow, H. F., 32, 204
Harris, A. J. R., 50, 192
Harris, C., 3, 179
Harris, E. H., 44, 204
Harris, G. T., 50, 112, 116, 192
Harris, R., 10, 214
Hart, S. D., 6, 49, 186, 189
Harte, J. M., 130, 193
Hart-Kerkoffs, L., 9, 211
Hartman, C. R., 15, 182
Hartmann, U., 84–85, 198
Hastings, T., 13, 15, 192
Hathaway, S. R., 128, 193, 203
Hay, D., 110, 120, 128, 200
Hayes, S., 7–9, 196
Haynes, M. R., 6–7, 15–16, 184, 204
Hazan, C., 32, 193
Heaven, T. R., 102, 190

Heim, C., 75–76, 80, 193
Heit, S., 75, 193
Heller, S. S., 31, 181
Helmeke, C., 75, 193
Hemphill, P., 13, 15, 192
Henggeler, S. W., 158, 193
Hent, J. P. M., 130, 193
Herkov, M. J., 4, 12, 115, 117, 193
Herpetz, S. C., 46, 193
Herrmann, D. J., 4, 178
Hertsgaard, L., 78, 193
Hertz, M., 130, 194
Hervé, H., 44–45, 49, 51, 112, 116, 194, 206
Hess, E., 21, 23–24, 201
Hietala, J., 76, 196
Higgitt, A., 138, 160, 188
Hill, N. L., 17, 44, 183
Hillenbrand, E., 160, 191
Hiller, J., 136, 194
Hilliker, D. R., 10, 184–185
Hilton, M. R., 4, 194
Hindy, C. G., 32, 194
Hinshelwood, R., xvi, 194
Hirschamn, R. D., 100, 103, 180
Hirvonen, J., 76, 196
Hodges, J., 16, 113, 194, 209
Hodkinson, S., 7, 93, 202
Hoffman, K. C., 149, 189
Hoge, R. D., 4, 17, 36, 125, 190, 194, 209
Holloway, J., 4–5, 9–10, 12–13, 112, 185
Holmes, J., 24, 43, 194
Holt, S. E., 44, 194
Hooke, M. T., 62, 197
hormone(s), xxviii, 6, 32, 47–48, 74, 76, 78–79, 81–85, 87–89, 153
Horowitz, H. A., 32, 207
Horowitz, L. M., 26, 179
Horwitz, A. R., 80, 200
Houchens, P., 5, 191
Howard, M., 62, 197
Howard, N. G., 107, 135, 200
Hsu, L. K. G., 10, 194
Huang, J.-M., 85, 205
Hubbs-Tait, L., 14, 194
Hudson, S. M., 3, 7–8, 10, 36–38, 93, 111, 117, 119, 178, 194, 202, 206, 208, 212
Huffman, L., 31, 185
Hughes, K. P., 14, 194
Hughes, S. A., 13, 194

Hull, E. M., 82–84, 195, 200
human content (H), 97–99, 106, 112, 126, 131, 145
human experience variable (HEV), 95–98, 102, 106, 108, 127, 131–133, 145
Hunter, J. A., 5–6, 15–16, 195
Hutchinson, D., 16, 37, 210
Hyatt-Williams, A., 56, 60–61, 138, 162, 195

Imhof, E. A., 127, 178
Insel, T. R., 81–83, 195, 213
intervention(s)
   early, 8, 118, 120, 174–175
   intensive, xxvii, 168–169
   psychoanalytic, 138, 155, 168
   psychodynamic, 158–159
   psychological, xvi, xxix, 90, 157
   psychotherapeutic, xxvii, 76, 90, 119, 158
Iwasa, K., 133, 195

Jacobs, W. R., 13, 195
Jay, V., 78, 195
Jenkins, S., 175, 195
Jensen, P., 44, 198
John, O. P., 81, 207
Johnson, G. M., 13, 195
Jones, E., 169, 199
Jonson-Reid, M., 14, 195
Jurist, E. L., 33, 40, 151, 153, 162–164, 188

Kachele, H., 158, 188
Kaemer, B., 128–129, 182
Kahn, T. J., 10, 13, 195
Kahr, B., xi, xiv
Kalander, J., 76, 196
Kankkonen, M., 15, 192
Kaplan, M. S., 11–12, 15, 112, 115–117, 179–180, 196
Kaplan, N., 22, 26, 190, 201
Karlsson, H., 76, 196
Karnolz-Langdon, H., 79, 196
Katsoyannis, P. G., 81, 186
Katz, R. C., 11, 15, 196
Kaufman, K. L., 10, 184–185
Kaufman, L., 12, 59, 209
Kavoussi, R. J., 11–12, 15, 112, 115–117, 180, 196

Kear-Colwell, J., 8, 36, 38, 117–118, 196, 208
Keenan, K., 14, 208
Keenan, T., 111, 212
Kelly, T. P., 14, 206
Keltner, D., 81, 207
Kempton, T., 116, 196
Kennedy, R., 30, 32, 117, 188–189
Kennedy, W. A., 13–14, 180, 195
Kenny, D. T., 4, 6–13, 15, 17, 40–41, 110, 112, 115–116, 120, 158, 178, 196
Keogh, T., 4, 6–15, 17, 40–41, 48, 58, 60, 62, 110, 112, 115–116, 120, 144, 175, 196–197
Kernberg, O. F., 33, 54, 56, 60, 62–63, 65, 197
Kershaw, C., 5, 188
Kessler, R. C., 6, 204
Kessler, R. M., 85, 182
Keverne, E. B., 81, 197
Kiehl, K. A., 46, 197
Kimerly, R., 6, 183
King, J. A., 6, 197
King, R. P., 5, 192
King, S., 6, 197
Kjaer, T. W., 76, 197
Klein, M., xii, xiv, xxi–xxiii, 55–56, 68, 197–198
Klim, S., 17, 210
Knet, P., 169, 198
Knight, R. A., 4, 10, 13–16, 195, 198, 214
Knop, J., 44, 198
Kobak, R., 34, 183
Kobayashi, J., 7, 10, 198
Kohut, H., 68, 198
Koivisto, E., 46, 199
Korosi, A., 74, 198
Koscis, J. H., 169, 190
Kosson, D. S., 139, 189
Kourt, M., 175, 197
Kraemer, H. C., 6, 185
Krafft-Ebing, R., 67, 198
Krauth, A. A., 10, 12, 198
Kreutzer, T., 30, 210
Kroger, J., 35, 198
Kroll, L., 4–5, 9–10, 12–13, 112, 185
Kruger, T. H. C., 84–85, 198
Krugman, R. D., 3, 6, 10, 15, 94, 114, 207
Kumari, V., 76, 198
Kumka, G., 44, 191

Laakso, M. P., 46, 199
Laaksonen, M. A., 169, 198
Lafond, M. A., 10, 195
Lakey, J. F., 3, 11, 112, 116, 120, 199
Lalumière, M. L., 3–4, 9, 11–12, 17, 72, 109, 115, 208
Lamb, W., 169, 199
Lamont, A., 5, 199
Lane, S., 4–5, 11, 207
Lang, P. J., 47, 205
Lang, R., 13, 128, 199
Langevin, R., 13, 37, 128, 199
Långström, N., 5, 49, 199
Lanyado, M., 113, 194
Larose, M., 50, 188
Layando, M., 16, 209
Leadbeater, B. J., 31, 179
LeGrand, S., 15, 211
Leguizamo, A., 8, 10, 13, 16, 120, 199
Leibing, E., 158, 199
Leichsenring, F., 158, 169, 199
Leigh, T., 30, 32, 117, 188–189
Leitenberg, H., 3–4, 10–11, 185
Leon, A. C., 169, 190
Leschied, A. W., 4, 209
Leversee, F., 4–5, 11, 207
Levinson, A., 30, 189
Levy, D. M., 55, 200
Levy, K. N., xxv, 181
Levy, R. A., 158, 169, 200
Lewis, D. O., 11, 200
Li, R., 85, 182
Lichtenberg, J. D., 21, 173, 185
Liddle, P. F., 46, 197
Lilienfeld, S. O., 107, 134–135, 158, 178, 200, 213
Lim, M. G., 7–8, 40, 191
Lindblad, F., 49, 199
Lindfors, O., 169, 198
Lindman, R. E., 47, 178
Lindsey, R. E., 12, 110, 200
Linney, J. A., 7, 11, 13, 189
Liu, D., 74, 200
Loeber, R., 9, 110, 120, 128, 200, 211
Longo, R. E., 15, 200
Looman, J., 14, 177
Lorberbaum, J. P., 80, 200
Loredo, C., 11, 191
Lorenz, K. Z., 23, 200
Lorrain, D., 83–84, 200
Losada-Paisey, G., 13, 200

Lotke, E., 6, 200
Lou, H. C., 76, 197
Lovelace, L., 46, 201
Loving, J. L. J., 8, 59, 101, 133, 201
Lueke, W., 15, 189
Luh, K. E., 46, 180
Luyten, P., 111, 163, 165, 188
Lydiard, R. B., 80, 200
Lyons-Ruth, K., 14, 23, 31, 120, 201

Macdonald, R. R., 158, 186
MacLean, P. D., 79, 201
Magagna, J., 63, 201
Mahler, M., 57, 201
Mailoux, D. L., 49–50, 208
Main, M., 21–24, 26, 190, 201
Major, K. A., 158, 186
Malcolm, P. B., 49–50, 208
Malloy, P., 80, 203
Mandansky, D., 6, 197
Manocha, K. F., 10, 201
Markianos, M., 47, 87, 190
Markkula, J., 76, 196
Marsh, A., 133, 201
Marshall, L. A., 48, 201
Marshall, W. L., 7–8, 10–11, 32, 36–38,
    50, 93, 110–111, 117, 120, 184, 202,
    208, 212
Masterson, J. F., 165, 202
Mattlar, C. E., 134, 202
Mattoon, G., 32, 117, 188
Matuszewich, L., 83–84, 200
Maurish, M., 127, 178
Mayer, J. B., 13, 195
McArthur, M., 46, 85, 206
McBride, M., 44, 191
McCormack, A., 15, 182
McCoy, M. E., 50, 202
McDougall, A., 132, 205
McDougall, J., 68, 70–71, 141–142, 151,
    202
McDowell, C. J., 130, 202
McEntee, B. K., 129, 202
McFarlane, K., 10, 197
McGauley, G., 138, 202
McKinley, J. C., 128, 203
McMillan, D., 16, 209
McNulty, J. L., 129–130, 203
McWilliams, N., 58, 62, 119, 162, 203
Meany, J. M., 74, 200
Meany, M. J., 6, 74–75, 78, 82, 203, 212

Meck, W. H., 84, 203
Mega, M. S., 80, 203
Meloy, J. R., 8, 37–38, 44, 47, 49, 57,
    59–60, 98, 102, 106, 116–117, 130,
    134, 145, 149, 190, 194
Meloy, R., 44, 47, 54–57, 59–60, 62, 65,
    102, 133, 138, 142, 149–150, 164,
    203
Meltzer, D., 68, 71, 173, 203
Mendrek, A., 46, 197
mentalization, 30, 40, 59, 65–66, 142,
    155, 159–166, 174
mentalization based therapy (MBT),
    xxvii, xxix, 118, 138, 155, 157,
    159–162, 165–168, 174
Metzner, J., 3, 6, 10, 15, 94, 114, 207
Meyer, G. J., 135, 203
Mezey, G. C., 4, 10, 194, 201
Mikulincer, M., 34, 203
Miller, A. H., 75–76, 80, 193
Miller, D. L., 4–5, 9–10, 14, 16, 182
Miller, T. A., 6, 203
Millon, T., 45, 49, 203
Milloy, C. D., 17, 208
Milrod, B. L., 169, 190
Miner, M. H., 11, 13, 203–204
Minnesota Multiphasic Personality
    Inventory for Adolescents
    (MMPI-A), 95, 97, 99–100, 105–106,
    108, 127–129, 133, 144, 148–150
Minzenberg, M. J., 47, 204
Mirsch, P., 4, 11, 211
Mitchell, I. J., 81, 83, 180
Mittleman, M. S., 5, 177
Miyoshi, T. J., 3, 6, 10, 15, 94, 114, 207
Moellenhoff, F., xii, xiv
Molnar, B., 6, 204
Monachesi, E. D., 128, 193
Monaco, L., 49, 204
Monahan, J., 138, 209
Monastersky, C., 11–12, 14, 16, 187,
    209
Monck, E., 4, 11, 211
Monto, M., 10, 214
Moon, D., 5, 188
Moran, T., 46, 183
Moriarty, L. J., 125, 191
Mortensen, E., 44, 198
Moss, E., 14, 204
Mulvey, E. P., 138, 209
Murphy, S., xviii, 3, 204

Murphy, W. D., 6–7, 15–16, 184, 204
Murray, J., 10, 197
Muschamp, J. W., 82, 195
Myers, W. C., 4, 12, 44, 49, 115, 117, 193, 204

Nachmias, M., 78, 193
Någren, K., 76, 196
narcissism, 35–36, 49, 53–57, 59–62, 66, 69, 71–72, 106, 144–145, 151
  aggressive, 54–55, 145
  malignant, xvii, xxiii, xxvi, xxviii, 35, 40, 53–54, 56–60, 62, 66, 69, 71–72, 116–117, 165–166, 173
  personality disorder, 54, 60
neglect, 11, 14–16, 26, 48, 65, 142, 146
Nemeroff, C. B., 75–76, 80, 193
Ness, C. M., 12, 204
neurotransmitter(s), xxviii, 32, 78, 81–84, 86, 88
  dopamine, 47, 76, 82–86, 88–90, 151
  dysfunction, 47, 76
  serotonin, 47, 76, 82–86, 88–89
New, M., 16, 209
Newman, G., 16, 37, 210
Newman, J. D., 80, 200
Newman, J. P., 46–47, 180, 204, 211
Newport, D. J., 75–76, 80, 193
Nezworski, M. T., 134–136, 213
Noller, P., 32, 187
Novak, M. A., 32, 204
Nunberg, H., xii, xiv

object, xvii, xxi–xxiii, 33, 40, 54–55, 57, 62–63, 66–67, 71, 86, 114, 142, 146–147, 150, 152–153, 164
  relations, xvii, xix–xxvi, xxviii–xxix, 23, 27, 32–33, 54–56, 60–61, 63, 69, 71–72, 110, 112–114, 117–118, 120, 132, 145, 149–150, 154–155, 157, 164–165, 167, 173
  self-, 56–58, 60–61, 63–65, 70–71, 142, 150, 163–164
O'Brien, M., 4, 113, 117, 120, 204
O'Callaghan, D., 11, 205
Ogawa, T., 133, 195
Ogden, T., xx, xxii, 34, 67, 205
Olweus, D., 44, 48, 205
O'Neil, J. N., 10, 184–185
Openshaw, D. K., 4, 10, 191
O'Shaughnessy, R., 44, 191

Osofsky, J. D., 14, 194
Owens, E. B., 14, 208

paedophiles/paedophilia, 15–16, 37–38, 40, 67, 70–71, 83, 86–87, 90, 114, 119, 143, 147, 154, 165, 167, 174–175
Page, I. J., 15–16, 204
Pai, C.-Y., 85, 205
Paitich, D., 37, 199
Pape, E., 32, 184
Paperny, D. M., 5, 185
paranoid, 44, 54, 65, 103, 108, 116, 166
Parekh, A., 112, 183
Parent, S., 14, 204
Parkes, C., 30, 205
Patrick, C. J., 47, 205
Patros, R. L., 5, 192
Pearson, D., 74, 200
Pearson, J. L., 32, 184
Peed, S. F., 11, 115, 183
Penglase, J., 10, 197
Peralta, P., 31, 187
Perkins, P., 169, 190
Perry, W., 131–132, 205
personality disorder, xviii, 43–44, 169
  see also: narcissism
  antisocial, 48, 120, 146
  borderline (BPD), 6, 160–161, 165–166
phantasy, xxi, xxiv–xxv, 23, 70, 126, 166, 169, 172
Piaget, J., 23, 205
Piccini, P., 76, 197
Pickering, A. D., 84–85, 205
Pincus, J. H., 11, 200
Pine, F., 57, 201
Pinel, P., 40, 205
Piotrowski, C., 127, 178
Piotrowski, Z., 130, 205
Pithers, W. D., 5, 191
Plotsky, P. M., 74, 200
Poeck, K., 80, 205
Poeggel, G., 75, 193
Poe-Yamagata, E., 3, 5, 209
Polaschek, D. L. L., 119, 206
Ponder, J. I., 49, 206
Porges, S. W., 78, 206
Porter, S., 51, 112, 116, 206
Portman Clinic, 55, 60, 170
Power, K. G., 158, 186

Prentky, R. A., 4, 14–16, 124, 198, 206, 208
Preston, D., 49, 178–179
Price, C., 5–6, 207
Pridmore, S., 46, 85, 206
Print, B., 11, 205
psychopathology five scales (PSY-5), 95–96, 100, 103–106, 108, 127, 129, 145, 149
psychopathy
    level of, xix, 7, 50, 94, 102, 107, 110, 117–118, 157–158, 173
    score(s), 54, 101, 105–107, 116, 129

Quilty, S., 10, 197
Quinn, K. M., 3, 206

Rabung, S., 158, 169, 199
Ralston, C. A., 124–125, 186
Rapaport, D., 130, 206
rape/rapist, 4–5, 12–16, 35, 37–39, 50, 67–68, 70–71, 87, 93, 101, 111–114, 116–117, 119, 143–144, 173–174
Rasi-Hakala, H., 76, 196
Read, S. J., 32, 183
recidivism, xxvi–xxvii, 5, 41, 45–46, 48–51, 93, 98, 115, 118
    sexual, 40, 49–51, 88, 110, 112, 116–117
reflection response, 106, 135, 145, 150
regulation see also: self
    affect, 80, 101, 138, 160, 174
    emotional, 74, 103, 118
Reich, W., 55, 206
Reid, W. H., 11, 206
Reitzel, L. R., 158, 206
Repo, E., 46, 199
Ressler, C., 81, 186
Rice, M. E., 50, 112, 116, 192
Rich, P., 124, 206
Richards, L., 15, 211
Richardson, G., 14, 206
Righthand, S., 124, 206
Rilke, R. M., 109, 206
Riolo, J., 83–84, 200
Riviere, J., 141, 206–207
Robbins, L., 16, 37, 210
Roberts, C. W., 81, 186
Robertson, P. J., 10, 208
Rodrigues, S. M., 81, 207
Romboletti, R., 13, 194

Ronis, S. T., 10, 14–16, 214
Roose, S. P., 169, 190
Rorschach, H., xxv, 49, 59, 95–97, 99, 102, 105–108, 112, 123, 127, 130–136, 144–145, 149–150, 207
Rosen, L. N., 5–6, 207
Rosenfeld, H. A., 54, 56, 60, 62, 68, 207
Rosenstein, D. S., 32, 207
Rosenthal, R., 136, 194
Roth, A., 138, 160, 188
Rothbard, J. C., 30, 207
Rousseau, D., 14, 204
Rowe, W. E., 17, 208
Rowland, M. D., 158, 193
Russell, W. F., 8, 59, 101, 133, 201
Russon, A. E., 37, 199
Ruszczynski, S., 34, 44, 59, 65, 207
Ryan, G., 3–6, 10–11, 14–15, 94, 114, 207

Saas, H., 46, 193
sadism, xi–xii, 35, 44, 54, 56, 58, 62–64, 67, 69–71, 86–87, 112, 139, 143
sadomasochism, 57, 62, 68–71, 112
Saintong, J., 14, 204
Salainen, L., 46, 199
Salekin, R. T., 119, 138, 174, 208
Sales, B. D., 3, 7, 10, 179, 198
Salloway, S., 80, 203
Salminen, J. K., 76, 196
Santos, R., 31, 187
Sarkar, S. P., 138, 202
Saslow, L. R., 81, 207
Sass, H., 44–45, 187
Sato, S., 82, 195
Saunders, E. B., 7, 10–12, 16, 178, 208
Sawle, G. A., 8, 36, 38, 117–118, 196, 208
Schafer, R., 130, 206
Scharff, D. E., 154, 187
Schedlowski, M., 84–85, 198
schizophrenia, 11, 103, 128, 132, 148
Schmal, H., 160, 191
Schmitt, W. A., 47, 204
Schoenwald, S. K., 158, 193
Schore, A., xxvii, 160, 208
Schram, D. D., 17, 208
Schuengel, C., 78, 211
Schwartz, J. C., 32, 194
Schwartzman, A. N., 85, 182
Seckl, J. R., 74, 212
Segal, H., 55, 208
Seghorn, T. K., 15–16, 208

Seidler, K., 4, 6–13, 15, 17, 40–41, 75, 110, 112, 115–116, 120, 193, 196
Seidman, B. T., 10, 208
selective serotonin re-uptake inhibitors (SSRIs), 83, 90
self, xx–xxiv, 35, 54, 56–57, 61–63, 69, 71, 114, 143, 146, 150, 157, 162–163, 165, 168
  -esteem, 12, 29, 54, 110, 115, 149
  -reflective, xxiii, 30, 40, 173
  -regulation, 76, 78, 101
  sense of, xxi–xxii, xxvi, 34, 45, 58, 63, 65, 70–72, 114, 142, 146, 152, 157, 160, 162–164, 172
Serin, R. C., 49–50, 178–179, 208
Seto, M. C., 3–4, 9, 11–12, 17, 49–50, 72, 109, 115, 178–179, 208
sexual see aso: abuse, aggression, behaviour, fantasy, recidivism
  assault, xxvii, 5–6, 125
  experience, 15, 33
  perversion(s), xxviii, 51, 53, 66–72
sexuality, xv–xvi, xxiv, xxviii, 3, 21, 31–35, 40, 67–68, 71, 80, 88, 142, 147–148, 150–151, 171
sexualization, xvii, xix, 39, 53, 68–71, 78, 86, 112–113, 126, 141–143, 150, 164, 167, 172–173, 175
Shanock, S. S., 11, 200
Sharma, S., 74, 200, 212
Sharp, D. M., 158, 186
Shaver, P. R., 30, 32, 34, 193, 203, 207
Shaw, D. S., 14, 208
Shedler, J., 158, 168–169, 208
Shelby, E. S., 85, 182
Sheldon-Keller, A., 30, 212
Shill, C. T., 4–5, 9–10, 14, 16, 182
Shipley, S., 45, 178
Shiva, A., 55, 203
Sickmund, M., 3–5, 209
Siegert, R. J., 37–38, 94, 119, 206, 211–212
Siekert, G. P., 13, 204
Siever, L. J., 47, 204
Silberg, J. K., 6, 185
Simmons, R. J., 14, 191
Simonsen, E., 45, 49, 203
Simpson-Taylor, D., 4, 178
Sinourd, D. J., 4, 209
Sjodin, A., 83, 210
Sjögren, B., 81, 209

Skeem, J. L., 49, 138, 186, 209
Skuse, B., 16, 209
Sluga, W., 87, 180
Smallbone, S. W., 32, 36, 38, 209
Smith, A. M., 12, 46, 59, 197, 209
Smith, C. E., 85, 182
Smith, K., 5, 188
Smith, W. R., 11–12, 14, 16, 187, 209
Sniffen, C., 5, 209
Snyder, H. N., 3–5, 182, 209
social brain, xxviii, 73, 76–77, 119, 146
Soderstrom, H., 83, 210
sodomy, 4, 12, 116–117
Soininen, H., 46, 199
Solomon, J., 23–24, 201
Spaccarelli, S., 17, 210
Sperling, M. B., 14, 22, 29, 31, 58, 110, 210
Spiegal, D., 6, 185
splitting, xx–xxiii, 61, 68, 116, 150
Sroufe, L. A., 30–31, 110, 182, 186, 210
St. Laurent, D., 14, 204
Stalenheim, E. G., 47, 210
Starzynski, J., 10, 194
Stasch, M., 160, 191
Steele, H., 30, 32, 117, 188–189
Steele, M., 30, 32, 117, 188–189
Steinberg, L., 87, 110, 180, 210
Stejskal, W. J., 135–136, 213
Stermac, L., 36–37, 210
Stern, D. N., 157, 166, 210
Stevenson, J., 16, 209
Stevenson-Hinde, J., 30, 205
Stirpe, T., 36–37, 210
Stoller, R., xvii, 40, 68, 113, 210
Strack, S., 44, 194
Swan, J. M., 81, 186
Symington, J., 59, 210
Symington, N., 59, 210
Szyf, M., 74, 212

Tannebaum, B., 74, 200
Target, M., 30, 32–33, 36, 40, 117, 151, 153, 162–164, 188–189
Tellegen, A., 128–129, 182
texture responses (T), 95–98, 102, 106–108, 127, 133–135, 145, 149–150
Thase, M. E., 169, 190
Thoennes, N., 5, 210
Thomas, S., 4, 12, 115, 117, 193

Thornton, D., xxvi, 210
Tiihonen, J., 46, 199
Tingle, D., 16, 37, 210
Tinklenberg, J. R., 10, 13, 211
Tjaden, P., 5, 210
transference, xx, xxii, xxv, 34, 56, 62, 65,
     67, 161, 166–169
  counter-, xxv, 57, 65, 67, 127, 139, 146
Treadway, M. T., 85, 182
Troyer, R., 5, 181
true response inconsistency (TRIN), 99,
     103, 128
Truscott, D., 5, 210
Tyler, L., 17, 44, 183

Uvnäs-Moberg, K., 81, 209

Vaidakis, N., 47, 87, 190
Valliant, P. M., 5, 12, 210–211
van Horn, J., 10–11, 115, 211
Van IJzendoorn, M. H., 78, 211
Van Ness, S. R., 14, 211
Van Wijk, A., 9–11, 13, 115, 211
Vaurio, O., 46, 199
Veneziano, C., 15, 211
Veneziano, L., 15, 211
Vermeiren, J., 9, 211
Vermeiren, R., 11, 13, 211
Viglione D. J. Jr., 99, 131–133, 182, 201,
     205
Vinogradov, S., 10, 13, 211
Vitale, J. E., 47, 211
Vizard, E., 4, 11, 211
Von Knorring, L., 47, 210
Vondra, J. I., 14, 208
Voss, W. D., 47, 204

Waddell, M., xv–xvi, 211
Wagner, D., 76, 80, 193
Wall, J. K., 9, 211
Wall, S., xxiv, 21, 23–24, 177
Wallace, J. F., 46, 180
Ward, T., 7–8, 36–38, 94, 111, 117, 119,
     194, 206, 211–212
Ware, L. M., 14, 194
Waters, E., xxiv, 21, 23–24, 177
Way, I., 14, 195
Weaver, I. C., 74, 212
Weenink, A. G. M., 130, 193
Weigert, E., 53–54, 212

Weiner, I. B., 130–131, 134–135, 187, 212
Weiss, J. M. A., 45, 212
Welldon, E., xiii, 61, 212
Wenet, G. A., 5, 185
West, M., 30, 212
West, S. G., 136, 213
Westwick, A., xi–xiv
Wheeler, E. E., 31, 181
Whitaker-Azmitia, P. M., 83, 212
White, G., 12, 208
Wide, L., 47, 210
Widlocher, D., 22, 212
Widom, C. S., 6, 212
Widström, A. M., 81, 209
Wilcox, M. M., 75–76, 80, 193
Williams, A., 129, 213
Williams, C. L., 128–130, 182, 203
Williams, R., 16, 209
Wilson, J. S., 37, 114, 133, 181
Wilson, R., 36–37, 210
Winnicott, D. W., xv, 33, 60–61, 68, 213
Winslow, E. B., 14, 208
Winslow, J. T., 81–83, 195, 213
Wong, S., 118, 174, 213
Wood, J. M., 107, 134–136, 200, 213
Wood, M., 15, 178
Woodward, N. D., 85, 182
world
  emotional, 151, 154
  internal, xvii, xix–xxi, xxiii, xxv–xxix,
     3, 54, 57, 59, 66, 73, 75, 94, 99,
     109, 111–113, 118, 123, 126, 130,
     146, 159, 171–172, 175
Worley, C., 119, 138, 174, 208
Worling, J. R., 4, 6, 12–13, 15–17, 93,
     119, 125, 213

Yang, C.-H., 85, 205
Young, L. J., 15, 32, 81, 178, 195, 214
Yuille, J. C., 44–45, 49, 194

Zakireh, B., 10, 14–16, 214
Zald, D. H., 85, 182
Zaragoza, M. S., 100, 103, 180
Zeanah, C. H. E., 21, 23, 214
Zeanah, C. Z., 31, 181
Zeki, S., 86, 179
Zgourides, G., 10, 214
Zhang, Z.-W., 85, 205
Zuckermann, K. J., 11, 110, 178